1980

The Decorative Thirties

THE DECORATIVE THIRTIES

Martin Battersby

Walker and Company · New York

Acknowledgements

My grateful thanks to all those who have racked their memories for first-hand information about their work and experiences during the thirties and in particular to Raoh Schorr; Miss Brown; Frederick Mayor, who allowed me to consult his records of the Mayor Gallery; Herman Schrijver whose reminiscences of both decorators and clients in the thirties are diverting but, alas, too often unrepeatable; Oliver Messel; Mrs Reco Capey and Mrs Curtis Moffat, each of whom placed her husband's records at my disposal; Mr and Mrs Digby Morton; and Winnafreda, Countess of Portarlington. I must also thank Jonathan Joseph of Boston who so kindly searched for and sent me copies of contemporary magazines; Anne Urquhart for photographs of work done by Smyth, Urquhart and Marckwald; PEL, Best and Lloyd and The French Line for catalogues; Philip Dyer for help in tracing ballet photographs; the staff of Brighton Reference Library and the Director and Staff of Brighton Museum for their assistance in photographing pieces in the collection; and a special word of gratitude to Josephine Hickey for all her help in bringing order out of chaos.

Dollar and sterling equivalents in brackets in the text are approximate and based on the 1971 standard exchange rate of £1 = $2.40.

Cover illustrations

Front cover Drawing by Charles Martin for *Harper's Bazaar* August 1931 of jewelry by Maubousson

Back cover Entrance hall for Gayfere House, London by Oliver Hill for Lady Mount Temple, about 1931

First published in the United States of America in 1971
by the Walker Publishing Company, Inc.
Library of Congress Catalog Card Number: 70-159516

ISBN: 0-8027-0353-4

Photoset by BAS Printers Limited, Wallop, Hampshire, England
Printed in Italy by Alfieri and Lacroix S.p.A.

Contents

Preface   7
The background   10
The Depression and its impact on the decorative arts   24
The modernist decorative style   33
Art and industry   48
Decorators   62
Interior furnishings   91
Decorative painters   129
Period revivalism   165
Fashion   185
Hollywood style   198
Envoi   203
Bibliography   204
Index   206

Preface

To write a book about the twenties is an objective experience. When a period is sufficiently removed in time to place it in the area of history with most of its creative protagonists vanished, in some cases even from memory, the distinctive feel or atmosphere has to be reconstructed by patient research and a piecing together of fragments of information gleaned from the books and magazines of the period. The thirties is another matter. My direct involvement in the decorative arts in the 1930s, both as a member of the studio of one of the leading firms of decorators in London and later freelance as a mural painter and theatre designer, has both advantages and disadvantages. It is not possible to be entirely unbiased but at the same time actual experience of the conditions of the period gives a viewpoint which can shed a revealing light.

The thirties was far from being an ideal time to start a career in the decorative arts – if there has ever been such a time. Opportunities were limited, recognition difficult to achieve and the rewards less than meagre. For the young hoping for careers in architecture, painting or any branch of the decorative arts the prospects were bleak, with preference inevitably going to older and more experienced exponents with established reputations and even the fact of being young considered a disadvantage. Even an older generation with a record of solid achievement reaching back perhaps to the days before the Great War found it hard to make ends meet in the drab years of the Depression and anyone fortunate enough to be in a safe and congenial employment took care to hold on to his position at any cost. Few if any painters, for instance, could earn enough by the sale of their works alone and many an artist who has since become well known was glad, in the thirties, to paint decorative flower pieces or screens for interior decorators at say £10 ($24) a time or to design china or textiles if the opportunity occurred.

Aesthetic theories played little part in practical creative life during the thirties, as anyone with actual experience of that period will testify. Herbert Read, John Gloag, John de la Vallette and others in England preached the gospel of fitness for purpose in books, lectures, articles and even broadcast talks, but their efforts met with indifference on the part of a buying public which resented being either instructed or patronized concerning the artefacts they were able to spare the money to purchase. Manufacturers were equally loath to add to their overheads by engaging outside designers with little experience of the required techniques – an understandable reaction when factories were closing down and banks were refusing to lend the money to finance new ventures. When the majority of manufacturers were learning to live with the idea of bankruptcy they had neither the means nor the inclination to further any revolutionary theories about design. The position of even established firms of interior decorators was precarious, threatened as they were by an increasing number of freelance competitors. In this field in particular the client was all-important and what the client wanted the decorator had to provide. Even if the Bauhaus, by some turn of fate, had managed to survive throughout the thirties, it is extremely doubtful that its theories would have had more than a local influence and the decorative arts in England, France and the

United States would probably have pursued their own course unaffected. As it was, few in England were aware of its existence – the recent spate of books and exhibitions concerned with the work of the Bauhaus has probably made more people aware of its work and aims than at the time of its existence – and any interior decorator rash enough to try to persuade a client to embody its percepts in a decorative scheme would have met with short shrift, that is, assuming the highly unlikely fact that the decorator himself had heard of the Bauhaus. The excessive and frequently boring simplicity of many interior schemes of the early thirties was often a case of making a virtue out of a necessity – rooms were sparsely furnished because many people – young married couples, for instance – simply could not afford to fill them with unnecessary furniture and accessories, however decorative. Then there were those, of course, who found this trend towards simplicity (advocated by so many contributors to the *Architectural Review* and similar periodicals) very much to their taste, whatever their income. Simultaneously, however, there was an even greater number of people who found bare rooms devoid of decorative objects unsympathetic and preferred to cover every available flat surface with ornaments – if not perhaps quite to the degree fashionable in the twenties or earlier periods. And it was this second trend which became increasingly prevalent as the decade advanced.

Inevitably any survey of the thirties must contain constant references to the Depression and to the state of political uncertainty which preoccupied the minds of many. But at the same time, despite these clouds, the thirties was a period of creative activity which is only now beginning to receive its just appreciation and in retrospect a time when more originality and freedom of expression was permissible than is generally realized. It is to be hoped that this volume, though written from a personal point of view and experience, will help to eliminate many of the misconceptions which have arisen about a decade which tends to be overshadowed by the more spectacular achievements of the twenties.

'It's rather sad', she said one day, 'to belong, as we do, to a lost generation. I'm sure in history the two wars will count as one war and that we shall be squashed out of it altogether, and people will forget that we ever existed. We might just as well have never lived at all, I do think it's a shame.'

'It may become a sort of literary curiosity,' Davey said. 'People will be interested in it for all the wrong reasons, and collect Lalique dressing-table sets and shagreen boxes and cocktail cabinets lined with looking-glass and find them very amusing.' (Nancy Mitford, *The Pursuit of Love*, London 1945)

Cocktail cabinet, about 1932

The informal cocktail party became accepted to a greater degree during the thirties as a form of hospitality and in the smaller apartments and servantless households imposed upon many by the prevailing economic conditions it was both a more convenient and a less expensive way of entertaining than a formal dinner party. During the twenties antique bookcases or lacquer cabinets had been gutted and adapted to contain the numerous bottles needed but the specially designed cabinets, such as this example, designed to harmonize with modernist interiors, were made in some quantities during the thirties.

The background

The thirties were born prematurely and disastrously on Thursday 24 October 1929 when the New York Stock Exchange closed its doors. The events of that day were to affect the lives of millions, directly or indirectly, for years to come. The previous decade for all its reputation of hectic gaiety had had its realities of disillusion and hardship and to many the depression of the early thirties spelt out the end of any hopes they may have had. But for others – and they were in the majority – the bright bubble of a false prosperity vanished overnight, leaving them in a seemingly endless twilight of poverty and hopelessness. The arts survived as they always do, for there were still a number of rich patrons who were either unaffected by the recurring financial crises or even richer as a result of those same crises.

It is the aim of this volume to trace the progress of the decorative arts through the thirties, a progress leading from the austerities of the early years of the decade to the more prosperous times before the Second World War when for a brief period romanticism and fantasy were triumphant.

In the years following the First War the trend of taste in the decorative arts was dictated by the artists and designers active before 1914 and on the cessation of hostilities the natural thing for them was to continue where they had left off – a return to the conditions prevailing before the war. Money was plentiful with the emergence of a new class of war profiteers anxious to enjoy their new wealth, and for a considerable period the problem for the luxury trades was not a shortage of clients so much as a need for skilled craftsmen and materials. In some trades a new generation of workers had to be trained and in France hundreds of factories in the battle areas had been destroyed. The luxury fabrics, for instance, upon which France depended for her supremacy in fashion were in short supply. The lack of well-seasoned timber for fine furniture was general. Trade and export, particularly to the United States, were of prime importance to countries faced with colossal war debts and a return to something approaching normality was essential.

In each country the problem of catering for the prevailing taste was different. In France the devotion to the furniture and decoration of the eighteenth and to a lesser extent the early nineteenth centuries was as strong as ever, tempered with that desire for novelty which led the Parisians to be compared with the Athenians of classical times. The brief reign of art nouveau from the mid-1890s to the early 1900s, a period of little more than ten years, produced a sharp reaction even among its most enthusiastic supporters and came to be regarded with as much disdain in France as it had generally been in England. This essentially linear style lyrically described by Raymond Cogniat as 'irises, water lilies and convolvulus – precious flowers languorously decomposing in tender harmonies' was succeeded after a brief hiatus by another style equally linear in which the sinuous curves of art nouveau were controlled into circles and ovals, the naturalistic flowers formalized into geometric patterns and the delicate nuances replaced by vivid tones of cerise, orange, violet, emerald and lapis. This style, referred to as art déco as early as 1935, has since become generally known by this name, an abbreviation of the title of the Exposition des Arts Décoratifs et Industriels held in Paris in 1925, an exhibition so successful that in the ensuing years it came to be used as a standard of comparison for subsequent exhibitions.

The sources of the style were various. Its vibrant colouring came from the Russian Ballet and the designs of Leon Bakst, in particular his setting and costumes for *Scheherazade* when it opened in Paris in 1910. The leading couturier Paul Poiret was producing a wealth of fantastic, sometimes bizarre, designs in a similar vein. The decorative motifs owed more than a little to the Austrian designers Dagobert Peche, Josef Hoffmann and Bruno Paul. Interest in their work had come about as a result of the 1910 Exhibition of Applied Art from Munich which had earned the disapproval of Parisian critics but had nevertheless been sufficiently popular for mounted police to be brought in to control the crowds waiting for admission. These three designers had been among the many in Germany and Austria influenced to a considerable extent by the work of that flawed genius Charles Rennie Mackintosh. Fifteen years before, his work had been ignored in France where artists and designers had been preoccupied with their own elegant and sophisticated variations on art nouveau themes. After a period of time, however, and when the decorative imagery of Mackintosh had been transmuted through Germany and Austrian sources, Parisians were captivated.

The sometimes wayward and perverse outlines of art nouveau furniture were replaced by a more controlled style which had its origins in the Directoire and Consulate styles created during the revolutionary period (and in essentials simplified versions of Louis XVI) with a suggestion of the more ponderous Empire period which followed. Equally, the fashions of the years around 1910 as depicted by Paul Iribe and Georges Barbier show the Directoire influence in their long straight lines combined with applied ornaments of Oriental motifs. After the Armistice the designers of both dress and interiors resumed where they had left off five years before. Many architects and decorating concerns were still preparing for the exhibition which originally had been planned for 1915, had been postponed owing to the war and after several delays finally took place in 1925.

Two of the leading figures during the period that art déco was at its height were Paul Poiret and Jeanne Lanvin. Poiret has often been erroneously described as being the arbiter of taste before the First World War with a decline in power during the twenties, but in fact his influence was even stronger during most of the twenties, as a result of the décors and fabrics designed in his Atelier Martine, and his period of decline dates from the very end of the decade, when his financial problems became serious. During the twenties his *salon de couture* was a meeting place for rich, elegant women with aspirations to be regarded as leaders of fashion, his passion for collecting paintings brought him into contact with new and promising artists, while the perpetual need for new ideas and inspiration brought most of the young designers into his orbit at one time or another.

Jeanne Lanvin was in a similar position as a leader of taste – celebrated as a couturière and a decorator though not to the same extent as Poiret. Besides these two there were a number of designers supervising the decorating departments of the big Parisian department stores – Paul Follot whose work in the art nouveau style had been featured at La Maison Moderne at the turn of the century and who was now designing in the art déco manner for the Atelier Pomone at Bon Marché; Maurice Dufrêne, similarly adapting to a new idiom as the head of La Maîtrise at the Galeries Lafayette; Louis Sognot at Printemps and Kohlmann at the Magasins du Louvre. Eugène Sue and André Mare, like André Groult, were creating interiors and furniture based on the forms of the late eighteenth century while Emile-

Jacques Ruhlmann, a dominant figure during the twenties, became more and more inclined to follow the traditions of the heavier and more sombre Empire style.

Considerable misunderstanding has arisen as to the exact use of the terms 'art déco' and 'modernist' and the two names are often incorrectly applied. At its best the effect of art déco was one of elegant luxury, of a delight in ornament for its own sake, while the rather restricted range of decorative motifs gave an over-all unity of style which made it applicable to anything from the façade of a building to the decoration of a vanity case, and an immediately recognizable character. In the 1925 Exhibition art déco was seen at its most luxuriant.

This exhibition was however at once the apogee and the finale of art déco – a curious parallel with art nouveau can be found, for this style too was seen at its best in the exhibits for the 1900 Exhibition and suffered, with a few exceptions, a sharp decline in public favour very soon after. Possibly the artists and designers working in each style – and there were a number who adapted from one to the other and whose work appeared in both exhibitions – experienced a revulsion of feeling on seeing the particular decorative idiom which they had helped to create commercialized and cheapened by unintelligent plagiarism. The changing and often illogical movement of fashion will have played its part. In the case of art déco, which had been flourishing since before the Great War, a change was overdue, especially in the rapidly moving times of the postwar period. Like art nouveau it was a fashion directed almost exclusively towards women, applied to the rooms they used and the objects which surrounded them. But in the early twenties women were beginning to rebel against the role imposed upon them and were no longer content to remain passive decorative objects extravagantly dressed and hatted and posing like odalisques in exotic surroundings reminiscent of the *Arabian Nights*. The shortage of manpower which resulted from the war gave many women opportunities for more active and useful lives. The pursuit of a career in business or even in sport became possible to women. The new feeling was for freedom and simplicity combined with a somewhat hectic gaiety symbolized by the prevailing rhythms of jazz and this new feeling found expression in the angularities of modernism.

Even before 1925 there had been signs of a reaction against the sensuous curves of art déco. The creative ferment which first manifested itself about 1905 in cubism and its elaborations of analytical, synthetic and orphic cubism and a consequent interest in negro art, was reinforced by the postwar development of purism, a movement exemplified by *Après le Cubisme* published in 1918 by Ozenfant and Le Corbusier. The authors accused the followers of cubism of allowing it to degenerate into decoration, and advocated an impersonal art stripped of ornament and even individuality, owing its inspiration to the machine. The Russian concept of constructivism propagated by Vladimir Tatlin, Naum Gabo and Anton Pevsner, with its insistence on abstraction and the use of new materials such as perspex, had a considerable influence on architecture, theatre design and sculpture and its ideals were taken to Paris in 1921 by Pevsner and to Germany by Gabo. The collaboration of these two artists in the ballet *La Chatte* with its décor of transparent talc and black American cloth was instrumental in bringing constructivism to a wider audience, and demonstrated the desire of Serge Diaghilev to break away from the exoticism of the earlier ballets such as *Scheherazade*, *Thamar* or *Le Dieu Bleu*. A similar rejection of ornament and an insistence on elementary colours and linear abstraction were the tenets of those following De Stijl, a Dutch movement originally founded by Theo van Doesburg

House by Professor Adolf Rading, 1932

The architect's brief was to build, on a strictly limited budget, a modest house, unostentatious, incorporating 'spiritual values'. Decorative effects were to be obtained by the use of space and colour. The main room illustrated was basically olive green with the doors painted red, the linoleum floor in squares of white, blue, red, grey and black. The decorative metal construction was the work of Oskar Schlemmer and was described as 'a space-enlivening element'.

Chair by Mies van der Rohe for Thonet, before 1934

and named after the magazine launched by him in 1917.

The most notable of these movements was that developed at the Bauhaus founded in 1919 by Walter Gropius at Weimar and after 1925 situated in Dessau. The teachings covered all branches of art from architecture to typography, with the aim of amalgamating the best of craftwork with the needs of industry. Among its teachers were Paul Klee, Oskar Schlemmer, Moholy-Nagy and Mies van der Rohe. But these revolutionary ideas current in Holland, Germany and Russia were for the most part ignored in Paris and London during the twenties.

France has always been the home of the *avant-garde* – within limits. As an acknowledged leader of fashion Paris has always had a reputation for luxurious elegance and the country's economic balance has depended largely on the maintenance of this reputation, which has always, and particularly in the twenties and thirties, attracted the rich and discriminating from many other countries. Their patronage meant the livelihood of a vast number of artists, designers and craftsmen whose aim was to divert and astonish with masterpieces of invention and skill.

The ideas of mass production and of designing simple handsome objects which could be produced in indefinite quantities by machinery, with a consequent loss of individuality, ideas which lay behind most of the theories advanced by the Bauhaus, for instance, would be abhorrent to any French person priding himself on his taste during the twenties and thirties. In addition the mere fact that these ideas emanated from countries whose reputation for taste had never been highly regarded in France was enough to put them out of court. It was only when these concepts were filtered through the work of *avant-garde* French designers that they became acceptable to French patrons. Ernest Tisserand writing in *L'Amour de l'Art* in 1929 on the controversial question of steel furniture implies that the first steel chair was a French creation and nowhere in his article mentions the name of Marcel Breuer, who was actually responsible for the first steel chair in 1925.

The older generation of designers in Paris were too established easily to change their conceptions of design. Some had already experienced their own revolt against art nouveau a quarter of a century before and could not adapt to yet another style, and in addition they had a faithful clientele who could see no virtues in modernism. The critic Guillaume Janneau did not conceal his scepticism of the importance of contemporary German trends. Reviewing the exhibits at the autumn Salon des Décorateurs in 1930 and, in particular, the specially invited German section, he commends Gropius and Breuer as 'daring moderns, informed and courageous in the expression of their ideas', but continues: 'French artists have revealed themselves as very impressed by the strength of impulse they feel to be behind this section. If they had ever visited Germany, the new Germany that has arisen during the ten years since the war, they would discover a complete native absence of this formula. In actuality, it is something of a hot-house plant. It would be just as false to judge the activities of modern Germany by the theories of this numerically ill-equipped vanguard as to judge our own by the opinions of a few of our already outmoded theorists. In fact, before two years were out, wearied of this application and the ineradicable monotony of effect it must produce we would joyfully return to little porcelain flowers and mother-of-pearl inlays.' Janneau's words were prophetic.

It was the younger generation of architects and designers, including Robert Mallet Stevens, Robert Printz, Pierre Charreau, Francis Jourdain, René Herbst, Charlotte Perriand, Le Corbusier and his cousin Pierre Jeanneret, who were able, against considerable hostility, to impose their ideas, but after a first enthusiasm for the austerities of steel, glass and bare walls, even these designers found their clients inclined to temper the clinical atmosphere with fur, velvet and lacquer.

The best method of showing the difference between art déco and modernism is by comparing an art déco shop front, for instance, with one designed in the modernist manner. Azema, Edrei and Hardy's design for the façade of the hair-dressing establishment Girault in the Boulevard des Capucines employs practically every motif in the art déco repertoire. The lavish use of wrought ironwork contrasts with stone, the metal with its profusion of conventionalized flowers being treated almost as a lace curtain. Closer examination reveals the use of the spiral (a form natural to the techniques of wrought iron), either as a termination of a graceful curve or as a repeated motif. The metal flowers include the characteristic formalizations of roses, sunflowers, dahlias and zinnias set upon smoothly sinuous stems to create an effect of elegance and luxury. The octagonal panel which appears time and time again in art déco designs is here found in the centre window of the mezzanine floor and the only motif which is not incorporated is that of the elongated oval. The lettering of hammered iron, although not altogether happy in design, is gracefully appropriate, while the two female heads in relief on the pilaster and the mysterious half-mask over the entrance door are reminders that this is the façade of a temple of femininity – despite the announcement 'Coiffeur pour Messieurs' and the masculine toiletries displayed in one window.

This shopfront, dating probably from the early twenties, is in complete contrast with that of Covanna, designed by Patout in 1927. Curves have been banished in

Art déco shop-front by Azema, Edrei and Hardy for Girault, Paris, early twenties

Modernist shop-front by Patout for Covanna, Paris, 1927

favour of a rigidly balanced geometric arrangement of shapes, and, except for the cross-hammered frames of the three upper windows and geometrical ventilation panels under the two ground-floor windows, the intricate ironwork has disappeared too. The fundamental simplicity of the design is made more interesting by the shadows caused by the projection and recession of the various elements such as the deep cornice and the raised lettering. The broad band of coloured geometrical ornament – possibly made more obtrusive by the effects of photography – is reminiscent of the *simultané* designs of Sonia Delaunay.

In England there was a deep attachment to historicism, for the inclination was to regard taste as having ended somewhere around 1780 and new houses both large and small together with their interior decorations were conceived in the styles of the sixteenth, seventeenth and eighteenth centuries. A Tudor cottage, sham if the real thing were not available, was considered to be the ideal home in the country and if it were half-timbered and with a thatched roof so much the better, especially if furnished with more or less 'Tudor' antiques. Alternatively, Georgian or neo-Georgian houses were permissible as being rather more convenient and comfortable, and having the advantage that furniture in the Chinese taste could be incorporated in the decorative schemes to lend an air of genteel exoticism.

When materials and labour became available vast quantities of furniture were made in the Tudor, Queen Anne and Chippendale or Sheraton styles and although most of these pieces were obvious pastiches, enough of considerable quality and accuracy of period detail emerged to double – at the most moderate estimate – the number of 'antiques' on the market in the following decades. The word 'modern' meant only one thing – the piece to which it was applied was a contemporary reproduction of an antique. The nearest approach to a contemporary idiom in furniture design was in the worthy but, it must be said, somewhat dull, beautifully handmade pieces in the style of the arts and crafts movement (then still in existence but losing ground as a decisive influence) and even these had strong traditional features. The attitude of looking back at the past was fostered by the large firms of decorators who had a virtual monopoly of such interior decoration as was not considered the province of the architect. The individual decorator exploiting his own personal taste and knowledge and working in a close consultation with the client was almost unknown. Those with an individual taste and able to plan original and striking backgrounds for their lives needed neither architect nor decorator. In the main, however, the advice of the salesmen in the large decorating establishments was sought, whether for the entire redecoration of a house or the choice of a piece of fabric for a cushion, and as most of these firms carried a large stock of antique or reproduction furniture together with fabrics reproducing old patterns, the client was induced as a matter of course to perpetuate the cult of historicism.

The designer Paul Nash in *Room and Book* has a number of caustic comments to make concerning this nostalgia for the past: 'There exists in the English character an extraordinary sentiment, which baldly stated is that everything new is ugly

Dining room by Doris Howard Robertson for Mr and Mrs Digby Morton, about 1934

A conversion of a small early-nineteenth-century Chelsea house. The original mantelpiece has been removed and replaced by an inset electric fire.

and everything old is beautiful'; elsewhere he remarks 'the craze for the antique is bred in snobbery and survives in lazymindedness or is imposed on the ignorant and credulous by ignorant tradesmen.' *Room and Book* was published in 1932 when efforts had already been made to improve the taste of the general public and the gospel of design through fitness for purpose put forward by a number of architects and designers. So far their efforts had met with little success in weening away the public taste from the olde worlde and Nash comments: 'It must be admitted that at the present time in 1932 the taste for the antique is the favourite flavour of eighty per cent of the population or at least is supposed to be by the builder and furniture makers . . . there have been certain cross currents persistently flowing, by far the strongest of which is the Lethe-like stream of the Antique. These waters of forgetfulness roll down their preposterous logs of old oak, rosewood, and mahogany to some undefined limbo of dead things where no doubt a herd of white elephants will carry them wherever they are going. For antique furniture is the possession and often the product of people who wish to forget they are living today, the symbol of a sentimental nostalgia fostered by dealers in ghosts.' In his view the English taste could be summed up as a 'gabled house with bogus beams and lattice windows, a sham inglenook and a gas log fire; Old English chintz and Persian carpets . . . a teacosy of Jacobean design . . . an endless dance of ancient masks like a fearful fancy dress ball composed of nothing but travesties of the Jacobeans and poor Queen Anne.'

An advertisement of 1930 for antique furniture, published by a London department store, incorporated in the caption a gem of unconscious humour. 'Place on top of an Old English desk a gem of a Queen Anne mirror and you have a dressing table a queen or an American would envy'; and the fact that both table and mirror even in the photograph are obvious as reproductions adds a further twist.

Herbert Read's championship of Walter Gropius and the ideals of the Bauhaus took the form of a lecture to the Design and Industries Association which was reprinted in the *Journal of the Royal Institute of British Architects* in May 1934 and his book *Art and Industry* was written 'to support and propogate the ideals expressed by Dr Gropius', but the results were minimal in England. Apart from a few illustrated articles in the *Studio* and the *Architectural Review*, little notice was taken of the work of the pioneers on the Continent and a traditional attitude left no room for new concepts, except to a very limited extent in architecture. The *Architectural Review*, as its name implies, was published for the architectural profession: its editors, whenever possible, reported and illustrated the best contemporary work on the Continent, and as a result a number of English architects picked up the superficial elements and mannerisms of the more extreme European examples which they superimposed on traditional plans. The case is on record of a well-known firm of architects who had been commissioned to build a large country house in the neo-Georgian style for a millionaire: just as the plans and elevations were finalized, their client visited an international exhibition, and, bemused by the modern architecture, decided to have his house built in the contemporary style instead. The architects simply eliminated all ornament and mouldings from the façades, substituted horizontal steel windows (to the later chagrin of the interior decorators) and had the brick surfaces covered in stucco. The theories of Le Corbusier, Gropius and other masters of modern architecture on the relationships of space, of the interior to the exterior or of the suitability of the building to its surroundings need never have been formulated.

'Where is your vorticist?' asked Wyndham Lewis in 1934, 'a handful of

'Skyscraper' bookcase by Paul Frankl, 1930

modernist villas have been put up; a few big factories have gone cubist . . . one shop in a hundred has acquired a chromium-plated façade but only in the big cities.'

The word 'modernistic' itself had its detractors, despite its practical value in indicating the difference between contemporary design and a pastiche of the antique. Paul Nash, while offering no alternative, described 'modernistic' as a 'repellent title' and regarded commercial modernism as the most formidable obstacle to the new movement, adding that 'just as at an earlier date persons and things were referred to as "so artistic", now they are described as "quite modernistic" and in such case one knows only too well what to expect. The modernistic craze is kept lively by the same stimuli as the antique vogue – snobbery and delusion.' Here Paul Nash in his writings reflects an attitude common among the advocates of what he describes as the 'new movement' – the belief that because many people preferred to live surrounded by the artefacts of a past century they were at best snobs and at worst the mindless slaves of fashion. He and many others seemed unwilling to accept the fact that a love of the antique could be genuine.

American interior design changed in every aspect during the thirties. Commenting on the state of design in the United States in 1930 the *Studio* made the point that 'the modern furniture movement is only a little more than four years old', although there had been a few courageous pioneers earlier, and in a review during the same year of an international exhibition of glass and rugs at the Metropolitan Museum the opinion is given that 'American exhibits cannot bear comparison with those from other countries', with the significant addition that France and Sweden, both prominent in these fields, had refused to cooperate for fear of plagiarism. The American designer Paul Frankl in *New Dimensions* published in 1930 explains that, 'the only reason why America was not represented at the exhibition of decorative arts held in Paris in 1925 was because we found that we had no decorative art. Not alone was there a sad lack of any achievement that could be exhibited,

Miniature room by McMillen Inc., 1932

but we discovered that there was not even a serious movement in this direction and that the general public was quite unconscious that modern art had been extended into the field of business and industry. On the other hand we had our skyscrapers, and at that very date (1925), they had been developed to such an extent that, if it had been possible to have sent an entire building abroad, it would have been a more vital contribution in the field of modern art than all the things done in Europe added together.'

But by 1937 the *Studio* is recording that in America 'professional designers of interiors not only influence fashion but control the purchases of two hundred thousand influential clients.' No reference was given for this figure but it indicated that in a short space of time the profession of interior decorator had become very much a part of American life.

As in England and France there was – and still is – a certain number of wealthy patrons with a preference for the styles of the past and if all these people were not able to buy the antique furniture and paintings imported by Joseph Duveen or Elsie de Wolfe, they still preferred to live in surroundings reminiscent of the past epochs of England, France, Spain or Italy.* Modernism was not allowed in the house beyond the bathroom or the kitchen and their tastes were untouched by passing enthusiasm for any 'amusing' revivals of periods not regarded as classic. And at the same time as the more advanced designers were working in a modernist idiom there were others who favoured an updated version of historic periods.

* It was solemnly announced in an American periodical that 'Mr Charles Duveen, the international decorator, will continue to purvey his originals copied from Chippendale and Adam and all the famous eighteenth-century craftsmen: Macy will have copies of the copies.'

20

A modernized version of Regency and Empire styles characterized the majority of a series of miniature rooms designed and exhibited by McMillen, Inc., early in 1932. Constructed to the scale of one and a half inches to the foot they were perfect replicas, even to the lighting fixtures, ornaments and a typewriter, of possible schemes of decoration for entrance halls, dining rooms, living rooms and bedrooms. A number of artists, including Jans Juta, the sculptor Boris Lovet-Lorski (who numbered Mary Pickford among his pupils) and Bernard Boutet de Monval, created miniature works of art, decorative features or replicas of portraits for the various rooms. In the living room illustrated the pared-down simplicity of the decorations, the three-quarter columns without capitals or bases and the limiting of decoration to bands of fluting suggest rather than reproduce a period style, at the same time providing a harmonious background for the black and gold Regency furniture, reproduced in miniature with painstaking craftsmanship and probably replicas of actual pieces in stock at the time. A number of interiors in a similar style, a compromise between modernism and Regency, appeared in periodicals in the early thirties, some of them showing an obvious debt to the designs of Sir John Soane – an architect much admired in Scandinavia.

But in spite of the Depression – or because of it – there was a growing taste for modernism, a streamlined expression of the American spirit in glittering chromium plate, mirror and tubular lighting – a realization of a new machine-made world of drive and efficiency, not uninfluenced by the movies and far removed from the harsh realities of economic strains, a reflection of the comparison, made in 1933, that 'while English interiors are domestic and reticent, the French had an air of feminine luxury and the Germans stark and utilitarian, the American interior was different, had something exhilarating in its use of new forms and was occasionally theatrical'. This may be largely attributed to the fact that a number of the leading designers in America, Lee Simonson, Norman Bel Geddes and Joseph Urban for instance, were also simultaneously working as stage designers.

Electric clock by Gilbert Rohde for the Herman Miller Clock Company, before 1937

Neo-Regency interior, American, about 1931

An early example of an exercise in Regency themes, achieving a cool elegance by its restraint. The reproduction of the plaque by Thorvaldsen became a favourite feature of rooms in this manner and the Copenhagen porcelain reproductions of his sculpture, especially the *Ganymede and the Eagle*, were much sought after.

22

Modernism, with a growing emphasis on the machine as a source of inspiration for design and an often exaggerated stress on the dubious virtues of 'streamlining' had in the late thirties brought about the emergence of a new figure – the industrial designer. His role became one of vital importance in the long years of the Depression when 'styling' became one of the integral features in sales promotion. A newly styled object or piece of household equipment became something to be acquired as a status symbol and a proof that the owner was unaffected by the Depression – at least until the manufacturers produced a restyled model which made the previous one old-fashioned and obsolete. There must have been many English designers who read with astonished envy of the fees commanded by their opposite numbers as recorded in *Fortune* and quoted in an English periodical. Norman Bel Geddes was said to obtain a flat fee ranging from $1000 (about £415) to $100,000 (about £41,500) plus royalties for designing such items as a radio or a gas range; Walter Dorwin Teague, the designer for advertising and interiors, worked on a retainer of $12,000 (£5000) to $24,000 (£10,000) and Raymond Loewy could ask sums in a similar range. The English equivalents of the corporations for which these and other designers worked were, of course, with a limited market for their products, on a far smaller scale, but even taking this into consideration the sums they expected to pay for new designs were infinitesimal in comparison – even when they considered a designer necessary.

America took to modernism with an enthusiasm unequalled in England. 'Our age is one of invention, machinery, industry, science and commerce . . . modern furniture has several strong characteristics. It is built in flat surfaces and strong lines. The angles are decided and sharp. The proportions are well considered and the finish is beyond reproach. Sentimental* moulding and panelling are avoided as much as possible in order to gain the effect of extreme and severe simplicity', wrote Paul Frankl in 1930.

In many ways the Bauhaus ideals found their fullest expression in the United States. Many of those associated with the Bauhaus found refuge in America after its closure by the Nazis in 1933 and their teachings undoubtedly influenced the more *avant-garde* design in that country to a greater extent than anywhere else.

---

* The description of a moulding as being 'sentimental' seems as curious to a present day viewpoint as the comment of Frederick Everard, the head of the drawing office in a London firm, who wrote to the *Studio* complaining that 'Modern furniture is finished in an extremely effeminate and aesthetic tone . . . today we are letting the atmosphere of the Continental Casino invade our homes.'

The Depression and its impact on the decorative arts

The Wall Street Crash of October 1929 brought about a world-wide depression which directly and indirectly affected the lives and fortunes of most people, whatever their occupation, until 1935. For about two years before there had been a wave of speculation in the United States, a gambling fever which manifested itself in an optimistic but ignorant investing in stocks and shares. The prices of shares rose or were driven up by unscrupulous operators to unparalleled levels until the inevitable time when shares were unloaded to take advantage of the prices and the market finally crashed. In twenty-four hours the value of shares fell to approximately their normal level and hundreds of thousands of speculators lost their investments. A rush upon capital in the banks proved too much for their resources and in the confusion a number of small banks closed their doors and in so doing placed the resources of the larger banking combines in jeopardy. In the following month it looked as though the downward movement had eased and a small amount of cautious buying of shares started but again the market broke, a pattern to be repeated in the following spring of 1930 and again six months later. By some mysterious process incomprehensible to laymen the financial experts maintained that in fact no real loss of wealth had occurred and that the gold reserves of the United States were actually greater than before but these statements gave little consolation to the ruined investors and the millions of unemployed. The stories of bankrupted financiers throwing themselves in despair from the windows of their offices in skyscrapers, of the family of millionaires who embarked on a liner at New York *en route* to Paris and found themselves destitute on landing at Cherbourg, of Americans living in Paris who had to borrow money from their French servants, have become part of American folklore and, true or apocryphal, they illustrate the dramatic suddenness of the ruin which marked the end of the twenties.

England had suffered a financial setback on a far smaller scale in September 1929 when the collapse of the Clarence Hatry financial bubble had shaken the economic structure. The postwar boom in the United States had not been equalled in England and with less loose money for investment the English stock market was less affected by the fever of speculation raging across the Atlantic. But if the English were spared the immediate disaster they could not in the long run escape the results of that disaster.

The panic cancelling of all projects in America immediately hit the luxury trade and the art world. Art dealers in London and Paris who had enjoyed prosperous years exporting old masters found that their market in the United States had vanished overnight, with the additional blow that many of the works of art delivered were not yet paid for and were not likely to be paid for. Cartier's had so much jewelry in America that it was necessary to send a member of the firm to collect those pieces for which there was no possibility of payment.

The many Americans who had led a carefree existence in Paris where, owing to a favourable rate of exchange, they could live on a far higher scale than in the States, hastily left for America and with them departed the market for paintings by hundreds of second-rate painters of the Ecole de Paris.

The efforts of French couturiers, hoteliers and shopkeepers to retain the American market are wryly described by Mieda Monro, an American resident in Paris and a contributor to *Town and Country*. She relates how in 1932 all the dressmakers had slashed the prices of their models – Chanel halving her prices – while maintaining the standards of quality of fabric and workmanship, a drastic reduction which must have given some of the shrewder American patrons of the couturiers food for thought. Shops devoted to luxury goods in the rue Saint-Honoré broke the custom of closing on Monday and went further by reducing their prices on that day to compete with the big department stores which remained closed.

Chanel and Schiaparelli designed evening dresses of cotton, a revolutionary step viewed with dismay by the silk manufacturers. A hotel was specially opened out of season for a single American family and the most celebrated restaurants advertised *prix-fixe* luncheons including unlimited wine.

Early in 1930 the Depression had had little effect as yet upon the English economy and it was not necessary to be rich to have an apartment in Paris as well as one in London. Rents were, if anything, lower in France than in England – a bachelor apartment in the Palais Royal could be had for £125 ($300) a year furnished, and a ten-room apartment with a view over the Seine would entail an outlay of £300 ($720) a year. Towards the end of 1930, however, only the richest English or Americans were able to maintain the luxury of a second home in Paris.

But France was probably less affected by the Depression than the United States or England. Though the luxury trades suffered from the sudden loss of the English and particularly the US market there were still many rich clients from other countries, like India and South America, partly to compensate. And even in the United States, after the first panic had subsided, there were people rich enough to order costly work in quantity. So, for example, although the demand for decorative lacquer panels and furniture – necessarily expensive through the skill and patience required in their making – should have been one of the first casualties, the lacquer worker Jean Dunand seems to have been unaffected by the general depression of the early thirties.

Also, the policy of the French government to encourage any skill or craft in order to foster prestige helped many branches of the luxury trades to survive. Major sources of work for French craftsmen in the thirties were commissions for such symbols of national prestige as the luxury liner *Normandie*.

The *Normandie* was launched in 1932 and put into service with a maiden voyage in 1935. She was conceived and designed in terms of superlatives, for under the stipulations of the contract between the French line and the government the new vessel 'had to be not less than equal to the best foreign ship in commission or under construction'. This condition entailed the construction of a liner larger than any other afloat – a statistic much quoted to the press was that the length of the *Normandie* was greater than the height of the Eiffel Tower. And the boat had to exceed in luxury of decorations as much as it did in size the same line's *Ile de France* which had made its maiden trip in 1927. The *Normandie*'s gross tonnage was nearly twice as much as that of its predecessor and with this amount of space at their disposal the designers of the public rooms were enabled to achieve spectacular results. The author Ludwig Bemelmans was a passenger on the maiden voyage and his comment on the *Normandie* was that 'she leaned to excesses in her décor – there was something of the fatal woman'. The main dining room, 305 feet

Main dining room on the *Normandie*, with glass panels by René Lalique, 1935

in length, 46 feet wide and 25 feet high, had walls sheathed in hammered glass panels and seven hundred passengers could dine by the light of thirty-eight wall panels, two gigantic chandeliers and twelve decorative standard lights, all the creation of René Lalique. Additional embellishments were four 20-foot-high panels of gilded plaster representing aspects of life in Normandy and a twice-life-size statue of *La Paix* in gilded bronze by Dejean. Off this vast room led eight private dining rooms each decorated with mural paintings by leading contemporary artists and an extra banqueting room with bas-reliefs by Janniot.

The main lounge, slightly smaller than the dining room, contained four panels by Jean Dupas representing the history of navigation (see page 27). Each panel, 50 feet wide and 22 feet in height was executed in a complicated technique which involved etching and painting the designs on the back of the glass, an arduous process which entailed working in reverse. The gilded furniture by Goudissart was covered in tapestry representing the flowers of the French colonies in tones of red, orange and grey; the carpet by the same designer was claimed to be one of the largest ever woven in one piece and the windows were covered at night by embroidered silk curtains.

The transatlantic liners served the purpose, apart from transporting passengers quickly and comfortably, of providing a showcase for the work of the best designers of the country and the smoking room of the *Normandie* was devoted to the creations of Jean Dunand, long esteemed as one of the finest craftsmen in France. The walls were covered with panels, 22 feet high and 27 feet wide, of lacquer carved in relief after the style of Chinese Coromandel screens, and depicted various sporting activities treated in a quasi-oriental manner, one composition of life-size galloping horses being particularly handsome. To avoid damage to the

26

Main lounge, *Normandie*, 1935

precious lacquer by the movement of the ship, each panel was divided into smaller sections framed in copper. The small occasional tables and the frames of the brown morocco-covered chairs were also lacquered by Jean Dunand and completed the scheme of dark rich tones of sepia, black and gold. Equally arresting were the walls of Algerian onyx with decorations of hammered glass and gilded metalwork by Raymond Subes in the main entrance hall, the silver leaf walls of the theatre, claimed to be as large and as well equipped as many theatres in London and Paris, the 75-foot long swimming pool, the corridors lacquered in old rose and silver and the winter garden arranged by Madame de Vilmorin and Emile-Jacques Ruhlmann. Numerous ornate suites, consisting of a drawing room, bedroom and dining room, were designed by the leading decorators of Paris and like the smaller staterooms featured walls covered in leather, woven straw, panels of etched glass or engraved metal, suggesting 'some rich jewel casket rather than a prosaic bedroom'. Two staterooms with metal walls and metal furniture were from the designs of Ruhlmann and of Madame Klotz.

The decorations of the second- and tourist-class sections though less sumptuous were conceived on an equally grand scale and it is remarkable that throughout the liner the schemes were in the contemporary manner and only two of the private suites were in the eighteenth-century style.

The liner was deprived by a piece of pettifogging beaurocracy of a scheme which would have added to the richness of its decorations. Raoul Dufy was invited to ornament the walls surrounding the swimming pool with painted panels on any subject he might choose. It is tempting to imagine that he might have used the yachting themes he explored so brilliantly in many paintings and drawings and particularly in the backcloth for the ballet *Beach*, a charming light *divertissement*

Lacquer panels by Jean Dunand in the smoking room of the *Normandie*, 1935

The lounge, S.S. *Orion*, designed by Brian O'Rorke, 1935

The *Orion*, like the *Queen Mary* and the *Queen Elizabeth*, was decorated in a subdued modernistic manner which never achieved the style or splendour of the contemporary French liners or even of the Dutch *Nieuwe Amsterdam*. However, this interior at least shows a break from the traditional 'period' treatment; for it was not until the mid-thirties that contemporary decoration came to be considered suitable for a British liner, and the tendency was still to incorporate Tudor panelling with plaster ceilings and fake mantelpieces.

choreographed by Leonide Massine to music by Jean Françaix which was presented by the Ballets de Monte Carlo in 1933. However the ruling was that although Dufy had been decided upon to receive the commission, there must, for reasons which have been forgotten, appear to be some sort of competition. Dufy therefore, must ostensibly be the prize winner in an open competition, but he refused to take part in this charade and the swimming pool was decorated by another hand.

Dufy's pleasure in depicting the freshness and gaiety of yachts, brilliant sunshine and the deep blue of a Mediterranean sea was marred by a degree of misfortune where boats were concerned. The large panels commissioned by Paul Poiret to decorate the three barges *Amours*, *Délices* and *Orgues* which were a feature of the 1925 Paris Exhibition were met with such critical indifference that it is not possible to determine with accuracy the exact number of paintings, and search has revealed no photographs of the interiors of the barges moored on the bank of the Seine. Indirectly, one of these panels was to affect the lives of one man and countless women. This panel, depicting a map of Paris, was bought from Poiret by a young man dabbling in art dealing. In the early thirties this young man, desperately hard up, sold his Dufy painting and with the money was able to exist until the time his fashion designs earned him sufficient to live upon. That young man's name was Christian Dior.

There is a certain irony in the statement in the commemorative booklet issued to mark the launching of the *Normandie*: 'The French line were determined that their splendid new liner the *Normandie* should approach as nearly as possible to a 100 per cent fire proof ship . . . the possibility of catastrophe by fire on board this vessel is a very remote possibility.' The *Normandie* caught fire in New York Harbour in 1942, sank during the salvage operations, was raised after the war with a view to reconditioning but was found to be too damaged and was scrapped. Thus the most luxurious liner of its day terminated its short life of seven years.

The situation as regards the decorative arts was rather different in England. The luxury exports to the United States were on a far smaller scale – for while Americans appreciated the tradition associated with England it was in France that they found the chic and elegance for which they yearned and which they were unable to find at home. The longer-term effects of the Wall Street Crash were on a more mundane level which indirectly affected the decorative arts. The general disorganizing of world markets brought about serious unemployment, and in addition in late 1929 the Australian government suspended all immigration, blocking a traditional escape route for those who could not find work in England. The various remedies attempted by English governments during the early thirties were ineffectual in stopping the downward trend which had reached such proportions that no government could do anything really constructive, and the only results were reductions in prices and incomes, a lowering of production and a consequent rise in unemployment – a conservative figure of three million out of work was given. For most people these factors led to a considerably lower standard of living.

To prevent the drain of money abroad, tariffs of ten per cent upwards were imposed on all imports except meat and wheat, a campaign to 'Buy British' was launched and attempts were made to improve the almost non-existent export trade. John de la Valette opened his introductory chapter to *The Conquest of Ugliness* with the statement that 'The Glory of God and the joy of men are the constant sources of beauty. To extol the one and give voice to the other are the aims to which art aspires', but a more practical view can be observed in the preface by the Prince of Wales: 'a greater attention to the artistic side of industry is essential if our manufacturers are to develop their domestic and overseas markets. Proof is not lacking that tariffs, however high, fail to keep foreign goods out of a country if they possess qualities which the domestic article lacks.' The slogan of fitness for purpose had a sharply practical reason. The conquest of ugliness, 'the introduction of decency and beauty into the lives of the people, expecially at the lower end of the social scale' were admirable desires and John de la Valette's sincerity in formulating them should not be questioned, but the fact remains that behind the idealism lay the urgent necessity to sell more goods at home and abroad.

The picture dealers, jewellers, antiquaries and other branches of the luxury trades were, as we have seen, among the first to feel the effects of the Depression and in their case the impact was immediate. However, many of them either had sufficient financial backing to tide them over for quite a while or they had enough clients unaffected by the Depression to enable them to keep in business even if on a reduced scale.

Among the worst hit were the studio craftsmen and the artworkers. Large numbers of these had set up in business after the war, eking out a day to day existence on slender financial resources and even more slender talents. Many of these were women who had lost husbands or fiancés and were hoping to augment pensions or small private incomes by making and selling handicrafts: others were reluctant to relinquish the newly found independence they had experienced by working in factories or in the services during the war and equally hoped to earn a living even if they had no particular skills which would enable them to find a regular job in an overcrowded labour market. When about 1930, as the side-effects of the Crash began to be felt, there was a general decrease in spending, these handicraft workers and the shops selling their products found that there were fewer and fewer people able to buy hand-thrown pottery, painted lampshades, leathercraft or craft jewelry. At the same time the fashionable bare rooms – and this at least was a fashion people could afford to follow – dictated that the flat surfaces, tops of bookcases, tables, sideboards and other pieces of furniture should be free and uncluttered by a host of knick-knacks. Thus the creators and purveyors of these harmless trifles were added to the growing numbers of unemployed. Only the best craftsmen were able to survive and even they, during the thirties, had a hard struggle to keep going. When it is possible to discover the original price of a piece of pottery thrown and fired by a master craftsman the profit margin seems to have been negligible.

It needed a sense of complete dedication or a private income to keep head above water in these circumstances. In consequence there was no influx of new blood into the crafts which had already been diluted by amateurism in the twenties and brought into a somewhat contemptuous disrepute which found expression in the dismissive term 'arty crafty' with its implications of homespun tweeds and morris-dancing – the latter a particular target for satire in revues during the thirties.

The confusion of design in the late twenties and early thirties can perhaps best be illustrated by citing the state of affairs in an actual decorating firm during that period. Established in the early years of the century, this firm situated in London, had, like so many others, specialized in period reproduction designs of furniture and interior decoration. Patronized by royalty, it had had an impressive list of clients and its work had been represented at all the important international exhibitions. The standard of craftsmanship was impeccable, which meant that a considerable number of pieces of reproduction furniture made in its workshops have since become 'genuine antiques' including a version of an eighteenth-century pine-panelled room which eventually found a resting place in a museum. The design policy of the firm was controlled by the head of the drawing office who held the equivalent of the rank of director of the business. He had gained this position by seniority rather than by talent and during the twenties his staff numbered a dozen or more. By 1930 and the beginning of the Depression this had dwindled to four. Helped by the standard reference books, these draughtsmen could design and do the full-size drawings for a piece of furniture from any period from Elizabethan to late Georgian. Competent draughtsmen and versed in period ornament as they were, they had no interest at all in any other branch of the arts and even if their long working hours had permitted, felt no urge to visit exhibitions of painting, sculpture or even contemporary industrial art. In the prosperous days of the twenties, in the unlikely event of a client expressing a wish for a modern scheme the salesman would either have talked him out of it, or if unsuccessful, have sent him elsewhere. In the early thirties the picture had changed. Clients were few and far between and the financial position of the firm – even its existence – was threatened, for not many people could afford elaborate period schemes any longer. Modernism with its inexpensive simplicity was finding admirers whether through choice or necessity. This situation placed the drawing office of this firm in a dilemma. With no sympathy or training for modernism the designers had to copy examples from the few available volumes of contemporary decoration – mostly dating from the 1925 Paris Exhibition. The simple built-in furniture presented few problems but if a panel of ornament was needed they had no precedent. Consequently motifs, art déco or geometrical, were borrowed from other sources and combined into a composition which was modern in that it had no references to the periods with which the draughtsmen were familiar. This case of a real firm (with which the author had personal experience) was repeated many times elsewhere and the same circumstances applied to the firms of metal workers, plasterers, wood workers and decorative sculptors sub-contracted by architects, particularly on public buildings.

In firms such as these the design aspects of the work produced was firmly controlled by an older generation of draughtsmen and craftsmen who had entered the business before the First World War – even before 1900. Since then they had been turning out continually the same designs year after year, uninfluenced by fashion and completely unaware of developments on the Continent. With the coming of the Depression they retained their positions by virtue of long service, while junior members of the staff were dismissed or left of their own accord to branch out in other directions. Left with a staff unable to keep up with changing tasks, many of these firms foundered or were amalgamated with other concerns.

The modernist decorative style

The historicism which pervaded design in England during the twenties showed signs of giving way about 1929 to influences from the Continent and in particular from France. The few exhibitions of French or French-inspired furniture at Shoolbred's and Waring and Gillow's had introduced English designers and public alike to a version of art déco diluted with the modernism which was already superseding it on the Continent; and for a brief period there were indications of the beginnings of a distinctive English style in which the period references so dear to English taste were minimal though not entirely absent – a style which tended to dissipate as the effects of the Depression made themselves felt, though some designers, like Oliver Hill, were continuing to produce examples in this style even at the end of the decade. The use of gold and silver leaf applied to walls and ceilings had been seen in the twenties, a range of certain colours in decoration, black, jade green, coral and lemon yellow, dated from the immediate postwar years but these elements had hitherto been used in conjunction with period or reproduction furniture to create an effect which, charming in its own way, was still rooted in the past. The new feeling in the work of, for instance, Basil Ionides and Oliver Hill came from brilliant colour and specially designed furniture – even in some cases steel furniture – and a lavish use of mirrors, plain and coloured, and of metal foil. Period mouldings, cornices, dado rails or skirtings, hitherto regarded as necessary adjuncts, were either dispensed with completely or replaced with stepped mouldings or bands of fluting – a motif which in later and more austere designs became the sole relief from plain surfaces. There is however one motif which appears with variations in the work of a number of designers and in fact persists to the end of the thirties and of modernism, particularly in association with mirrors. The contrasting curves found in the walnut frames of early-eighteenth-century English mirrors and occasionally in the panelled doors of bureau-bookcases were adapted to the coloured mirror surrounds to decorative looking glasses, and in some cases for the tops of alcoves.

The renovation of 'a gloomy Early Victorian building' at Cambridge by the Australian architect Raymond McGrath was a typical example of this style and received much critical acclaim in decorating magazines. Both the exterior and the interior of the house were transformed – with the exception of one or two of the original mantelpieces – into a tribute to a legendary Scottish queen, 'Finella', 'credited by tradition with having contrived a palace all of glass and having leaped to her death in a fathomless waterfall'. Beyond renaming the house 'Finella' and incorporating a pool with a totem pole of concrete covered with Pictavian designs and carved with a double head of the queen from whose mouths jets of water sprang, the tribute was inconspicuous. A contemporary description of the entrance hall indicates the use of coloured glass and metal – 'the mansard ceiling is of silvered ribbed cast glass of a jade green colour. The pointed arch which divides the silver-leafed vault from the hall proper springs from pilasters of cast glass lit from within, the axial door has a surround of gold mirror, the walls are

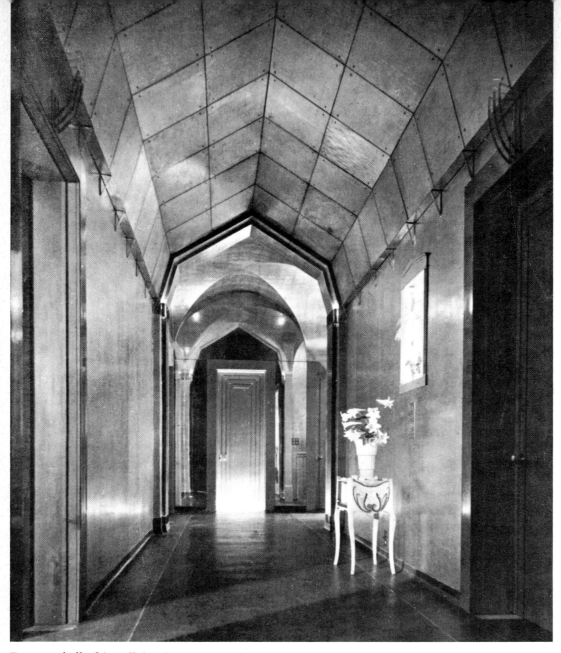

Entrance hall of 'Finella' redecorated by Raymond McGrath, 1930

The illuminated niche contains a T'ang pottery figure of a horse and rider.

silver leaf lacquered green, the floor is of black induroleum composition with a border of blue and a line of gold mosaic.'

The two pink-walled living rooms were divided by folding doors faced with copper Plymax with large handles of black nickel, set in burnished silver-leafed architraves, while the architrave of another door was replaced by a surround of black glass. The staircase featured a contrast between lemon-yellow mirror and lavender doors.

The impersonality of the larger public rooms in hotels, which can so easily become portentous, was lightened by decorators working in this style by a lavish use of shaped and engraved mirrors whose glittering faceted reflections gave an impression of animation no matter how few people were in the rooms. Oswald Milne's schemes for Claridge's Hotel have become inevitably altered with the passage of time but enough remains to indicate the luxurious elegance which characterized them when they were new in the early thirties. The primrose walls,

Lounge at Claridges Hotel, London, redecorated by Oswald P. Milne, 1930

Oswald Milne's redecoration of Claridge's Hotel with its compromise between art déco – the elaborate mirror 'drapery' and the decorative lighting ornament in wrought iron; and modernism – the geometrical design of the black and cream carpet by Marion Dorn, the angular treatment of the two smaller mirror panels and the cubist design of the furnishing fabrics – is typical of a number of interiors created about 1930 and can be compared with Oliver Hill's scheme for Gayfere House and Raymond McGrath's redecoration of 'Finella'. The specially designed carpets and the lavish use of expensive materials and accessories were conceived at a time before the effects of the Depression were being felt.

silver-grey cornices, ebonized woodwork, floors of Roman stone and black marble, the wrought-iron doors by Byron Inison incorporating glass panels by Lalique, and the boldly designed carpets contributed to a general effect eminently suitable for a luxury hotel.

A bedroom designed by Elwes Ltd and illustrated in the *Studio Year Book of Decorative Art* for 1931 further demonstrates the use of metal foil and intense colour. The caption describes 'walls hung with specially made paper in rich blue-green, mottled to represent Persian pottery: ceiling silver: floor black inlaid with silver: doors, mantelpiece and furniture of mirror. The bed is gold, hangings in blue-green shot silk lined with cerise satin.' Even this caption gives no idea of the elaboration of the four-poster bed which extended in height from a dais to

35

Entrance hall, Gayfere House, London, by Oliver Hill for Lady Mount Temple, about 1931

The sleek contemporary porcelain cats contrast with the T'ang dynasty guardian figures of demons placed on the radiator cases.

the ceiling and had an intricately carved headboard, while the doors were ornamented with outlined vases with a scrolled ornament reminiscent of a Lalique scent bottle.

In another scheme of decoration for a house in London, Elwes Ltd combined the honey brown walls of the dining room with 'Italo-Spanish' furniture, stripped and waxed, brown carpet and curtains and table top, columns with urns for indirect lighting and a mantelpiece of imitation malachite. The walls of the drawing room were shaded from deep jade green at the skirting to pale green at the cornice and the furniture covered in gold fabric, while the bedroom had gold walls, gold, silver and brown fabrics, black mirrors, a cherry carpet and a ceiling painted to represent the midnight sky.

Of all the architect-designers working in this particular manner, and they included Guy Elwes, Basil Ionides, Edward Maufe, Symonds Lutyens and Lord

36

Drawing room designed by Oliver Hill for Lord Vernon, before 1935

In this room Oliver Hill effects a compromise between the period furniture, the collection of *blanc de chine* porcelain and the contemporary feeling for simplicity by clothing the walls in weathered sycamore and designing a modernized version of the traditional bolection moulding round the fireplace. This is in polished Perrycot Portland stone edged with slips of green African Budd stone which pick out the colouring of the leaves in the painting by Gluck.

The stepped picture frame was the invention of the painter, who held a number of extremely successful exhibitions during the thirties.

Gerald Wellesley, the name of Oliver Hill occurs most frequently in the contemporary press. All the exhibitions of the thirties devoted to design incorporated a major scheme by Oliver Hill – he designed the British Pavilion at the 1937 Paris Exhibition – and in addition he created for private clients numerous schemes varying in style from the luxurious to the expensively austere. His decorations in conjunction with Lady Mount Temple for Gayfere House were widely publicized throughout the thirties and here again an extensive use was made of mirrors. The bathroom in particular was the inspiration for many others on a less extravagant scale, and colour photographs appeared in a number of books on interior decoration. Its walls completely covered in grey mirror reflected a carefully placed collection of pale blue opaline glass, the floor was of black marble, the bath and wash basin of gold mirror with taps made of Lalique motor car mascots. It must have had considerable impact, especially when it was further decorated by vases of white madonna lilies.

Oliver Hill designed another bathroom at North House, Westminster, in a somewhat similar manner, with a marble bath, boldly fluted on the outside and lined with gold mosaic, set in an alcove defined with vertical strips of mirror. Grey mirror appears again in the dining room, used as architraves and other architectural features and accentuating the walls covered in white canvas stencilled with green floral designs and the ivory-lacquered furniture.

In a music room for Sir Albert Levy, Hill collaborated with the painter George Sheringham in a scheme which illustrates Hill's penchant for experimenting in

Dining room by Oliver Hill at North House, Westminster, London, 1932

Sitting room decorated by Eric Gill for Oliver Hill, 1938

A rather late manifestation of the modernist decorative style. It is at its least austere, combining Chinese porcelain and rugs, silvered fire-dogs of seventeenth-century design, exotic veneers, book bindings and the ubiquitous lilies. The white line-drawings under plate glass on the chimney breast were by Eric Gill and their near-eroticism recalls the fact that Gill's sculpture of the naked figure of Ariel – posed for by the talented young actor Leslie French who had recently had a considerable success in this role – had to be modified before it was unveiled as part of decorations of the new Broadcasting House, London.

new materials. Laminated wood was still regarded as a novelty and had hitherto been mainly used constructionally and painted or stained. In this case Hill used sheets of laminated wood, veneered with walnut, which extended from the floor to ceiling with no pretence of their being 'period' panelling but rather resembled large leaves of screens, an effect heightened by Sheringham's decorative paintings of Chinese scenes. Niches contained a collection of carved Chinese jades.

The more erotic aspects of the work of Eric Gill were given ample scope in Oliver Hill's own house. The Portland stone slabs incised with nudes by Gill, which decorated the dining room, had been adversely criticized when they were part of the Design in Industry Exhibition in 1935. The sitting room featured more of Gill's nudes; in this case they were drawn in white outline on the charcoal grey paper which covered the chimney breast and were protected by sheets of plate glass. A noticeable feature of this room was the panelling of cedar wood with strongly marked grain in ivory colours. The built-in fitment enclosing the chaise-longue covered in bottle green velvet was veneered with macassar ebony and contained a radiogram. The ceiling was pale yellow, the curtains of grey-blue shot taffeta, and the room contained an antique Chinese rug with a yellow ground and a charcoal-coloured alcove displaying Chinese porcelain.

Darcy Bradell and Humphrey Deane, the architects of the Hon. Henry Mond's house, provided a variation on the style in the treatment of the dining room. The *Architectural Review* commented that 'although the architectural ornament is of an academic pattern, the grouping and masses are not, so that the room as a whole cannot be described as a "period" one. It has been built in direct contradiction to that school of modern decoration which owes its birth to the influence of the "Ballet Russe".' The walls were sheathed in dull polished travertine marble carved with classic Greek ornament, the doors covered with sheet pewter studded with gilt *paterae* harmonizing with the massive nickel dining table by DIM placed on a cream rug with dark brown borders, the only ornaments being antique Greek sculpture and pottery, the only notes of colour the green horsehair coverings to the sycamore chairs. Concealed illumination in the cornice gave a range of lighting effects including that of moonlight. (See page 40.)

Basil Ionides, perhaps the most original of the designers working in this style, was given full scope for his fertile imagination in the decorations for the Savoy Theatre rebuilt on the site of a former theatre, uncomfortable and dilapidated, which had in its heyday been the home of the Gilbert and Sullivan operas. Raymond McGrath was full of praise for the completed theatre, writing to the *Architectural Review* that there were 'two kinds of architecture – architecture which is lasting, simple and monumental in form and permanent in material, and architecture which is of the moment, accurate, impermanent. It is stupid to build decorated architecture to last and it is stupid to think that decorative art is not as important as that which is more monumental. Without fresh, vital, contemporary decoration everywhere, the public becomes artistically anaemic and unintelligent. . . . What we have got is our Savoy and its influence will be immeasurable without a doubt. A great many people will wake up in the morning and begin to rhapsodize about stainless steel or neon light and thus overnight are victories won.'

If the opening of the theatre had not coincided approximately with the beginnings of the Depression, McGrath's prophecy as to the immeasurable influence of the Savoy decorations might have come true. But in the years to come there were few in a position to emulate the extravagance of the scheme. The auditorium was

Dining room designed by Darcy Braddell and Humphrey Deane at Mulberry House, London, 1930

Interior of the Savoy Theatre, London, designed by Basil Ionides, 1930

entirely covered in silver leaf lacquered in different shades of gold, the metallic sheen emphasizing the detail of the deep proscenium arch which projected and embraced the auditorium in a series of recessed panels enclosing modelled designs symbolic of the historic associations of the site. The seats and the curtain were in shades of red-brown, beige and coral, a gesture toward the traditional theatre colouring of red and gold. But before reaching this splendour – now after forty years bereft of its pristine freshness – the audience had passed through the entrance doors with their bronze handles modelled by Gilbert Seale into the foyer with its decorative light fittings (also by Gilbert Seale), its gold and silver carving and its décor of black marble and mirrors.

The Whitehall Theatre built at the same time for the comedienne Marion Lorne by her husband Walker Hackett occupied a much smaller site – the stage is one of the smallest and most awkward in London – but its decorations of silver leaf contrasted with black, red and green were no less elaborate than those of the Savoy. The architects, E. Stone and Partners, seem to have been inspired in the details by Swedish examples.

The new Cambridge Theatre, built by Wimperis, Simpson and Guthrie and

Cabinet designed by Robert Printz, probably about 1935

Cabinet in dark green lacquer, possibly by Jean Dunand, on a carcass of sycamore, the shaped supports of green-finished bronze outlining the surround to the cupboard and rising to support a plate-glass shelf. A decorative piece of furniture of the finest craftsmanship, combining lacquer, bronze and glass in an unconventional design owing nothing to traditional sources.

Teapot in 'Vogue' pattern by Shelley Potteries, 1930. Plate by Duncan Grant; cup and saucer by John Armstrong; jug by Graham Sutherland; all for Foley Potteries, 1934

Boxes by Reco Capey, exhibited at the British Art in Industry Exhibition, 1935

A group of boxes in various woods. The finial in the shape of a rabbit was the first piece of perspex to be carved for decorative purposes and was the result of an experiment by Reco Capey using a sample block of perspex sent to him by the manufacturers.

Interior of the Odeon Cinema, Leicester Square, London, designed by Weeden and Mather, 1937

The demolition of the historic Alhambra Theatre, a pseudo-Moorish fantasy somewhat in the manner of the Royal Pavilion, Brighton, was a cause of regret for many and at the opening of the new cinema in 1937 the first sight of the gold and veneered wood interior with its leopard-skin-upholstered seats did little to reconcile theatregoers to the loss of former splendours.

decorated by Serge Chermayeff, was equally lavish in its use of gold leaf, the curved interior of the auditorium being treated with gold of different shades, darkening in tone on the planes furthest from the proscenium. Compared with contemporary theatres the Cambridge was austere in its absence of decorative motifs in the auditorium but the clean lines and rich surface treatment – now unfortunately repainted – had a striking effect which did not, however, prevent criticism as to the lack of ornament.

These three theatres were examples of a type of contemporary decoration which had little or no reference to historic styles, but historicism triumphed in the Phoenix Theatre, built by Gilbert Scott, Crewe and Masey and decorated by Komisarjevsky. Here the decoration was relentlessly Italian Renaissance, incorporating facsimiles painted by Polunin of frescoes of the period.

Had the theatre managers had any idea of the grim times ahead of them it is doubtful whether these theatres would have been built, or if they had the decorations would have been on a more economic scale. The theatre had suffered from the advent of the silent film but over the years the situation had adjusted itself.

Believing that nothing could replace the live theatre, theatre managers maintained the view that the talkies were a passing phase, a novelty of which the public would soon tire; and, considering the indifferent direction, acting and sound reproduction of the majority of the early talkies, there was some justification for this opinion. The new theatres, designed to attract the public away from the cinemas and to equal in magnificence the often overblown décors of the big cinemas, were capable of being adapted into cinemas themselves in the worst eventuality – it so happened that those described remained as legitimate theatres. The Depression, however, began to make itself felt about the time these theatres opened and 1930 heralded a decade of economic stress for their owners.

The deplorable demolition of the entrance to the Strand Palace Hotel, a fantasy of decorative modernism in marble, chromium and plate glass, drew attention to its designer, Oliver P. Bernard. His autobiography, *Cock Sparrow*, published in 1933 and written in the third person, ends at the close of the Great War but contains information about his early working years. Like Frank Brangwyn, Bernard spent a number of years as a sailor but his artistic training was gained as a theatrical scene painter and later designer for opera. Bernard was commissioned by Covent Garden and the Boston Opera House – it was on a trip to Boston that he survived the sinking of the *Lusitania* – mainly to design for productions of Wagner and a reproduction of a setting for Wagner's *Ring of the Nibelungs* was illustrated in the *Studio* for 1926. The accompanying caption records that Captain Oliver P. Bernard was 'the decorator responsible for the most outstanding mural decorations (outdoor and indoor) at Wembley [the British Empire Exhibition of 1924] wherein he showed very great accomplishment as a colourist and evinced a happy fertility in humorous invention.'

Bernard's training and experience of the theatre necessarily coloured his outlook when he came to the task of designing interiors for hotels and restaurants during the early thirties. Accustomed to creating a striking visual effect and then working out a method of translating this effect in terms of paint and canvas, he was less fettered by practical considerations than, for instance, an architect whose training, particularly in the period under discussion, generally tended to stifle any imaginative flights of fancy. Only a designer working in a theatrical tradition could have conceived the decoration of a restaurant (the Corner House, Tottenham Court Road, now demolished) in terms of walls covered with tapestry-like views of mountain scenery with pine forests and waterfalls carved out in differently coloured marbles. It was perhaps this theatrical element which made his work popular with the proprietors of the popular hotels and restaurants he designed – a larger-than-life bravura quality which turned anything from a cocktail to a banquet into a festive occasion in glamorous surroundings.

The entrance staircase from the street to the foyer of the Strand Palace Hotel with its illuminated glass balustrades was a smaller but more solid version of the staircase found in the final scenes of a revue at the Folies Bergère or the Casino de Paris, glittering settings for the descent of the star in sequins and ostrich plumes. His design for the Empire Room at the Trocadero Restaurant – also demolished – was rather more restrained, although his use of repeated arched openings, filled with peach-tinted glass and gilded bronze traceries, of walls faced with blond wood panelling and a dividing wall similarly decorated, which rose from the floor to partition the huge banqueting hall into two smaller but still spacious rooms, had a decorative exuberance rarely found among his more sober contemporaries.

Foyer of the Strand Palace Hotel, London, by Oliver Bernard, 1930

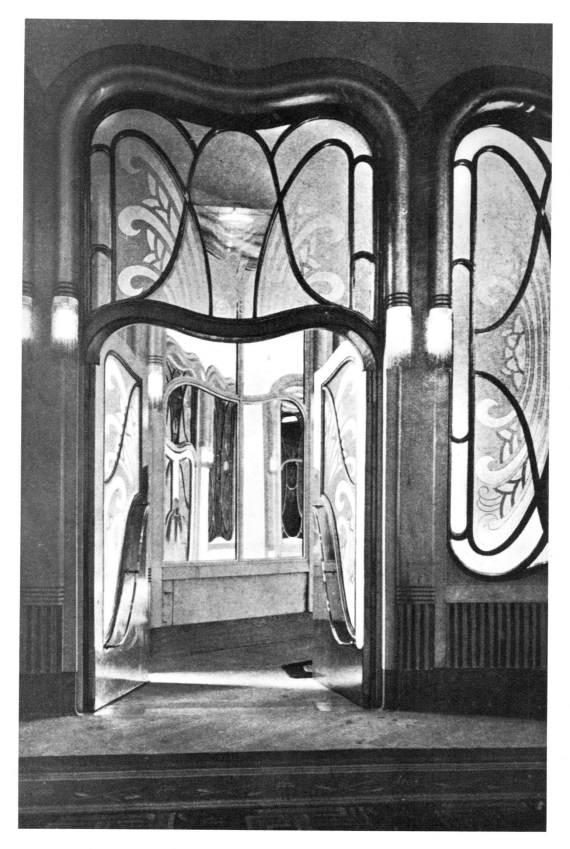

Entrance to the Empire Room, Trocadero Restaurant, London, designed by Oliver Bernard, 1930

Art and industry

Design in Modern Life was one of a number of books published in the early thirties at the height of the Depression, the effects of which upon the domestic and the export trade provided an opportunity for the advocates of a closer relationship between art and industry. More and more influential voices were to be heard preaching the doctrine that only by an increased standard of design could business improve and as the financial state of the country worsened more people were inclined to listen and to act upon their advice.

In view of the admiration for the exhibits in the Swedish Exhibition of 1930 the editor of the *Architectural Review* expressed what in his opinion were the reasons for the higher quality of decorative art in Sweden as compared to England. Apart from the benefit of having been neutral during the Great War with the advantages of being able to continue traditions of craftsmanship uninterrupted, there was a far closer degree of cooperation between Swedish designers and manufacturers than had ever been possible in England. There was also, he commented, the added benefit for the Swedes of having a royal family actively interested in the arts. The King and his brothers Carl and Oscar were all actively interested in theatre, another brother, Eugen, was a painter of considerable talent, the Crown Prince an archaeologist of repute, while Prince Sigvard designed silverware which was made by Georg Jensen. It was felt that in comparison the English royal family made a poor showing, their patronage being confined to the opening of occasional exhibitions. However, the Prince of Wales lent his support and in several speeches

Composite plywood chair by Alvar Aalto, before 1934

Upholstered chair by PLAN, before 1934

stated bluntly that 'if British trade is to hold its own in the markets of the world it must do more than maintain the technical excellence in which it has so long enjoyed leadership: it must raise the standard of design in its products, for in design it is outstripped by other countries.' Such an opinion, even coming from one who on his own admission was far from being an authority on the arts, carried weight if only because of his personal popularity.

Whether it was the result of the Prince of Wales's influence is problematical, but the practical step was taken by the government of forming a committee under the chairmanship of Lord Gorell to deal with art in industry. Their findings and recommendations were published in 1932 in what came to be generally known as the Gorell Report. Among the numerous suggestions made were that special buildings should be provided for exhibitions of industrial art in London and the provinces, each exhibition to last for at least six weeks with a permanent show of the best products of contemporary design, that there should be travelling exhibitions in both Britain and in foreign countries and – here followed the most difficult idea to implement – that there should be an improvement in the status of industrial artists, together with an active encouragement of manufacturers to use first-rate designers. Finally it was stressed that there should be better art education and research into methods and needs of industry in so far as design was concerned.

The Gorell Report had a definite response from the Bournville organization founded by the Cadbury family. In 1932 this took the form of an offer of £1000 ($2,400) a year for artists for designs suitable for use on chocolate boxes – the lack of experience in the industry being of no importance. The standard of packaging of medium-priced confectionery had been for years on the lowest level of appeal, with a stress on appealing white Persian kittens or lush herbaceous borders, while the more expensive handmade chocolates were packaged in satin boxes hand-painted with ladies in crinolines or sprays of roses. 'Chocolate box prettiness' had come to denote over-sweet charm. In order to attract a more serious type of design a competition was announced with a prize of 100 guineas ($250) – in addition to the prizes (already offered prior to the Gorell Report) awarded each year in the annual Competitions of Industrial Design organized by the Royal Society of Arts. Several hundred entries were received and a considerable number subsequently purchased. Furthermore, a prestige range of boxes was planned and a number of well-known painters were invited to submit designs. They were given a free hand and of those invited only two were rejected as being unsuitable, the remaining eleven, after being exhibited at the Leicester Galleries, being reproduced and making their appearance in the confectioners' windows in 1934. The majority of the artists invited to participate were conventional in their approach to the problems involved, but two among them were in more academic circles still regarded as *avant-garde*. Mark Gertler's contribution was a still life of fruit and flowers, colourful but betraying the waning powers of a painter succumbing to ill-health and melancholia – he committed suicide in 1939. The 'Exotic' box with a spiritless tropical view framed by curtains bore the surprising name of C. R. W. Nevinson, the solitary English futurist and recorder of the devastation of the 1914–18 war but, like Gertler, of declining power during the thirties. Others were by Arthur Watts the humorous artist, Dame Laura Knight – two contributions, a circus scene and a forcefully drawn portrait of a ballerina – Philip Connard, a decorative painter who had executed murals in Windsor Castle, George Sheringham the talented theatrical designer, Edmund Dulac, illustrator of many fairy stories, Arthur Rackham and Dod Proctor and her husband Ernest.

Electro-plated coffee set, about 1930

Probably made for an exhibition, this service demonstrates the striving after novelty which was a corollary of the new modernism.

The constant propaganda similarly influenced the makers of Foley china (see page 43) and the directors of the Royal Staffordshire Pottery to cooperate in a presentation of pottery and glassware designed by a number of leading artists – Duncan Grant, Vanessa Bell, Dame Laura Knight, Graham Sutherland, Barbara Hepworth, Mary Crofts (Dame Laura's sister), Paul Nash, Ben Nicholson, Frank Brangwyn, John Armstrong, Dod Proctor and Albert Rutherston – who were given a free hand with no restrictions. Any adjustments necessary for technical reasons or due to lack of practical experience on the part of the designers were made only after consultation with the designer concerned. The actual painting of these designs on the ware was entrusted to Clarice Cliff, creator of the 'Bizarre' designs for A. J. Wilkinson Ltd. After two years' work the finished results were shown in 1934 in an exhibition of 'Modern Ware for the Table'. In an opening speech Sir William Rothenstein commented that since Flaxman's work for Josiah Wedgwood no British artist of any standing had been asked to design china. One reason for this long separation between artist and manufacturer was of course the circumstance that not since the days of Flaxman had there been conditions of financial and industrial depression severe enough to bring together the fine and applied arts from necessity on both sides. A critical comment in the *Studio* gives a clue to another possible reason: 'It must be admitted regretfully that some of the designs were quite unsuited to the purpose for which they were intended.'

The article did continue on a more optimistic note, 'The Exhibition was of great importance as it marked the inauguration of a policy which will no doubt be extensively followed.' But in general the constant exhortations to manufacturers to improve the standards of design which came from various official and unofficial bodies and the repetition of the slogan 'Design or decline – plan or perish' by the Prince of Wales in his speeches either fell on deaf ears or, if the members of a particular industry were feeling the effects of the general depression, posed

Grand Staircase of the Paramount Theatre, Newcastle upon Tyne, designed by Charles Fox, about 1930

The pattern books of ironwork and ornamental sculpture published in Paris and recording details of exhibits in the 1925 Paris Exhibition were the obvious sources of inspiration for the decoration of this cinema foyer and staircase by an American designer. The octagonal panels, the use of a spiral motif, the leaping deer and the nude nymphs surrounded by sunrays are directly taken from French examples. The elaborate chandeliers and wall brackets were made by Best and Lloyd Ltd. The conservatory palms were probably the idea of the cinema manager.

problems which seemed insuperable. It was all very well to emphasize the importance of design but the real question was where did the manufacturers find the designers capable of creating work original and arresting enough to tempt new customers at home and abroad. Designers of little or no talent could assemble 'period' motifs with not much effort provided they had sufficient technical knowledge, but the new wave of 'modernism' was another matter.

'Manufacturers and dealers, snuffing the prevailing wind, call up their hack designers and command them to "jazz things up a bit" ', wrote Paul Nash in *Room and Book* and in many cases this jazzing-up process consisted of pirating designs from French pattern books – for there were no English equivalents from which they could adapt examples. Several examples can be found in *A Survey of British Industrial Arts*. The hammered iron grilles and the bronze balustrades carried out by Gardiner and Sons for the Forum Cinema, Bath, were obviously inspired by examples of the work of Edgar Brandt and Raymond Subes in *La Ferronerie* – a volume issued to commemorate the wrought iron and metal work in the 1925 Paris Exhibition. The conventionalized flower forms, the use of spirals and the flat bands twisted to look like crumpled ribbon are direct copies from the French prototypes and similarly a carpet by John Crossley and Sons illustrated in the same book is a coarsened version of one by Da Silva Bruhns.

Elsewhere one can find many examples of fabrics and wallpapers adapted from designs by Edouard Benedictus, Madame de Andrada and other French designers whose work appeared (reproduced in colour by the *pochoir* process) in French pattern books, despite warnings against breach of copyright. That their work would be pirated must have occurred to the artists and to the publishers but the pity is that it was usually done with such insensitivity and in such a way as to destroy all the original style and elegance.

Curtis Moffat, an American photographer who had in 1929 opened a gallery in Fitzroy Square and one of the few disciples of modernism active in England, played an important role in the British exhibit at the international exhibition at Monza in 1930. The *Studio* had proudly announced in the issue of July 1929 that the magazine had been entrusted by the Italian government with the task of organizing the British section. This was at a time when Mussolini was still generally regarded in a favourable light and the editorial staff of the *Studio* was anxious to

Cocktail cabinet by J. C. Pritchard, exhibited at the Monza Exhibition, 1930

An experimental effort to use the metal-covered plywood 'Plymax' in furniture. A somewhat unfortunate resemblance to a kitchen stove seems to have inhibited any further attempts in this direction. Plymax was however used to a certain extent architecturally – usually for interior doors.

introduce British manufacturers and their wares 'to a great and friendly nation, keenly interested in British productions, an importing and exporting country which, under the new regime, has awakened to an unexampled vigour and the prospect of brilliant developments in every sphere'. On the surface the British section appeared to have made a successful showing with exhibits by the Rowley Gallery, Edinburgh Weavers, Doultons and Gordon Russell as well as Curtis Moffat; and Mussolini congratulated the organizers after being shown round. Cook's tours were organized to bring visitors from England and it was agreed that the general standard of design was an improvement on the British exhibit at the 1925 Paris Exhibition. But an acid note creeps into the comments by the editor of the *Studio* and suggests that difficulties had been encountered in finding an adequate selection. The cooperation between manufacturers and artists common on the Continent was almost unknown in England: it was found for example, there were commercial printers in Paris who had fifty artists on their staff, whereas in England it was unusual to find even one. Several pages of photographs of the exhibits were featured in the *Studio* but even the most chauvinistic critic could not have described them as being particularly impressive, and this mediocre showing undoubtedly gave an impetus to efforts to bring about a closer cooperation between art and industry – efforts which were to culminate in the Royal Academy Exhibition of 1935.

For several seasons, since the beginning of the decade, the Royal Academy, under the presidency of Sir William Llewellyn, had organized important exhibitions during the winter of the arts of the past or of other countries. Those of the arts of Persia and of China proved particularly successful, the former revealing aspects of the artistic tradition of the Middle East which had never been shown to the general public before, while the latter, which included the greater part of the Eumorphopoulos collection, displayed a series of masterpieces of Chinese art of all periods which confirmed the long-held interest of the English in the culture of that country. This series of historical exhibitions was interrupted in 1935 when 'British Art in Industry' was chosen as the theme for the winter show. Organized under the joint auspices of the Royal Academy and the Royal Society of Arts the published theme of the exhibition had a familiar ring . . . 'to impress upon the public the importance of good design in articles of everyday use; to show not only to our own people but also to other nations that British manufacturers in cooperation with British artists are capable of producing in all branches of industry articles which combine artistic form with utility and sound workmanship; to encourage British artists to give to industry the benefit of their talents and training so that the objects with which we are surrounded in our daily lives may have an appearance which is not only attractive but is based on genuinely artistic principles.'

A great deal was written on the subject of art in industry about the time of the Burlington House Exhibition and some of the arguments put forward were optimistic in the extreme. John Milne, the chairman of the Medici Society, advanced the view that 'In so far as greater beauty in his products is achieved by the manufacturer when his wares are brought among a growing public, joy and happiness will be spread in wider and wider circles. At the same time there will take place an improvement in the average level of taste. This will in its turn lead to a demand for further improvements in all goods and wares. Thus the small beginnings of good taste and enthusiasm for beauty introduced by the more progressive manufacturers and salesmen will have the effect of leavening the

Writing desk designed by Alistair Maynard and made by Betty Joel Ltd, exhibited at the British Art in Industry Exhibition, 1935

Made of sycamore with parchment top and ivory handles, this desk is an example of the veering away from stark functionalism towards a more decorative idiom, a tendency which characterized many of the exhibits at Burlington House and which aroused sharp criticism in the case of the more extreme examples. The fluting motif was used by Alistair Maynard in another exhibit, the case for a radio-gramophone, also in sycamore, designed for His Master's Voice and made by Betty Joel Ltd. Fluting, whether concave or convex, was a device used by a number of other designers as a comparatively economical means of breaking up plain surfaces.

whole process of production and distribution and will tend towards the diffusion of greater happiness among the people through a wider appreciation of beauty.'

Such idealism inevitably drew a cynical reaction, and admirable as the aims of the organizers may have been, they were no more successful in convincing the public, artists or manufacturers than those of previous exhibitions. The annual Ideal Homes Exhibition organized by the *Daily Mail* provided a popular and

Bedroom by Alistair Maynard, 1938

An opulently feminine interior of the late thirties, modern but with period references. The painted bed with head and footboard of buttoned satin and a bedspread of quilted satin – a fabric repeated in the curtains and upholstery – the panels of mirror and the mirror-covered bedside table create an effect of luxury which is both perilously close to excess and at the same time has the impersonality of a hotel bedroom.

Alistair Maynard had a career in the British Army culminating in an appointment of ADC to the Governor of Bengal. In 1935 he opened a decorating and furnishing business in Grosvenor Street, London, and through his contacts was able to create many schemes for maharajahs' palaces in India and for their houses in London. Furniture to his designs was made by the workshops of Betty Joel Ltd.

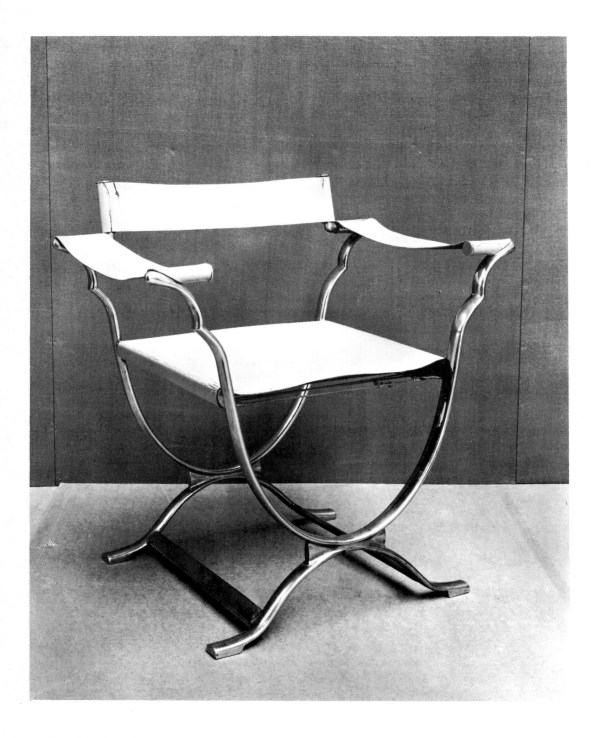

Steel and leather chair by Sir Ambrose Heal, exhibited at the British Art in Industry Exhibition, 1935

The critic Herbert Read, who found little or nothing favourable to say about the exhibition in general, in an article in the *Architectural Review* compared this chair with those designed by Marcel Breuer. Disregarding the fact that Heal may have had a completely different concept of metal furniture, Read commented that 'the beautiful curves of the Breuer chair, its simplicity and functional efficiency are replaced by senselessly scalloped arms and bowed legs, sharp points, dust traps and more than a suggestion of antiquarianism and the price has gone up to 10 guineas [$25.20].' Read had conjectured that the Breuer chair, if mass-produced could be marketed for approximately 2 guineas ($5).

Left Carpet by Ronald Grierson, exhibited at the British Art in Industry Exhibition, 1935

Right Rug in tomato pink and white, by Betty Joel, exhibited at the British Art in Industry Exhibition, 1935

spectacular opportunity for manufacturers to show their latest products to the general public but while every care was taken by the sponsor to present a lively, entertaining display, the fact remains that the exhibition was a commercial venture and any firm able to afford the hiring of a stand would be allowed to exhibit, no matter how low the standard of design of the furniture, china or fancy goods. To avoid this, the organizers of the 1935 exhibition decided that merit alone would be the deciding factor for inclusion. The unavoidable result was hostility on the part of those firms whose work had been rejected, who were naturally disinclined to learn any lessons from it. And the efforts of the organizers were received with caustic comments from the popular newspapers and from journals more directly connected with the arts and design. They could draw small comfort from the comment in the *Studio* that 'the exhibition marks a great step forward and will lead on to further advances', while *Reynolds' Illustrated News* was describing it as 'an attempt to humbug the public' and Anthony Blount in the *Spectator* was informing his readers that 'it comprised the vulgarity of Tottenham Court Road, the sham modernity of Wigmore Street, the expensiveness of Bond Street', and that it was 'a shock to find that almost every quality which disfigured industrial objects of the nineteenth century was here'. The decorative setting for the exhibition, widely publicized as having cost £20,000 ($48,000), a considerable sum of

BETTY JOEL

OF
KNIGHTSBRIDGE
(SLOANE 8205)

MODERN FURNITURE

A BETTY JOEL EXHIBIT AT THE ROYAL ACADEMY EXHIBITION OF BRITISH ART IN INDUSTRY

Bed by Betty Joel, exhibited at the British Art in Industry Exhibition, 1935

This scheme was the butt of considerable criticism which may have been caused by Mrs Joel's comment that 'the Royal Academy Exhibition of 1935, if it manages to steer clear of being an exhibition of the work of certain architects already known, should have a very far-reaching effect.' Mrs Joel designed and made the furniture for a number of film sets during the thirties, including *Love and Let Love* in collaboration with the art director Alfred Junge.

money in the thirties, and as having required the services of thirty-one experts, came in for its share of adverse comment. 'Eastern bazaars', wrote a critic in *The Times* 'about which it would have been more appropriate to boast if only £500 [$1200] had been spent.' The contribution of one of the thirty-one experts, Rex Whistler, whose reputation as a decorative artist was rapidly growing, was dismissed as 'an icing-sugar fantasy' while that of his colleagues was as severely castigated. Three of the exhibits in particular seem to have aroused the hostility of the critics. Oliver Hill's garden dining room with its engraved marble walls, marble floor and 'marble-stuc' chairs was described as 'a piece of heartless and extravagant snobbery' – a contrast to the praise which had met a rather similar dining room with engraved marble walls designed by René Lalique for the Paris Exhibition ten years before. An eccentrically shaped bed on a revolving circular platform designed by Betty Joel earned general condemnation as 'a dislocated hip-bath' while Robert Lutyens's breakfast table consisting of a circular plate-glass top suspended from the ceiling by three metal rods was greeted with a storm of abuse.

The critics seem to have taken exception to these three exhibits in particular as typifying a tendency on the part of the organizers to include the expensive and the fantastic for, in their view, 'industry should imply mass production', a conception which certainly could not be said to include marble walls, revolving beds or hanging tables. For the organizers it must be pointed out that the previous exhibitions had been financially rewarding in spite of the costs of transporting and insuring the precious objects and paintings and the attendance figures had increased with each show. They realized that the public would not flock with equal enthusiasm to a display of mass-produced articles however well designed – the practical lily had to be gilded with a certain amount of novelty to attract publicity and to give the exhibition a popular appeal. But harsh as the critical comments were – and they were not balanced by praise – there was some justification for them. A writer in the *Architectural Review* commented on the pottery, porcelain and glass sections that 'The pottery section shows a complete lack of life; there has been no improvement on the traditional forms which originated in the eighteenth century and perhaps these forms cannot be improved upon – why then lower the quality of the design by excluding them from the exhibition? . . . the decoration is timid and ineffectual', while with reference to the glass section the writer continues 'everywhere timidity, lack of inspiration, refusal to let the material have its way', ending with the faint praise that 'there is a commendable lack of cut glass of the prickly variety'. One of the organizing committee, H. S. Goodhart-Rendel, the vice-president of the Royal Institute of British Architects, gave a clue when he wrote that the idea before the selecting committee could be summarized as 'no copies and no stunts'. The exclusion of copies of past styles had been one of the rules of the Paris Exhibition of 1925. There was no clear definition of 'stunts' and some rectangular dinner plates in the pottery section were included simply because of 'their popularity in the market'. The next year the Royal Academy reverted to a historical exhibition for its winter season, though the annual exhibition of contemporary painting remained one of the highlights of the summer season.

The two associations which could have been influential in persuading or even forcing manufacturers to improve their standards of design were, in the opinion of John Gloag, so ineffectual as to be negligible. Writing in 1934, when the need for an improvement in the quality of design in British goods for export was as pressing as ever, he gives his reasons in the opening chapter of *Industrial Art Explained*. The Royal Society of Arts with a history going back to 1754 was founded for 'The Encouragement of the Arts, Manufacturers and Commerce of the Country' with rewards for inventions and improvements in industry, applied science and art, agriculture, chemistry and engineering. A later development was to inaugurate a Fund for the Preservation of Ancient Cottages. Though the RSA was the first body to identify the existence of industrial art, 'it suffers from a diversity of intention . . . it cannot encourage "the Arts, Manufacturers and Commerce of the Country" unless it is prepared to lead industry.' 'The Design and Industries Association', Gloag declared, 'could never have been formed in a really civilized country because no civilized country would have permitted industry to get into a condition in which its products were so fantastically inept that many manufacturers had to be reminded that fitness for purpose was a basic principle of design in everything.' Founded in 1915, any progress it might have made was crippled for lack of funds, though it had some small influence through propaganda for the doctrine of 'fitness for purpose'.

The basic tenets of 'fitness for purpose' were, of course, perfectly sensible. Obviously a teapot, for instance, should pour without dribbling, hold the heat of its contents and be easy to clean (although, incidentally, some of the square tea-pots designed in the new spirit failed to do any of these things), and so on with all objects made for a functional purpose. But the propaganda tended to harp too much upon industry, to mention too often the word machine, and in the public mind associations were aroused with the film *Metropolis* with its alarming (at the time) world of machinery and servant human robots or with the much-publicized phrase of Le Corbusier 'a home is a machine for living in' and other slogans connected with design, and particularly with architectural design, which were circulated 'to comfort bright young people who wanted to be aesthetically modish without the fatigue of thinking'. The logical argument that because an article was made by a machine it should not look as though it had been made by hand became slanted to the view that it should look like a machine. As Gloag pointed out, 'mechanical forms are used as patterns for textiles and wallpapers: they provide inspiration for the mechanistic baroque style of a decoration but they do not represent a real industrial contribution to design.' The reformers and advocates of fitness for purpose condemned the mass-produced ornament applied during the nineteenth century after the Industrial Revolution and were resistant to the fact that, however wrong it may have been in theory, in practice much of it had great charm. Unhappily they had no substitute to offer. Simple unadorned geometrical shapes, whether in furniture or pottery, had a limited appeal for the English buying public which, in the main, dearly loved a nice pink rose, and patriotism itself had to be used as a selling point, for instance in the case of the 1931 advertise-ment by Best and Lloyd, whose modernistic table lamp is captioned 'Modern – but English'. It is ironic that at the time when the purists were condemning Victorian designers as being the original culprits for the poor standards of design current in 1930, fashion was already turning its attention to Victoriana. Curtis Moffat denounced the reconstruction of the Victorian room as 'an amusing exercise in horror' in 1931. In the same year an article in *Vogue* was entitled 'The Victorian Age Returns' – and within a few years many of Curtis Moffat's clients were to be enthusiastically collecting buttoned furniture, papier-mâché and shell flowers under glass shades.

Another fact that the enthusiasts for fitness for purpose tended to forget is that an original piece of design, however theoretically functional that design may be, is still a reflection in some way or another of the time in which it was made and consequently governed by the laws of fashion. This does not apply to objects the design of which is the result of decades or even hundreds of years of use, where the form and design have been evolved by constant modifications or imperceptible alterations. Anything from a piece of furniture to an egg-cup fashioned according to the theories of functional design in, say, 1932 will look old-fashioned a few years later, no matter how chaste the form or how little ornamented, and it was this factor that made many people hesitate to favour modernism to any great extent – apart from the fact that such a step would entail their getting rid of posses-sions which were likely to interfere with the over-all functional look. Consequently when Regency and, at a later date, Victorian furniture and ornaments emerged from the no-man's-land of unfashionableness and were once more allowed to become objects for admiration – even if that admiration had a flavour of amused patronage – they were acclaimed because the question of their being dated or old-fashioned no longer applied any more than it did to Queen Anne or Chippendale furniture. By collecting Victoriana one demonstrated an awareness of trends without running the risk of finding oneself living in *démodé* surroundings – the Victoriana could only become more antique and consequently respectable with time.

Meanwhile in America the Metropolitan Museum of New York was indefatigable in its efforts to further a *rapprochement* between fine and industrial art, from its first Exhibition of Industrial Art in 1917 when most, if not all, of the exhibits were designed with objects in the museum collection as inspiration. For the next eight years the same principle was followed but in 1924 it was noted that there were a small number of pieces which owed nothing to historical references and in 1925 the museum purchased a selection of the best exhibits from the 1925 Paris Exhibition. In 1927 the display was limited to American products designed and made by American residents while two years later the exhibits were custom-made contemporary pieces. Possibly as a result of the Depression, from 1930 the exhibition consisted entirely of artefacts obtainable on the market and in 1934, as a result of the cooperation of nineteen leading architects and designers, the strictly contemporary designs on exhibit proved so popular that no less than 139,000 people attended the exhibition.

Decorators

During the twenties the profession of interior decorator in the sense of one who specializes in designing or choosing the decorations, furnishings and lighting in agreement with the client, whether for a new building or for an old one, was too new a conception for most architects to accept with any seriousness. Many architects of an older generation specializing in domestic design were given the responsibility for the design of the interiors by their clients. Alternatively this was entrusted to designers attached to the big decorating firms – this was especially the case where the fashionable reproduction period panelling was concerned. As for the furniture, the clients would either possess all that was necessary, whether genuinely antique or, as was more likely, reproduction, or they could order it from one of the big decorating firms. The postwar boom in low-priced building brought a new generation of architects whose main interest was confined to the external appearance of the house and in making a pleasing arrangement of windows or other architectural features on the outside they often paid little attention to the effects such a treatment might have on the inside. In a neo-Georgian house, for example, a formal drawing room could have the windows or doors asymmetrically and awkwardly arranged, the chimney breast could be out of centre or – a very common occurrence – the windows placed right in the corner of the room with no room left for curtains. Rarely if ever was there any consultation between the architect and the interior designer before the plans were finalized.

The purpose underlying the competition announced in the *Architectural Review* in May 1930 was to interest architects in the practical aspects of interior decorating and also in the possibilities of using the work of contemporary design-craftsmen, some of whom had had a struggle to survive during the twenties and whose working existence was threatened by the Depression.

Rarely has a competition stipulated so many conditions for the entrants to contend with; though, as will be seen, the rules were not too strictly observed. However, the prizes of £100, £50 and £25 ($240, $120, $60) were considerable inducements in 1930 and in addition the prizewinners were promised the prestige and publicity of having their designs built and exhibited in Waring and Gillow's showrooms. The competitors were required to design the decorations and furnishings for a drawing room and adjoining dining room (which could be either separate or combined in one large room) for an imaginary client, Lord Benbow, a Clydeside shipbuilder ennobled for his public services to the City of Glasgow. The rooms were to be part of his London home in bachelor apartments near Curzon Street where on occasions his sister acted as hostess – his lordship being a widower.

Born in a London suburb some sixty years before, Lord Benbow had spent many years in Glasgow and was thus acquainted with the work of Charles Rennie Mackintosh, though this enthusiasm for the work of the Glasgow school had changed into a devotion for the later developments of the modern movement. Here it must be pointed out that it was unusual to consider in 1930 that the work of Charles Rennie Mackintosh was something to be admired. In order to spread his patronage as widely as possible Lord Benbow wished to commission several artists to collaborate. Some furniture by Thomas Hope might be incorporated; and, as Lord Benbow was the owner of a stud farm and a racing stable, the portrait of a Derby winner could be included as well. It was hoped that the effect achieved would be 'gracefully sporting'.

The conditions of the competition have been quoted at length as a reflection of the common tendency of the time to accuse schemes designed by interior decorators of lacking personality or being designed in accordance with the decorator's taste rather than that of the client. This was undoubtedly true of some of the modernistic interiors of the early thirties, but with the imaginary Lord Benbow the organizers of the competition posed problems that would have taxed the ingenuity of the most experienced professional designer.

Any hopes that new talents would be discovered were dashed when the announcement was finally made, for the first, second and third prizewinners were all designers whose names and work were very familiar to regular readers of the journal, though only the first had had any architectural training, the others being painters and textile designers.

The first prize was awarded to Raymond McGrath, whose scheme included rugs by McKnight Kauffer, fabrics by Paul Nash, paintings and wallpapers by Edward Bawden and sculpture by Maurice Lambert, and the jury made little comment on what was a pleasant but not outstanding conception which, like the designs of the other prizewinners, made only the slightest acknowledgement to the tastes of Lord Benbow.

Paul Nash's second-prize-winning design with furniture and fittings by Denham Maclaren, paintings by Edward Wadsworth and textiles by Paul Nash, received the comment that it was a 'design made faintly ridiculous by the fact that the artist either misunderstood the purpose of the remarks regarding Lord Benbow's sporting tastes or surrendered to his sense of humour'. Certainly the treatment of the doors, the wall brackets in the shape of cricket stumps made from tubular lights, the electric radiator disguised as a football, the armchairs designed as cricket pads and the folding screens of tennis netting suggest Nash had his tongue in his cheek and here again there is no sign of the Derby winner, the Thomas Hope furniture, or Charles Rennie Mackintosh. (See page 64.)

The choice of the scheme submitted by Vanessa Bell in collaboration with Duncan Grant for the winner of the third prize is surprising in view of the editorial comment that 'the competitor has shown a still greater contempt for the plan produced by Lord Benbow and one feels that with very little alteration the same scheme could be carried out in almost any kind of room.' Mrs Bell's décor, with carpets and curtains by Humphrey Slater, sculpture by John Skeaping and furniture and light fittings by Robert Medley, was more reminiscent of Bloomsbury than Mayfair, of the Omega Workshops than the racing stable, and it goes without saying that in this scheme also there was no provision made for the portrait of the Derby winner. After the bare announcement of the winners' names and the comments of the judges, the *Architectural Review* seems to have considered the matter closed and there is no record of the winning designs ever having been built or exhibited.

In the same year the *Studio* took a more practical step by giving its readers a summary of 'The 1930 Look in British Decoration', featuring the work of three decorators, each working in a completely different manner from the others and each with an individual approach to the subject.

The designs of Francis Bacon, described as 'a young English decorator who has

Paul Nash's entry for the 'Lord Benbow' competition in the *Architectural Review*, 1930

worked in Paris and in Germany for some years and is now established in England', were demonstrated by photographs of his studio 'formerly an uninteresting garage' and now completely transformed with its windows curtained in white rubber sheeting. The furniture, its horizontal accents marked by long tubular steel handles somewhat reminiscent of towel rails, was painted in shades of grey with tops of black and white glass and shows the influence of De Stijl. The two large unframed circular mirrors lit by tubular glass bulbs were probably the forerunners of the many circular mirrors incorporated in modernistic dressing tables during the thirties. The tubular steel stools and tables with circular tops of half-clear, half-mirror glass had a chill chic and bring to mind the caption under a photograph of steel furniture in an advertisement published by Heals in 1930 – 'Suggested ideas for the Highbrow'. Displayed on the walls were rugs designed by Bacon in tones of grey, beige, brown and black, handsome rugs described as owing nothing to traditional or Oriental styles – 'they are purely thought forms'.

In contrast to this was 'a room of outstanding beauty, rich in colour, harmonious in design', the dining room decorated by Duncan Grant and Vanessa Bell for Lady Gerald Wellesley. Mainly grey in colouring, the room had six large panels with two smaller panels flanking the fireplace, freely painted with alcoves in which nude adults and children were grouped. The octagonal table, the chairs and the mantelpiece, were decorated in characteristic designs and borders of coloured spots and circles. It cannot be said that these paintings were Duncan Grant's most successful works, the painted alcoves are too low for their width with the consequence that the figures fit uncomfortably into them.

The third scheme, representing another aspect of British decoration, was the sitting room and dining room designed for his own home by Serge Chermayeff, the Director of the Modern Art Department at Waring and Gillow's. This was a

Rug by Francis Bacon, 1930

conversion of what appears to be the ground floor of an early Victorian house, the two rooms separated by sliding doors veneered in walnut, with the grain horizontal as in the rest of the fitted cupboards and the ubiquitous round-ended cocktail cabinet. A mural by Alexander Bayes on a theme popular in the early thirties as an appropriate one for modernist interiors – that of the skyscraper of a city of the future – filled the wall over the flush electric fire. An interesting contrast was provided by the dominant horizontal of the figured wood and the circular motifs of the rugs, the lampshades and the small table. The dining room, which could become a part of the other room when the large sliding doors were open, had plain walls and tubular steel chairs.

This contrast between rectangular shapes and circles can be seen again in a room designed by David Pleydell-Bouverie and dating from 1930 – a room which like so many of the period gives the impression that its purpose was to be perpetually filled with people drinking cocktails, the women in sleek bias-cut dresses outlining the figure and ornamented solely by a pair of geometrical diamond clips, the men in dinner jackets with smooth brilliantined hair and the Bulldog-Drummond air of weariness from a long day playing polo. Everything has been reduced

Interior by David Pleydell-Bouverie, 1930

to a basic simplicity, the design of the walnut furniture pared down to essentials with even the grain of the veneers selected for its lack of exoticism: the plain tweed upholstery repeats the deep amber of the walls but in a slightly darker tone. What might have resembled the impersonality of a superior dentist's waiting room is, however, brought to life by the bold design of McKnight Kauffer carpets which bring together the rectangular and circular shapes of the tables and chairs in a geometrical composition carried out in *tête-de-nègre*, beige and sand colours.

Raymond Cogniat, in an article on the decorative arts written in 1932 for the magazine *L'Amour de l'Art* put forward the theory that during the nineteenth century the decoration of interiors was dominated by cabinet-makers and upholsterers, in 1920 by dressmakers and in 1930 by architects. This was certainly true at the time Cogniat wrote his article, though architects were to be ousted from their leading positions in a very few years time, to be replaced by designers for the theatre, dressmakers and the new generation of interior decorators.

During the thirties the rapidly changing social conditions brought about the end of the monopoly of the decorating profession by the big firms of furnishers and decorators and the triumphant rise of a new profession – that of interior decorator. In the previous decade voices had been raised, notably those of contributors to the *Studio*, deploring the influence over their clients of the salesmen in the big firms, salesmen dependent upon augmenting a minimal wage by commission on sales. With a vested interest in selling antique furniture, whether genuine or reproduction, and in persuading their clients to order expensive panelling and elaborate plasterwork as a setting for their furniture, they were naturally the enemies of any innovations in style. In the hard times of the thirties, these big establishments found it increasingly difficult to maintain their overheads, with the consequence that the staffs in the drawing offices, as well as the less persuasive salesmen, found themselves redundant. Many of these drifted into other forms of employment or to a life on the dole, but the younger and more adventurous ones with a small capital set up as freelance decorators. Added to these were young people with artistic leanings who ordinarily might have become painters or sculptors but with hardly anyone buying pictures or sculptures by established names, let alone by unknown beginners, interior decoration offered an attractive alternative. Rents were low and premises with good addresses readily available. The requirements were few: a good appearance – ugly interior decorators had to rely upon talent – a fund of small talk, the ability to last out at interminable cocktail parties and a reputation for that mythical quality 'natural good taste', which was regarded as a substitute for ability. The rewards could be an active social life, a circle of wealthy clients and even a rich wife or husband. These decorators were described by Paul Nash as 'charming young men and formidable ladies . . . hopping backwards and forwards between England and the Continent on the benefit of the Exchange. In their homeward flight they seldom failed to carry back something for the nest, a piece of stuff from Paris, a German lamp, a steel chair or just a headful of other people's ideas.'

If these charming young men and formidable ladies had some ability for drawing and painting they could alternatively earn a meagre living as decorative artists under the patronage of interior decorators, or dealing directly with their clients. As few interior decorators could draw, let alone design, there was always a need for renderings in watercolour of proposed schemes of decoration or of single pieces of furniture to give the client an approximate idea of the finished result. Others existed by painting furniture with decorative floral arrangements or with landscapes, especially in the later thirties when honest pieces of Victorian furniture were painted in the fashionable pastel shades, decorated with baroque motifs and treated to give a *craquelure** to the paint. There was also the occasional commission to paint a four-fold screen with a design in the manner of Rex Whistler, but the fashion for silk lampshades painted with a reproduction of the design on the *famille rose* or Meissen vase converted into a lamp had, in the main, died with the twenties.

If anything Paul Nash understated in using the word 'formidable' to describe the women interior decorators. The generation of women who in the postwar years had been desperately and hopefully trying to earn a living from the decorative arts were mostly inexperienced in business and totally unprofessional, gentlewomen to the last with their sad leather bookmarks, pixie ornaments made out of pine cones, powder bowls decked with barbola flowers, rolled-paper bead necklaces and photograph frames decorated with swirls of sealing wax. There were a few skilled craftswomen whose talents were considerable enough to enable them to survive into the thirties: Stella Crofts who modelled vigorous and unsentimental animals in pottery; the textile printers Dorothy Larcher, Enid Marx and Phyllis Barron; Sybil Dunlop whose silver jewelry set with multicoloured semiprecious stones had – and still has – echoes of the Italian Renaissance and Ashbee's School of Handicrafts, and Dorrie Nossiter whose jewels were described as 'Poetry made precious'. But these were exceptional and the majority of the pathetic courageous figures had faded with the twenties. In their place appeared a new generation of lady decorators who, from necessity as much as inclination, developed qualities of toughness that would have embarrassed Attila. Some had social connections through birth or marriage, some, even more advantageously, had titles, but all had an unshakeable belief in their own taste and talent. Ruthless with their clients, they were often completely unscrupulous in their dealings with the cabinet-makers, upholsterers, painters and other technicians they employed – craftsmen who in the hard days of the thirties could not afford to offend no matter how often requests for settlement of long-outstanding bills were loftily ignored. Woe betide a client who bought anything from a rival decorator – by the lift of an eyebrow they could insinuate that the object was a shoddy fake, an error of taste, absurdly expensive and that the morals of the rival decorator were highly suspect.

The rivalry and mutual distrust between decorators at this period can be summed up in a true story in which the protagonists must, of necessity, remain anonymous. A celebrated woman decorator, whom we will call x, had her premises immediately opposite those of another decorator, y. Finding her stock of choice pieces of decorative furniture running low, x would on occasion cross the road and in y's absence choose some of his best pieces to the tune of, say, £1000 and they would immediately be transferred to her own showroom. Knowing perfectly well from past experience that x had little or no intention of paying without actually being sued, y would, in his turn, wait until x had gone to lunch and then select from her stock items to the value of £1100, leaving a cheque for the difference.

Paul Nash's comment about 'a headful of other people's ideas' pinpoints a problem which became increasingly pressing after the date (1932) when he wrote. For professional reasons a decorator was anxious to have a recently completed scheme, whether for one room or a whole house, featured at some length in one or more of the prestige magazines. The editors of these journals were only too

* See page 81.

glad to collaborate if the work had been done for a celebrity, as they found that their readers gained a vicarious pleasure from a peep into the homes of the famous – it was during the late twenties and thirties that it became socially acceptable for titled women to endorse beauty products in fashion magazines, for a fee. But at the same time readers took these pictures to their decorators with the request that a piece of furniture, a fabric or decorative effect, should be copied and, as a result, the first decorator and his client found to their dismay that original creations were being widely and often badly plagiarized.

Arundell Clarke

It would have been difficult, however, to find much to copy in the few photographs which appeared in periodicals advertising the interiors designed by Arundell Clarke. It is recorded that he exhibited his designs at the Ideal Home Exhibition of 1930 under the name of 'Charm', an inappropriate pseudonym which he soon abandoned. His original premises were situated at 71 Royal Hospital Road, Chelsea, but a growing clientele enabled him to make a move to a more modish address, 18 Bruton Street, Mayfair, where an all-white showroom displayed the widely publicized 'Arundell Clarke Easy Chair' capable, it was claimed, of accommodating five people at one time, two on each broad arm and one unfortunate person in the usual seat. This elephantine chair was sold in considerable numbers covered in the currently fashionable 'amusing' fabrics, off-white sailcloth or plain heavy cotton or woollen fabrics dyed dark brown, ice blue or navy blue, the last a colour much favoured by Arundell Clarke. Another speciality was a large square ashtray of cast glass which was sold for 7s 6d (90c).

The text of an Arundell Clarke advertisement widely published in 1933 is worth quoting as a reflection of the scarcity of money at the time: 'There are people who think that because the modern style of furnishing is so beautiful it must therefore be expensive. Nothing could be further from the truth. Modern design gets its lovely effect from the use of space and light and an intense simplicity of form and textures. I could furnish an entire "modern" room for what the Victorians would have spent on curtains and carpets alone! Write for my new catalogue or call. My shop is open until 7 o'clock.' The accompanying photograph shows the corner of a white room (actually one of the showrooms) entirely devoid of any mouldings, a bare polished floor, the windows draped with rather skimpy unlined curtains, the only furniture being a settee and one of the famous armchairs covered in white material, and a small plain table supporting a baluster-shaped china vase adapted as a lamp with a plain metallic shade. The only break in this almost monastic severity is offered by an arrangement of white lilies. Such a scheme was obviously Arundell Clarke's personal conception of the perfect interior and one which he was able to persuade some of his clients to commission, but judging from other examples of his work he was obliged to conform to the more general demand for built-in furniture, simple in outline and veneered with the decoratively grained woods so much in use. This aspect of his work was featured on a number of occasions by the German magazine *Innen Dekoration* edited by Alexander Koch.*

* Clarke and Ian Henderson were the only two English decorators of note whose work was examined in this periodical during the thirties – the French decorator Jean Royère was also the subject of several articles.

Emile-Jacques Ruhlmann

The sudden death of Emile-Jacques Ruhlmann in November 1933 robbed French craftsmanship of one of its finest exponents and one worthy of comparison with Weisweiler, Reisener or Jacob. The fifty-four-year-old doyen of decorators was at the height of his powers and still enjoying the reputation which had been anticipated in 1913 at the time of his first exhibition at the Salon d'Autumne and confirmed in 1919 when, in collaboration with Laurent, he opened in business. Throughout the twenties the name of Ruhlmann was synonymous with a luxurious combination of fine design, rare materials and consummate craftsmanship. The most precious veneers, exquisitely applied, were enhanced by ivory, coral, shagreen or the finest leather; these precious pieces of furniture were themselves displayed against backgrounds of silk, velvet, satin, damask or leather. His exhibit at the 1925 Paris Exhibition was much discussed as being a summing-up of the best of the current style, as Bing's Maison de L'Art Nouveau had been in 1900. He had his imitators as any great innovator has, but nobody came within measuring distance of his taste, style and elegance. Ruhlmann's clientele was extremely rich and he was totally uninterested in creating furniture and décors for any but the extremely rich – for him there was only the best in materials and craftsmanship. No less than sixteen draughtsmen were in his studio engaged in transplanting his sketches into reality. He employed only the most skilled workmen and retained their services by paying more than the usual rates – in return he expected them to be at the top of their form all their working hours.

The Depression made little difference to Ruhlmann's career. His work was constantly in demand by private clients as well as the French government which engaged him to design for their embassies – which, like the luxury liners, they regarded as showcases for the best in French art and craftsmanship. One of the last commissions he executed was the dining room in the French embassy in Tokyo, the long dining table showing the tendency toward the monumental which was characteristic of Ruhlmann's later works. During the previous year he had exhibited his latest models in conjunction with works of art of the seventeenth and eighteenth centuries to stress the classical quality of his furniture – a chromium and marble console supported a bust by Caffieri while an ebony cabinet was placed below a portrait by Largillière.

In the same year he created a décor for the theatre – possibly his only essay in this branch of decorative art. The play *Christine* by Paul Geraldy was presented at the Comédie Française in December 1932 and each act showed different aspects of the same room, which was represented by a curtain extending around the stage and looped up at different places to indicate various entrances or windows. To set off his furniture Ruhlmann insisted upon this curtain being of a certain shade of grey-beige and hundreds of yards of material was specially woven, dyed and presented to the production by Paul Rodier (for whom Ruhlmann had in 1931 decorated a library in oak panelling with macassar ebony furniture covered in tobacco-coloured velvet). In collaboration with Reco Capey, Ruhlmann designed the interior of premises in Old Bond Street for Yardley, the scent manufacturers. This scheme was replaced after the war but a number of pieces of the original furniture designed by Ruhlmann survived and were presented by Yardley to Brighton Museum to mark the two-hundredth anniversary of the firm.

In November 1934 Madame Ruhlmann organized a retrospective exhibition of her late husband's work at the Pavillon de Marsan. With no little difficulty she succeeded in gathering together examples of the most celebrated models he had

Entrance doors in gilt bronze by Reco Capey for Yardley, 1932

The lacquer work and textile designs of Reco Capey were recorded in the *Studio* during the twenties and thirties, and in the latter decade he was appointed artistic designer and consultant to Yardley. 'Junius' in an article in the *Architectural Review* for 1931 devoted considerable space to an appraisal of new compacts and bottles used by the firm, with the comment that the name of the designer was withheld by the managing director. In 1932 Capey collaborated with Ruhlmann in a complete scheme of redecoration for the offices and showrooms and although subsequent redecoration has taken place, some pieces of furniture are still in existence, in the Victoria and Albert Museum, London, and in the Brighton Museum.

Macassar and ebony table by Emile-Jacques Ruhlmann, about 1930; with a group of boxes by Reco Capey (for details see colour illustration page 43)

created during the past twenty-five years from the light, delicately inlaid and gracefully curved pieces of the early twenties to the last essays in the combination of steel, chromium, glass and wood.

Syrie Maugham

Syrie Maugham's name is invariably associated with all-white schemes and she is usually credited with inventing the idea of colourless rooms. Doubts and even forceful denials have since been expressed by contemporaries and certainly white rooms were being done by other decorators, including Arundell Clarke and Jean-Michel Frank, at the same time, though the difficulty, if not impossibility, of establishing the exact dates when comparable white schemes were completed leaves the question a matter of speculation. What can be established is that Basil Ionides in *Colour and Interior Decoration* in 1926 was giving advice about schemes which combined white or ivory walls, paintwork and ceilings with white or black floors, white curtains of satin, bolton sheeting or alpaca, white horsehair upholstery and ornaments and lamps of Leedsware, white Wedgwood, *blanc de Chine* and white opaque glass. Ionides, in the introduction to a chapter on white rooms, commented that with the improvement of modern paints, enamels and distempers 'the old saying that white decoration is the last resort of people with no taste can no longer be accepted as true'. From the evidence of many with first-hand information the impression is gained that Mrs Maugham was more of an impresario than an originator, combining a flair for adaptation with an acute sense of publicity.

Bedroom by Eugène Printz for the Princesse de la Tour d'Auvergne, 1930

This scheme was exhibited at the 1930 Salon des Décorateurs and drew from Guillaume Janneau the comment that such a 'remarkable combination . . . prompts us to query whether it is a drawing room or a boudoir. The pieces are designed in modern, rational forms: rare woods ingeniously allied with metal supports, lids that slide, tip or pivot, subtle colouring: the imagination of a *modiste* with the precision of an engineer.'

Such an exhibit exemplifies the custom, unknown in England, of French decorators allowing the general public to view either the actual scheme or a reproduction of work commissioned by distinguished patrons.

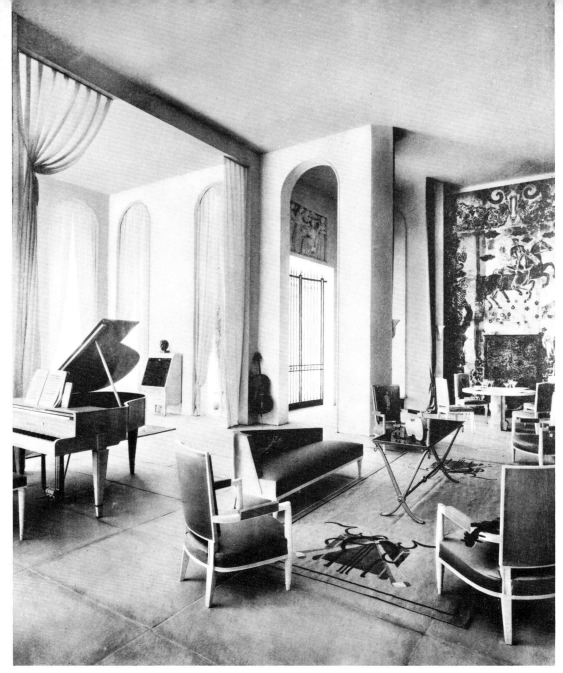

'Demeure en *Ile-de-France*' by André Arbus, exhibited at the Paris Exhibition, 1937

In 1931 André Arbus was the director of L'Epoque, working somewhat in the tradition of Ruhlmann but lacking the restraint and sobriety which characterized the latter's work. While more influenced by the past than by contemporary themes, Arbus's work was criticized on the grounds that the sinuous, calligraphic lines of his furniture were not always happily conceived, his chairs in particular often giving a somewhat precarious sense of balance. In the later thirties he adopted the more serenely classical style of the late eighteenth century and in some cases, particularly in some work he did in the theatre, appears to have been influenced by the designs of Ledoux.

Harper's Bazaar devoted an article in October 1929 to her Chelsea house, and Pollard Crowther illustrated it with soft-focus photographs reminiscent of those of Baron de Meyer – also a contributor to this particular issue. Entitled 'Mrs Somerset Maugham's White House', the article describes the music room as having white walls, white satin curtains, white satin slip covers to the furniture, white lilies, white velvet lampshades and a pair of white porcelain camellia trees about four feet high 'the joy of the owner's heart and the envy of her friends'. A corridor was enlivened with sheets of antique mirror and green and white painted wall hangings – a scheme almost duplicating one by Oliver Hill at North House.

Bedroom decorated by Herman Schrijver and executed by Elden (London) Ltd for Mrs Ernest Guinness, 1935

Herman Schrijver's interiors combined antique and modern furniture to achieve an effect of luxurious comfort. Discreet and without any strivings after theatrical effects, this type of decoration was, in fact, preponderant and strictly speaking has more claim than any other to the term International Style, for with minor variations this highly expert blending of new and old was created by the best — and least publicized — decorators in England, France and the United States during the thirties. It still has many adherents.

The stripped and waxed pine panelling of the dining room with its rock crystal appliqués was a setting for white-painted chairs, the dining table being covered to the floor with an ivory fillet lace tablecloth upon which were arranged white flowers and white porcelain — Mrs Maugham brought back into fashion white-porcelain-handled knives and forks. The furniture shown in the illustrations to *Colour and Interior Decoration*, *Simple Schemes for Decoration* by John Gloag and various articles in women's magazines of the twenties is invariably either 'brown' furniture — that is, of polished wood — or nondescript pieces of painted furniture of no particular character. Syrie Maugham conforms to this general pattern in the décors mentioned, except that some of the pieces are of Continental origin and the brown furniture like the panelling has been stripped and waxed.

Mrs Maugham's all-white drawing room which received considerable publicity in 1933 has more of the modern atmosphere, with its long plain settees upholstered in beige satin, a modern rug with a raised pile in a key pattern woven in two tones of cream by Marion Dorn and a striking tall screen made of very narrow panels of mirror set in chromium-plated frames. Three Louis XV chairs, painted and upholstered in off-white, form a group round a backgammon table and the problem of dealing with the grand piano is partly solved by concealing it behind

Entrance hall by Syrie Maugham, about 1939

Syrie Maugham here deviates rather markedly from her declared principle of elimination. With the exception of the large wall mirror nothing in this scheme has any claim to quality and every piece from the figures of blackamoors to the rope-stools – probably originally gilded – appears to have been ruthlessly repainted. The dolphin console table has been supplied with a faceted mirror top. The bold stripes of the *moiré* wallpaper and the profusion of furniture and ornaments indicate that Mrs Maugham had abandoned the simplicity of her all-white period.

a low eight-fold screen lacquered white. 'Such a scheme is practical and need not be expensive', wrote Derek Patmore in *Colour Schemes for the Modern Home*, although the practicability of such a white room in London could be doubted and the mirror screen which gave so much character to the room could not have been particularly inexpensive. According to one person who had acquaintance with it, this screen was a hazardous piece of decoration as the composition holding the long thin strips of mirror in position tended to melt if the room became warm, and pieces of glass would fall off without any warning.

Although Mrs Maugham's interiors were often described as including dead white and cream, these two shades were, according to a former colleague, anathema to her and during the all-white phase (which, in fact, lasted only a comparatively short time) she used every variation of white, ivory, pearl, oyster, parchment etc., except the hard and unflattering dead white, or cream with its associations of suburbia.

'Elimination is one of the secrets of successful decoration', Syrie Maugham is quoted as saying in an article in the *Studio* in 1933 but it was not a precept to which she adhered too strongly. With a staff and overheads, any interior decorator bent on eliminating everything unnecessary from a decorative scheme is headed for financial ruin – even Jean-Michel Frank's apparent simplicity masked a use of expensive materials. As the thirties advanced Mrs Maugham's interiors tended to become more and more filled with decorative furniture and ornaments which were charming and fantastic but were really superfluous, for instance the shell

Syrie Maugham's own drawing room, 1933

Bedroom scene in *Helen!* setting by Oliver Messel, 1932

Charles Cochran's version of *La Belle Hélène* was one of the notable productions of the decade. With new lyrics by A. P. Herbert and choreography by Leonide Massine, Max Reinhardt's production gave Oliver Messel a full-scale opportunity to decorate a production in the baroque tradition of the Bibbiena family and the bedroom scene in particular, executed entirely in white — as was most of the production — caused a sensation by its originality and elegance.

groups made by the Comtesse Hervé de la Morinière for which Syrie Maugham was the London agent in 1937. These were composed of several large polished seashells with clusters of smaller shells fixed into a group with green-tinted plaster and could be used as decorative centrepieces for dining tables, and for little else. They were however soon copied in quantity and enjoyed a considerable vogue.

1932 was the year when the white craze reached its height — a craze epitomized in the look of the film star Jean Harlow, who appeared to have been constructed of equal parts of snow, marble and marshmallow. White beach wear was *de rigueur* for holidays on the Riviera and white evening dresses formed the greater part of the Paris collections. Oliver Messel's white décors and especially the baroque bedroom scene, were a sensation in *Helen*, a memorable presentation by C. B. Cochran of Offenbach's *La Belle Hélène*.

By 1934 the all-white room had gone out of fashion, according to a writer in the *Architectural Review*. In that year Mrs Maugham sold her house at Le Touquet and concentrated on the interior decorating business which since about 1930 had been at 2 Wyndham Place, Davies Street, and finally moved in 1934 to Paradise Walk, Chelsea. For the next five years she was extremely active and extended

Spanish bed, about 1720

The eighteenth-century Spanish bed in the Victoria and Albert Museum served as a model for innumerable modern beds during the later years of the twenties and most of the thirties. Apart from direct copies of the original in mahogany with the headboard carved in relief with sprigs of flowers following the curved outline and with the curious double cabriole corner supports for the bedding at the foot (many of these copies can still be found on the second-hand furniture market), the shape of the headboard with its harmonious balance and contrast of curves served as inspiration for those of innumerable bedheads of painted wood or of a wooden framework covered in upholstered or padded fabric. A popular treatment was to cover the bedhead with a taffeta in one of the currently fashionable pastel shades of mushroom, pink, cream, ice blue or pale green, the material being deep-buttoned with a regular pattern, the edges finished with a matching caterpillar fringe.

Such a bed would be inevitably accompanied by a draped dressing table and the utmost ingenuity was exercised in the drawing offices of interior decorators and furniture manufacturers to create variations on the basic theme of a kidney-shaped table with a draped skirt. The origins of this table went back to the eighteenth century and similar examples can be found in English and French paintings and engravings of that period – modern additions being the cut-glass handles for the drawers and the plate-glass top to protect the fabric from lipstick or spilt face powder. On such a table would be placed a triple dressing mirror with a swinging centre section and adjustable side wings, sometimes bordered with glass in a colour to match the general scheme of the room while seating was provided by an x frame dressing stool, also covered in buttoned taffeta to match the bed.

her range to the creation of a number of pieces of furniture which became identified with her name. Painted in various colours, ivory with the mouldings picked out in pale pink, a deep green with white mouldings, indigo blue and a dark orange approximately the colour called tango in the twenties, they had an artificial *craquelure* finish.

The forms of these different pieces of furniture were inspired by those of the simpler pieces of eighteenth-century French furniture sometimes called 'provincial', but usually of an extremely elegant outline, simply executed with little or no carved decoration and left in the natural fruitwood or painted – furniture similar to that made by Nicolas Petit or Criaerd in the mid-eighteenth century.

Group of painted furniture by Syrie Maugham, about 1936

The telephone stand with shelves for directories is painted in a dark orange tone with a *craquelure* finish. The detail of the miniature cabriole legs and mouldings is particularly well conceived. The low chair, painted pale shell pink, has its original covering of satin. The side table is painted in sage green, also with a *craquelure* finish; the top has recesses for two oval metal containers for plants – an idea taken from French eighteenth-century models. The terracotta bust, white alabaster vase and flower painting by Billie Waters are typical of the decorative accessories favoured by Mrs Maugham's clients. Miss Waters's paintings particularly those of deer and fawns, were reproduced by the Medici Society as prints and were extremely popular. The mirror-glass frame is contemporary, although not the original frame of this picture.

Side tables with shelves and a drawer, sometimes with two zinc containers sunk in the top to take flowering plants; a triangular version of the same intended to fill the corner between a settee and another chair; bedside tables with a space for a tray and a raised part upon which a lamp could be placed, commodes based on Régence models with two drawers or with the drawer space left open to take large books; a finely detailed stand for a telephone with two lower compartments for directories — these were some of the models which became known as a 'Syrie Maugham' signature of a room.

No doubt these simple models were chosen in preference to the more ornate pieces veneered in marquetry designs and ornamented with bronzes because they were less expensive to make. Also, taste in the thirties tended to turn away from the elaborate Louis XV and Louis XVI furniture as being vulgar and showy — a criticism justified in the majority of cases. Such furniture was a drug on the market whether genuine or, as was more likely, reproduction of the kind almost mass-produced about 1900. Many decorators inspired by the example of what Lord Berners called 'Syrie Maugham's white furniture traffic' stripped off the bronzes and painted the carcasses of these inexpensive pieces of furniture. A genuine Régence commode had its inlaid marquetry panels covered in thick white paint and its rouge marble top similarly treated — fortunately in this case the bronzes, of a very high quality, were put back. Such an instance could be multiplied a hundred times at a period when antiques of certain periods were so plentiful and so cheap. An Aubusson carpet, at that time easily obtained and inexpensive although coming back into fashion, had its white background dyed violet by a new owner who applied household paint with disastrous results.

However, Mrs Maugham could hardly be blamed for the indiscretions of her imitators, though the poorly conceived copies of her white rooms undoubtedly influenced her to adopt more colourful schemes as the decade advanced. In 1936 *Vogue* recorded that Christian Bérard decorated Mrs Maugham's apartment but, although it would have been interesting to see the results of a collaboration between two people so influential in dictating taste during the thirties, no details of these decorations appear to have survived.

In addition to the individual pieces of furniture which were immediately recognizable as being Syrie Maugham creations, she had several characteristic treatments which were repeated time and time again. One was the use of fringe — a fairly long eyeglass fringe — where a gimp or braid would normally be used, for instance outlining the curves of a pelmet or around the arms of a sofa. Another was the use of a crackled finish on the paintwork of furniture. Mrs Maugham employed one craftsman in particular who specialized in producing this finish of crazing the surface of the paint, the minute cracks being filled in with black or a coloured pigment, an effect resembling the *craquelure* of some Chinese porcelains. The work was carried out in a cloak and dagger atmosphere of locked rooms and great secrecy, the craftsman not allowing even Mrs Maugham to discover the mysteries of his technique. He was not unique in producing this crackle effect but his particular secret was in knowing how to control the size of the crazing of the paint. When Mrs Maugham closed her establishment his services were used by the interior decorating department of a big store, but without Mrs Maugham's direction the crackle finish he produced on painted furniture became banal and commercialized.

In October 1939 Mrs Maugham sold the stock of her shop in Paradise Walk to Fortnum and Mason and went to Canada.

Interior by Lady Colefax, about 1938

A celebrated figure between the wars, Lady Colefax, working under the name of Sybil Colefax, was reputed to have financed her ambitions as a political hostess by her talents as an interior decorator. Harold Nicolson records in his diary that Lady Colefax 'tells me that she has made £2000 [$4800] last year by her own sole efforts' – a considerable sum of money in 1931. No more or less original than the majority of her semi-professional colleagues, she worked in an idiom of a blend of modern and antique, creating rooms with an atmosphere of expensive prettiness but which on closer examination are basically variations on the same theme. Characteristic of the fashionable taste are the spotted, striped and checked fabrics, the glazed chintz used for cushions and curtains, the white porcelain vase in the shape of a hand, the bouquet of shell flowers under a glass dome and the rather fussy Venetian mirror. The *trompe l'œil* wallpaper covering the screen was of French origin.

Jean-Michel Frank

Jean-Michel Frank was a designer whose highly individual approach to decoration and furniture found admirers on both sides of the Atlantic. The career of Jean-Michel Frank had started in the early twenties and his interiors had much in common with the most sophisticated classical rooms of Japan. To an initiated eye they might appear featureless – there is an apochryphal story that the bailiffs visited a financially embarrassed lady, gazed despondently at the decorations by Frank and departed remarking that there was no point in their remaining, as obviously everything had been removed by bailiffs who had arrived earlier. But to a discerning eye the virtues of the decorations were apparent, the delicate proportions of the furniture, the exquisite craftsmanship and above all the subtle varieties of the surfaces. Ivory, lacquer, vellum, shagreen, suede, calfskin, morocco, straw – these were among the favourite materials used by Frank to clothe and ornament the chaste lines of his furniture uncluttered by mouldings or carved motifs. Of all the woods his preference was for oak, preferably unstained and treated to make the grain stand out in relief. The rich dark markings of macassar favoured by Ruhlmann or the blond insipidity of sycamore used by so many of his contemporaries had no appeal for him. Another point of resemblance with Japanese rooms was the flexibility of arrangement of the furniture – he rarely included a commode or cabinet large enough to dominate the room or monopolize one position around which all the other pieces had to adopt fixed positions.

Left Chair by Jean-Michel Frank, about 1935
Covered in shagreen.

Centre Leather and lacquer chair by Jean-Michel Frank, about 1933

Right Table by Jean-Michel Frank, about 1935
Covered in parchment.

Left Plaster table lamp by Giacometti for Jean-Michel Frank

A collaboration between Alberto Giacometti and his younger brother Diego, also a sculptor, was probably responsible for a number of plaster lamps and decorative vases commissioned and sold by Jean-Michel Frank. The examples available are usually marked 'J.-M. Frank' and do not bear the signature of Giacometti. This lamp, intended to stand on a side table, has the light concealed in the central vase so that a picture can be illuminated. The design is reminiscent of the elaborately carved alabaster ornaments found in the tomb of Tutankhamun.

Right Lamp by Jean-Michel Frank, about 1935

Frank's work was to be found in Paris, South America, New York and San Francisco. In 1931 he decorated a houseboat for the Vicomte de Noailles, in white with white-lacquered furniture of deceptive simplicity and a dining room with panels by Christian Bérard. In 1935 he designed showrooms for the dressmakers Lelong and Schiaparelli – he had decorated the latter's apartment in a style which had made her rival Chanel 'shudder as though she had passed a graveyard', as Schiaparelli gleefully records in her autobiography *Shocking Life*.

In the United States Frank executed decorations for the Nelson Rockefeller apartment in New York and for the Templeton Crocker house in San Francisco, where he installed lacquered panels by Jean Dunand. Individual pieces of furniture designed in collaboration with Rodocanacchi and lamps designed for him by Diego Giacometti embellished houses on both sides of the Atlantic.

In 1939 Frank abandoned his usual subtle variations on the theme of white and beige and in a scheme for a ballroom for Baron de Roland de l'Epée indulged in a harmony of the confectionery colours favoured by Christian Bérard whose talents had been equivocally lauded in an article *Art Direction* as 'a genius for colour, a sense of arrangement, effeminate taste, morbid romanticism and perversity'. In this room each wall was painted a different colour, rose, blue, yellow and green with small settees upholstered in the same shades. Three of these were copies of Second Empire models while the fourth was that made from a design by Salvador Dali in the shape of Mae West's lips (see page 157). These were set off by a dark red carpet and in two corners of the room were curved pavilions draped with red velvet curtains and frames in white plaster barley-sugar columns. A screen painted by de Pisis completed the décor which was reminiscent of Bérard's décor for the ballet *Cotillon* with its arrangement of a series of boxes with red curtains against walls of white *faux marbre* (see page 146).

Curtis Moffat

In 1929 Curtis Moffat, an American photographer who had spent a considerable time in Paris, opened premises at 4 Fitzroy Square, London, a Georgian house which was modernized by the architect Frederick Etchells. The opening was marked by the issuing of an invitation card designed by McKnight Kauffer and the announcement that Curtis Moffat would henceforth be the London representative of DIM (Décoration Intérieure Moderne). Apart from a number of announcements in the press, no mention of DIM was made in subsequent publicity or in the numerous magazine articles which were written by Derek Patmore and others and it seems likely that hopes in this direction were disappointed.

Curtis Moffat's intention was to combine the most *avant-garde* decoration with Gothic and Renaissance furniture and objects and, perhaps most significantly, with negro sculpture,* of which he was an enthusiastic and knowledgeable

* Other collectors of negro art shared Curtis Moffat's opinion that its best setting was a contemporary one. The collector Ladislas Szecsi tried a number of styles from Louis XV to early Victorian as backgrounds for the collection of primitive masks he had amassed in Africa before coming to the conclusion that 'Negro masks are only in keeping in a modern environment. The mask being primarily a functional object is in harmony with furniture which is also functional, unbiased by aesthetic theory and without useless ornament.'

Invitation card designed by E. McKnight Kauffer for the opening of the Curtis Moffat shop on 4 June 1929

Upholstered chair by Curtis Moffat, 1931   Walnut table by Curtis Moffat, 1930

collector. In order to interest the widest public, the advertisements for the new gallery were carefully calculated to appeal to the readers of the various magazines, illustrations of a carved jade vase or an Italian shrine for the staider journals, and photographs of a gleaming glass abstraction for periodicals like *Vogue* and the *Architectural Review* which, in their own separate ways, were abreast of the fashions.

The opening was widely reported in the gossip columns and the adjectives 'modernistic', 'cubist' and 'futuristic' applied to the white rooms with doors faced in aluminium or copper, the curtains made of squares of chamois leather hanging from polished nickel rods, the profusion of modern cushions in geometric patterns of velvet or coloured leather, the steel furniture and the negro masks or bronze heads from Benin. Anyone who found the juxtaposition of a flower piece by Marie Laurençin in a faceted mirror frame and a carved wood figure from the Solomon Islands disturbing was reassured by a room with lettuce-green walls where ship models, antique leather drinking vessels and terrestrial globes were displayed.

Fitzroy Square and the neighbouring streets had been discovered in the 1920s and a number of social celebrities lived nearby. Curtis Moffat and his first wife, Iris Tree, the daughter of Sir Herbert Tree, were enthusiastic party-givers – Lytton Strachey was severely frightened by a snake at one of their parties – and it was not long before a trip to the Curtis Moffat gallery became a necessity if a birthday or Christmas present was needed. A wide choice could be found from rugs by McKnight Kauffer at 4 guineas (about $10) each, gold lacquer and diamond jewelry by Raymond Templier, 'amusing china animals by Robert Lallemand', cigarette boxes covered in leopard skin, silver cocktail sets by Desny or cupboards painted by Wyndham Lewis who may have been reminded of his comment on 'the amateur tastefulness of the Fitzroy tinkerers', made in 1919 about the earlier venture in the same neighbourhood – the Omega Workshops.

Occasional exhibitions were held of carpets by Marion Dorn, rugs by Evelyn Wild, furniture by Eyre de Lanux and Raymond Templier jewelry. Commissions for interior decorations were solicited in an advertisement in *Harper's Bazaar* in October 1930 with the injunction to the reader to 'Go into these rooms . . . you

Modernist rug by E. McKnight Kauffer, sold by Curtis Moffat in 1930

Chess set and table by Curtis Moffat, 1932

can breathe there and walk about . . . no longer decoration sickly with charm from which the spirit turns . . . here there is nothing of deception . . . the lie is a true one . . . the machine works.'

In 1930 Curtis Moffat designed the settings and supplied the furniture for two comedies, *Healthy Wealthy and Wise* starring an American actress, Mary Newcomb, and *It's a Boy* with Leslie Henson and Sydney Howard. The female impersonation scene by the two stars of the latter ensured a good run but Curtis Moffat was the only one to emerge with credit from *Healthy Wealthy and Wise*, an unamusing effort.

Curtis Moffat added a picture gallery to his decorating business – a venture commended as showing, in a way that no other gallery did, the function of pictures as furniture. Among the artists represented at the opening in January 1931 were Augustus John and Eve Kirk, for whose first exhibition John had written a glowing foreword to the catalogue. Eve Kirk's special genre was depicting, in a restricted range of cerulean blue, ochre and indian red, scenes of the Thames docks and – inevitably – Venice, with the paint laid on in a thick impasto applied

Silvered metal bowl by Desny, 1929

Advertised by Curtis Moffat.

Stool by Green and Abbott, 1931

Black-finished wood and printed calf skin.

Duncan Miller exhibit at the Dorland Hall Exhibition, 1933

The Dorland Hall Exhibition of 1933, held at a time when the Depression was at its worst, was, in some ways, a dress rehearsal for the larger exhibition held at Burlington House two years later. A leading part in this organization was played by the Design and Industries Association and it was intended to implement the advice contained in Lord Gorell's Report on Art and Industry. As can be seen in this illustration and in that of the all-glass scheme by Oliver Hall (see illustration page 109), the exhibits were conceived in a striking manner to drive home to the public and manufacturers alike the message that better design must be applied to interior furnishings if Britain's exports were to improve.

with a palette knife and drawn over with a brush handle. John's admiration for her work was shared by a number of critics and she was described (in 1931) as gradually establishing a position as one of the most important women painters in England.

The name John Duncan Miller appears at an early date in association with Curtis Moffat, draughting designs for decorative schemes, writing articles for magazines on various aspects of decoration, and as the designer of the Marquis

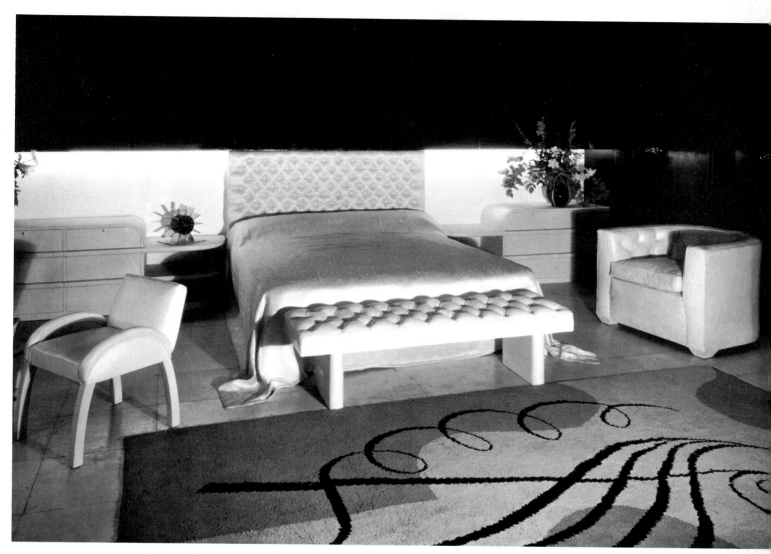

Interior by John Duncan Miller, 1937

Duncan Miller, in addition to his work as a designer, wrote two books published in the thirties by The Studio Ltd. *More Colour Schemes for the Modern Home*, which appeared in 1938 (a previous volume *Colour Schemes for the Modern Home*, from the same publishers, had been written by Derek Patmore), gives a cross-section of the various trends, ranging from the most austere modernism to fantasy baroque, prevalent in the decade. The twenty-four colour plates illustrate the practical advice given in the foreword concerning the use of colour in interior decoration and the author differentiates between the designer, 'architects and people whose chief interest is in the actual furniture of the room', and the arranger, 'the decorator who concocts a room out of ingredients already in existence'.

de Casa Maury's apartment in a style of modified modernism. The fireplace wall of the dining room was covered in sheets of mirror, reflecting the sky blue walls and ceiling and upholstery in shades of aquamarine and sapphire blue. The dining room had white walls and ceiling and dining chairs of Queen Anne design covered in aquamarine blue, while the top of the dining table was of thick pavement glass with a greenish cast of colour, a kind of glass much used by Curtis Moffat and other designers in the early thirties for table tops. The main feature of the dining room – and one much commented upon in the press – was the treatment of the curtains which were entirely covered in bronze, gold and silver sequins. 'Escape from convention is one of the main features of the furnishing fabrics of this second quarter of the twentieth century', wrote Olive Dent in the introduction to the catalogue of the 1930 *Daily Mail* Ideal Home Exhibition, 'Glittering sequinned material in geometrical patterns and two shades of gold [sic] acts as window hangings in one Mayfair drawing room.'

The Curtis Moffat venture lasted a bare three years but during that time its influence was considerable. Run on unorthodox and uncommercial lines – factors which caused its eventual demise – it brought to the notice of the public experimental work which would never have had a showing elsewhere. Its closure was brought about partly by the Depression and partly by Curtis Moffat's desire to devote his time completely to his first interest, photography.

Suzanne Talbot; Rose Cummings

The juxtaposition of negro sculpture and ancient Egyptian art in an extremely modern setting was employed by Suzanne Talbot in her drawing room in Paris and photographs of this striking décor were shown in *L'Illustration* in 1932. This room if reconstructed today, nearly forty years later, would have as contemporary an air as any to be found in the current decorating magazines and would not, unlike many of the rooms of the early thirties, appear in the least dated. The floor, the doors and some folding screens were covered in dull silver glass, contrasting with the white satin-finished cellulose paint on the walls. The upholstery of the steel chairs was in white leather and the bold stripes of zebra skins enlivened the floors and a divan. Two carved wood spirit stools from the Gold Coast and a number of Egyptian funerary vases contributed to the timeless atmosphere.

The apartment of Rose Cummings, a designer with a penchant for strongly decorative effects, was described in 1935 as having a bedroom in the Chinese taste with wallpapers painted by Avinoff in colours of lapis, Chinese pink, green and mauve, which provided a setting for a collection of Ming frogs and white monkeys: the adjoining bathroom had walls of pale silver with a design of delicate flowering trees while the black bath, sunk in the floor, was surrounded by a trough which was kept replenished with flowering bulbs and cactus plants.

Window box designed by Constance Spry for the coronation, 1937

Priced at 30s ($3.60). A noticeable feature in photographs of interiors of the early thirties are the vases of madonna lilies replacing the marigolds in black bowls of the twenties, which had in their turn ousted the carnations and sweet peas grouped in smilax or maidenhair fern of the Edwardians. Soon after 1930, however, the name of Constance Spry became known as the creator of 'flower arrangements' – not an entirely new concept but one which Mrs Spry presented with freshness and originality, revealing the beauties of hitherto unappreciated flowers grouped most often either in old vases or containers of unglazed white pottery.

Interior furnishings

Steel furniture

Possibly the most characteristic feature of modernist interiors in the early thirties was the use of chromium-plated tubular steel furniture and the main source in England was Practical Equipment Limited, more generally known as PEL. This firm was started from the chance placing in the newly decorated Strand Palace Hotel of two steel chairs of Continental origin – whether by Thonet or by Marcel Breuer is not recorded – by the hotel's designer Oliver Bernard. These attracted the attention of one of the directors of Tube Investments Ltd, who saw the possibilities of extending the activities of his firm in the field of prestige products. Bernard was placed under contract as a consultant designer between 1931 and

Chromium-plated tubular steel dining table by PEL, from the 1933 catalogue

'In definitely modernistic furniture a new development has been the introduction of equipment made of metal . . . metal furniture can be surprisingly attractive in appearance and in price it is reasonable', wrote Baseden Butt in a review of the furniture shown at the Ideal Home Exhibition of 1930. This table by PEL demonstrates the desire on the part of makers of steel furniture to abandon the severity of the earliest examples which had given rise to adverse comments and facetious references to operating theatres and to give tubular steel furniture a more decorative aspect which would make it suitable for the home and at the same time keep within the technical limits of the material, which, as John Armstrong pointed out in the *Architectural Review* in 1932 'prevent it from becoming stupidly ornate [and] tend to give it that confined perfection which is so irritating, like a woman who is too efficient and too good'.

Settee by PEL, 1932

Tubular steel frame covered in brown leather.

An early difficulty in bending the chromemolybdenum steel in curves of a small radius was that the tubing tended to flatten and to lose its circular section, but this failing was overcome by filling the hollow steel tube with pitch before shaping.

1932 and the PEL shop in Henrietta Place attracted an affluent and fashionable clientele by the novelty of the gleaming chromium-plated furniture – which nearly outshone the sapphire shirt-buttons of a frequent visitor, the Maharajah of Alwar. At this time individual pieces of furniture in steel and plate glass were made to the requirements of clients and architects, but as the technical processes improved more and more utilitarian furniture for offices and hotels was manufactured. Among the first clients for stacking chairs were the BBC, and barstools, luggage stands and traystands were made for the Savoy Hotel and Claridges. The field became ever wider with equipment for hospitals and canteens until the luxury pieces gradually came to be discontinued, partly because of a change of fashion but mainly because it was no longer practical to make them. The cantilever chairs were not cheap by the standards of the early 1930s, costing £6 ($14.40) – though the real leather covering could be dyed any shade to the client's specifications. Cox and Company, a rival firm founded soon after PEL and later incorporated in it, advertised chairs in 1932 at £5 5s ($12.60) if painted in enamel, £5 10s ($13.20) with a chromium finish, but it was estimated that with improved methods of mass production these prices would fall by 1935 to £2 ($4.80) in enamel with hide upholstery and an extra 10s ($1.20) for chromium plating.

Cheap mass-produced furniture

In addition to new furniture – modernist or reproduction of Tudor or Queen Anne – designed and made for a comparatively small but prosperous section, there was the numerically more common type of product intended for a cheaper market and sold through hire-purchase firms, big department stores or small furniture dealers. Of this type the greater part was still made in mock-Tudor style with grotesque melon-bulb legs and imitation curved panels of steam-pressed wood; second in popularity was a mock-Georgian style using spindly stock cabriole legs and lastly a version of modernism.

The cheap mock-antique furniture was characterized by a glittering French-polished surface and an over-indulgence in applied ornament masking a shoddi-ness of materials and workmanship which, unhappily for the customer but fortunately for posterity, ensured a short life. Its flashy finish had an immediate appeal to a public with no experience of or even interest in quality.

The 'designers' of the modernist furniture reckoned that there were two special characteristics of modernism. One was the use of steel, the other a tendency towards asymmetry. The latter was their solution to the problem of giving some originality to a piece of furniture when fashion dictated that there should be no ornamental details. So although the modernists advocated simplicity this 'modern-ist' furniture was often overloaded with asymmetrical decoration. Mirrors were made with freakish and unnecessary angles, while curtains, carpets and cushions had to be covered with stripes and spots in the manner of Picasso and Braque. Furniture was so angular and unusual that it was uncomfortable both to look at and use. An example is the dining room suite illustrated over page. The sideboard has chromium-plated curved supports which leave an awkward space and support

Left desk by Walter Dorwin Teague, 1933

The desk has a hardwood top and the rest is of rose lacquer sprayed silver, with the handle and support of chrome-finished tubing.

Right desk made by the John Widdicomb Company, exhibited at Chicago World's Fair, 1933

Left dining room sideboard; *right* dining table; both made of figured walnut with chromium-plated fittings, by A. Hermann Ltd, about 1934

two drawers which overhang the base more than the cupboard door at the other side. The dining table with its vaguely Tudor legs – in figured walnut – has curved chromium supports which are structurally redundant and inconvenient, but give an air of spurious modernism.

Thousands of suburban villas were happily filled by their proud owners with mock-Tudor dining room suites or modernistic bedroom suites bought on easy terms, all guaranteed to fall to pieces before the final payment was made unless handled with extreme care. Three-piece suites of elephantine proportions, covered in jazzy moquette hostile to the touch and occupying far more space than their seating accommodation warranted, were considered an absolute necessity for any young married couple setting up a home. R. Gardner Medwin in complaining that 'each year a shameless display at the British Industries Fair reveals the decadence of our furniture industry. . . . Grotesque novelty parades as "modern" ', gave vent to a *cricde oeur* that could have found echoes in France, Germany and the United States. 'Taste tends to be negative rather than bad', he continued 'and if the leading manufacturers would develop a conscience, would realize the advantage of employing skilled designers, public taste would soon be found to improve beyond measure.' The manufacturers he castigates must presumably have employed some designers, whether skilled or not, but with the passing of time any trace of these anonymous hacks, together with the furniture they designed, has passed into oblivion.

David Joel in his book *The Adventure of British Furniture* has a section entitled 'Chamber of Horrors', giving illustrations of cheap mass-produced furniture of the period between the wars. No source is given for the illustrations, some of which appear to have been redrawn in such a manner as to accentuate the ugliness of the furniture portrayed. Grotesque they certainly are, but it is impossible to suppress the thought that they often had – in the modernistic examples – a gusto and energy lacking in the work of many reputable designers whose efforts to rehabilitate good taste resulted in a rather anaemic and timid anonymity. An editorial comment in *House and Garden* described English contemporary furniture as 'sober and conservative', a definition calculated not to antagonize advertisers but adequate to explain why those with a taste for originality should have reverted to the Victorian or baroque styles.

Wall treatments

The natural setting for steel or other modernist furniture was plain walls. The disadvantage of plain walls however, especially in corridors or staircases open to the public, was that ordinary painted surfaces were liable to wear or scratching both accidental and deliberate. The appearance of a number of plastic paints marketed under various names such as 'Sankmar' provided a solution. The formula varied but basically was a mixture of powdered marble or mica combined with a powdered plastic. When mixed with water the resulting paste could be brushed on the wall and treated decoratively in a number of ways, a pattern incised in semicircles or shell shapes with metal combs or textures made by stipple brushes or wet rags. When dry the composition had a rock-hard surface impervious to cracking or peeling and could be painted. Unfortunately, in spite of an attractive surface texture when freshly applied, the drawbacks were apparent after a while. The incised patterns attracted dirt which lodged in the depressions and could only be cleaned with difficulty, and once the composition had set it was almost impossible to remove. The only way to restore the wall to a smooth finish was to re-plaster it entirely. It continued to be used in cinemas or similar public buildings but soon lost favour as a treatment in private houses when it was found that the incised designs could not be concealed under wallpaper when fashion veered towards more decorative treatments.

Painted or even distempered walls were to be found in the newer houses where the wall surface was fresh and needed no attention before the paint or distemper was applied, and the improvements in the quality and range of colours in the brands of washable distempers which could be applied by a comparatively unskilled decorator caused some concern to the wallpaper industry.

Wallpaper itself never ceased to be used, of course, as it was one of the cheapest methods of redecoration, and there was still enough demand for plain wallpapers to justify the production of textured papers, known irreverently as 'porridge', which were made in a seemingly endless range of tones of beige, cream and oatmeal in addition to extremely discreet pastel colours. These were enlivened by borders and corner motifs. The borders were between one and three inches wide – rarely wider – and were usually in sad colours in geometric or floral designs of quite notable mediocrity. The corner motifs or triangular shapes were cut out and applied near the ceiling and many a room in the early thirties – and for long after – derived any character it may have had from a spray of autumn leaves in appropriate shades of orange and brown or a modernist design in rich tones. Patterned papers were invariably geometrical in design, sometimes combined with discreetly conventionalized flowers or leaves, and these were printed in a technique which gave a curiously blurred over-all appearance. It was said that before putting a patterned paper on the market a sample wall was prepared and it was the job of an unfortunate employee to stare at this wall for days on end to detect any accidental hidden motifs which might reveal themselves, such as grimacing faces or worse. There was an apocryphal story that one firm had marketed several thousand rolls of a new paper before complaints flowed in that the pattern when applied to the wall resolved itself into unexpected motifs of astonishing eroticism. This type of paper was confined to the lower price ranges while at the other end of the scale there were the expensive damask papers of the type used in museums, art galleries and the drawing rooms of large period houses. There was so little demand for paper between these extremes that many firms destroyed the woodblocks dating from the mid-nineteenth century onwards, as it was considered that there was so little chance of their ever coming back into fashion that there was no point in continuing to store them. One firm used the blocks cut from designs ranging from Pugin to Marie Laurençin to construct a new wooden floor in the workrooms.

Sooner or later there was bound to be a reaction against the plain walls fashionable in the early thirties with a return to the use of patterned wallpapers. A contemporary reference attributes the revival of patterned papers – that is, the use of commissioned new designs – to American sources about 1934 or 1935. Corroboration for this can be found in the *Studio Year Book of Decorative Art* for 1935 where the only rooms featuring patterned papers are American – one designed by Ilonka Karasz for Donald Deskey and another in a dining room by Gilbert Rohde. By 1936 papers decorated with designs of flowers, shells and other motifs were in demand and one amateur decorator filled with misguided enthusiasm papered a room with a design in all its colour variations in alternating strips. With a larger production and better designers, the American manufacturers were in a position to export patterned papers to Europe, the London agent for Katzenbach and Warren and Richard Thibaut, Inc., being Kelso. It was not long however before the English manufacturers found it profitable to revive some mid-nineteenth century designs in view of the revival of Victoriana – one charming design of a large bouquet of mixed flowers, including cabbage roses, printed in clear tones, became particularly popular.

Lighting

The comments in several volumes written in the mid-thirties provide a striking reminder that electricity as a source of illumination was by no means common in England and, in those districts where it was available, it was expensive. In 1934 A. B. Read made the optimistic prophecy that 'to keep within the most convenient bounds of probability, the design of artificial illumination should be examined in terms of electricity. We are now at the beginning of a new age of power, the age of clean and abundant power for the Grid is completed and it is only a question of time before archaic methods of generating power and providing artificial light disappear. This will mean that our towns and cities and countryside will escape for ever from smuts and soot and fumes; that by day we shall get more and clearer sunlight, and by night more abundant light. Electricity will be available in most parts of the country at a reasonable cost in time.' But 'This cannot happen at once, unfortunately.' And indeed, 'it is not everyone who can afford, or who likes this form of illumination', wrote Mrs Darcy Braddell a year later.

A storm of protest had met the erection throughout the countryside of the pylons carrying the high-voltage transmission lines of the Grid, which was designed to reduce the cost of electricity and to bring new power to districts which had hitherto been dependent upon gas, candles or oil lamps as sources of illumination. The high cost of electricity imposed the need for utilizing it to the utmost once it had been installed, and bulbs were often left unshaded so that the light was not wasted. The tendency was however to disguise electric fittings wherever possible and purists in design fulminated against the 'nice little electric "candle" dripping with immovable wax', or 'the worst shapes of the earliest gas chandeliers incorporated in the design of electric lights'. In a majority of cases the concept of the traditional centre light was prevalent, even if the design of the fitting was in the latest idiom of chrome and pearl glass, and in the average home the advantages of more convenient and incidentally more flattering, table or

Standard lamp by Cox and Company, about 1934
Chromium stand, painted parchment shade.

standard lamps were not fully realized. Catalogues of the latest designs in fittings for domestic use throughout the thirties show a preponderance of centre lights, and wall brackets, usually in fan shapes of tinted glass, standard lamps being in the minority. The need for economy is reflected in the advice that 'it should be remembered that walls and ceilings must be coloured to help the lighting of rooms, if we wish to be intelligently economical. Clean pale colours reflect most light and it is expensive to supplement light in rooms whose surfaces are dull and dark in tone, while indirect lighting with the source of light altogether hidden practically doubles the consumption of current, and unless properly used it has rather a drowsy appearance.'

The arid appearance of many interiors of the early thirties and especially those put forward as examples of the new school of fitness for purpose is due in part to the institutional character of many of the 'functional' electric light fittings with their globes of opaque glass held in sockets of chromium steel. Designed to be practical, easy to maintain and clean, they succeeded in giving a dispiriting light to an interior and with the advent of period revivalism were relegated to serve a purely functional purpose in public buildings or institutions where the designs originating in the thirties can still be found.

For those to whom economy was not a pressing consideration or for those looking for more decorative light fittings, the recourse seems to have been to imports from the Continent, from Italy, France or Czechoslovakia. To judge from the large number still current, light-fittings of moulded glass by Lalique or Sabino appear to have been sold in England in considerable quantities. The chandelier

Chandelier advertised by Veronese, Paris, in 1934

Indirect lighting is concealed in the silvered bowl, and the curved ribbed glass strips have the effect of a decorative fountain.

illustrated was advertised by the French firm of Veronese in 1934 but was of traditional Italian, probably Venetian, manufacture with the design modernized to take electric light bulbs concealed in the base and replacing the candle sockets of the eighteenth-century models. Lampshades of pleated parchment, held together by silk cords or shades of vellum or parchment sewn on to a metal frame with leather thongs, had made their appearance in the twenties and became even more popular in the following decade, sometimes being painted with 'jazz' motifs. For the more conservative period interiors a decorative silk shade on a Chinese pottery or celadon vase or on a figurine of semi-precious stone was still considered essential.

Pendant light by Tony and Jacques Socard, 1930
Made of laminated glass panels.

Textiles

The majority of the 'modernistic' interiors featured in the periodicals of the first five years of the thirties have a sameness about them and a lack of character which makes it difficult to distinguish the work of one designer from that of another. The use of the same woods, the preponderance of built-in furniture, the use of strict geometric shapes, the lack of any ornament in the way of carving or even mouldings and the use of plain or only slightly patterned fabrics for curtains, and upholstery – all these factors tend to give the anonymous look of hotel rooms to most interiors. Very often the only decorative object is a rug or carpet, which almost invariably turns out to have been designed by Marion Dorn. Unfortunately it is not likely that many of her rugs have survived, as in the nature of things the floor coverings receive the most wear of the furnishing of a room, and also in the years of reaction against modernism her designs are most likely to have been rejected by interior decorators in favour of Aubusson or other period rugs. To judge from photographs her output must have been considerable and the standard of design extremely high. The prime requisite for a Dorn carpet – and the same applied to those designed by her husband E. McKnight Kauffer – was that the design should lie flat on the floor and that there should be no appearance of 'hills or valleys'. Three-dimensional effects were eschewed and the colours were kept in a subdued tonal range. Each season she produced a new range of designs and when a design had been repeated several times it was discarded – in this way each carpet became one of a severely limited edition. The colour range may have been restricted but within those restrictions the shades were extremely subtle and were chosen with great care from a range of five hundred specially dyed. Six shades of white and three of black were used in combination with dozens of browns, beiges and greys while blues, dull orange and red were sparingly employed for accents in a decorative motif. One design, woven in carpets up to

Opposite
Left print by Ronald Grierson for Campbell Fabrics, about 1934

Right rug by Ronald Grierson, 1935

Bottom rug by Francis Jourdain for Aubusson, 1932
Ivory background with brown lines and a yellow centre.

Left fabric design by Raoul Dufy, 1930

Right 'Fugue' screen-printed linen by Paul Nash, 1936

Fabrics screen-printed in a bold abstract design such as this and with a colour range limited for economic reasons to one or two colours enjoyed considerable popularity in the mid-thirties. Curtains in similar patterns were often the only decorative feature to ameliorate the bleakness of a modernist interior.

Left rug by Ivan da Silva Bruhns, 1930

Right rug designed and woven by Marion Dorn, for the Royal Wilton Carpet Company, before 1935

Bottom 'Mongoose' carpet by Joan Miro for Aubusson, 1932

Fabric by Duncan Grant for Allan Walton Fabrics, 1938

The work of Allan Walton and the Edinburgh Weavers in presenting the designs of artists as applied to printed and woven fabrics received considerable publicity in decorating magazines and articles. But the output of Allan Walton's workshops or from the studios of Phyllis Barron, was negligible compared to that of the big commercial mills where the sale of less than 10,000 yards of printed material meant that that design was a failure and a successful pattern was reckoned as selling more than 60,000 yards. For financial reasons modern designs were to be found mainly in woven fabrics – in 1936 it was calculated that ninety per cent of woven fabrics were of modern design – as the cost of the cards necessary for a new pattern on a Jacquard loom was a fraction of that of machine blocks for a printed fabric. There was a steady demand not only in England but also from America and Germany for the traditional floral patterns of the eighteenth or nineteenth centuries or for variations on these originals.

A number of designs by Duncan Grant were printed on linen or velveteen by Allan Walton and Grant was awarded a diploma for his textile designs at the Paris International Exhibition.

thirty feet square, was of a large all-over pattern reminiscent of Chinese Chippendale and executed in a technique of cut and uncut pile. Syrie Maugham used this pattern in a number of interiors in either off-white or dark brown.

Tapestry weaving in France had a hard struggle to maintain its existence in the thirties. For decades previously the reputations of the Aubusson, Beauvais and Gobelins works had been declining, a state of affairs which was due to the policies of the directors of these workshops. The policy followed was that of commissioning cartoons from the older generation of established painters, often from those with little or no experience of the techniques of tapestry weaving, painters who conceived a tapestry in terms of a woven version of a painting to be reproduced with absolute fidelity to the smallest nuances of colour and even brushwork. This tradition had been followed since the eighteenth century — the tapestries designed by Mignard, Coypel, Oudry or Boucher may be cited as examples — but by the early years of the twentieth century the standard of works commissioned or adapted had fallen to an extremely low level. Jean Lurçat records that in 1918 Gustave Geffroy, the director of the Gobelins factory, showed him with considerable pride a newly completed tapestry, *The Sleeping Beauty* by Jean Weber, the caricaturist of the comic journal *Le Rire* (though in fairness it must be added that at the same time Lurçat was also shown a tapestry from a painting by Odilon Redon).

This ignorance of technique on the part of designers had a direct affect on the financial state of the workshops. The technical dexterity in reproducing paintings led to the increase in the number of shades of colour required for each tapestry. The fourteenth-century masterpiece *The Apocalypse of Angers* used an extremely small number of colours — seventeen according to some authorities, twenty-two according to others. By 1740 the number used had risen to 333, fifty years later to 587 and in 1900 some nine hundred colours were available. In the early twenties a tapestry from a design by Paul Véra required 2667 shades and still later, through the experiments of the chemist Chevill, the Gobelins and Beauvais works were able to put at the disposition of their designers no less than 14,400 shades. The majority of these were of course of chemical origin and were found to be fugitive, so that with the passage of time many of the tapestries became travesties of the original design, large areas of the paler colours fading into a monotone. The most serious aspect of this proliferation of colours was that the cost of the tapestry became almost prohibitive, the minimum quantity of wool or silk to be dyed in a particular shade being often far more than was required.

The Gobelins and Beauvais works, under the direction of Gustave Geffroy and later of Guillaume Janneau, were subsidized by the government, but the Aubusson factory, an assemblage of private looms each working for its own clientele, was not so fortunate, and with the need to consider costs the weaving tended to be coarser than that of its rivals. The town of Aubusson with a small population of four to five thousand, a town difficult of access and one dependent on its tapestry workshops, was severely hit by the crisis of 1929 and the imposition of high customs tariffs by America and other countries to which it exported a large part of its production.

Cocktail bar by Kenneth Cheesman, 1935

An exhibition intended to show the decorative possibilities of the opaque glass manufactured by the British Vitrolite Company of London, combined with chromium-plated tubular metal furniture. The circular plaque of rough cast glass has a sand-blasted design by Siegmund Pollitzer.

But in 1929 an attempt to correct the decline of the Aubusson workshops was made by Madame Cuttoli. The wife of a French senator and a friend and patron of many of the younger generation of painters, some of whom were still struggling for recognition, she courageously invited a number of them to submit designs to be woven as tapestries. Among the first were Rouault's *Three Clowns* and works by Coutaud, Marcoussis and Lurçat. The last, who more than any of the artists invited became involved in the designing of tapestry, records that only he and Coutaud submitted cartoons that respected the limitations and techniques of the craft and implies that his colleagues merely submitted easel paintings which were reproduced with exact fidelity with the addition of a border simulating a frame. Between 1933 and 1936 tapestries by Matisse (*Papéete*) Léger, Derain, Dufy, Braque, Segonzac, Mirò and Picasso (*Two Seated Women*) were added to the collection of the Atelier Cuttoli which was exhibited in Brussels, London, Stockholm and in 1936 in New York (at the Bignou Galleries), Chicago and San Francisco.

The tours were a critical success. Many who had found it difficult to enjoy abstract painting could see a meaning, for decorative purposes, in the gay colours of these tapestries. 'The less definite outlines of woven threads made harmony out of discord for these few benighted ones who had not yet captured the full glory of the modern French painters' canvases' wrote an American critic and it is recorded that the Braque found a purchaser in Chicago and the Picasso and the Rouault in Philadelphia. Madame Cuttoli's own apartment in Paris – 'a modern Hôtel Sévigné' was used as a setting for the tapestries. Two floor-to-ceiling panels by Lurçat flanked a simple mantelpiece covered in mirror, two modern chairs covered in a beige tapestry also by Lurçat, a Louis XV table, a Chinese lacquer table and modern tables of glass, gilded copper and black lacquer were to be found in the salon whose walls of natural oak veneer were enhanced by smaller tapestries by Picasso, Braque and Rouault. In the dining room a large Hispano Moresque chest, a Louis XIII dining table and chairs were combined with a Dufy panel.

Several factors may have contributed to the new spirit which began to find expression in the Aubusson workshops and in the Gobelins and Beauvais works – the Manufactures Nationales – in 1936. By then the general feeling was that the years of Depression were over, restrictions were easing and doubtless the success of the Cuttoli venture was a cause for optimism. Reforms were inaugurated in both state and private workshops. There was a backlog of orders and assigned cartoons to be completed before the reforms could be fully realized but by 1938 a special laboratory was licensed to prepare vegetable dyes which like those used in the fourteenth and fifteenth centuries would hold their colour: plantations of madder-wort at Carpentras, yellow-weed in Normandy and woad in Albi were inaugurated and the number of shades to be used in the future was drastically reduced. François Tabard working with Jean Lurçat energetically started the reorganization of work at Aubusson just as the war started. A prisoner from 1940 to 1945, he was not able fully to realize his plans until the late 1940s when the great series of tapestries after designs by Lurçat, Dufy, Gromaire, Coutaud and others brought a new lustre to the Aubusson workshops.

Salon of Madame Cuttoli, 1937

Glass

The large plate-glass windows, often stretching from floor to ceiling, which characterized many of the buildings designed on the Continent or in America by Mies
van der Rohe, Hans Schumacher, Le Corbusier and their followers, were not popular in England. The implied lack of privacy and the climate of a country where it
was considered preferable to be out in the landscape rather than to sit and look
at it inhibited English architects from incorporating glass walls into the comparatively few examples of modern architecture erected during the thirties in England.
Even in public buildings the tendency was to design windows broken up into
smaller panes. Equally, the glass bricks used by many American architects do not
seem to have attracted the same attention in England or France, and the possibilities
of their being used as internal partitions or in place of clear glass windows to
mask an ugly outlook were ignored. Their structural strength and decorative
qualities were more than outweighed, in the view of most British architects and
builders, by the fact that they were not a traditional material and by their greater
cost.

Inside the house it was a different matter and architects and interior decorators
made full use of the new varieties of glass manufactured during the thirties.
There were many historical precedents for rooms with the walls and ceilings

covered in mirrors but limitations of size of the pieces of glass had required the provision of some sort of decorative framework to conceal the joins. With improved techniques of manufacture sheets of mirror glass could be made sufficiently large to give an uninterrupted reflection. In this way a comparatively small room could be made to appear twice as large by the aid of one wall covered with mirror – a desirable effect when, for economic reasons, people were tending to live in smaller apartments. Large areas of mirror were particularly useful in the small rooms which were a feature of the new blocks of apartments built in the thirties. The apparent size of the new one-room flats – a euphemism for a bedsitting room with attached bathroom – could be made to appear greater by judiciously placed sheets of mirror and at the same time the light which filtered through the net curtains, necessary in towns for reasons of privacy, could be reflected.

The dining tables made by Lalique and Sabino utilized glass in a different way, less to exploit the transparency of the material than for the sake of its decorative possibilities. The practical difficulties of invisibly joining a transparent table top to an equally transparent base are avoided by the use of an inconspicuous metal framework, finished in chromium plate, which supports a number of repeated glass units ornamented by sand-blasting, the single sheet of glass forming the table top being similarly treated on the underside.

Reeded and fluted glass, plain or silvered, was used a great deal in bathrooms. Probably the most publicized use of this type of glass was in the bathroom designed for Mrs Edward James (Miss Tilly Losch) by Paul Nash, where the walls were faced with panels of metallic purple, pale rose and black glass of different textures arranged in abstract designs. As no colour photographs of this scheme appear to be extant the decorative effect of this mingling of texture and colour is difficult to judge. Sigmund Pollitzer in England and Max Ingrand in Paris were among the designers of engraved mirrors or glass used for decoration in restaurants and private apartments, the former working in a calligraphic manner, the latter experimenting more widely in coloured textures of gold and black to enhance the engraved designs. Max Ingrand's work was widely used in France, America and England.

In America Joseph Urban, the Frankl Galleries, Donald Deskey and Gilbert Rohde all made use of a large frameless circular mirror, three to four feet in diameter and applied directly to the wall, to lend to a room the dramatic note which was already becoming a characteristic of American interior decoration.

Coloured mirrors, gold, gunmetal, green, blue, red, were extensively used in bathrooms and in restaurants but by far the most popular was peach mirror with its flattering reflections.

Pilkington Bros' stand at the Dorland House Exhibition, designed by Oliver Hill, demonstrated the many possibilities afforded by new types of glass, from the floor with its tiles of glass and mosaic patterns of gold and mirror to the walls of panels of ribbed and obscured mirror, with sand-blasted or engraved decorations, to the furniture, a chaise-longue, a dressing table and stool and a small table made from curved and shaped sheets of plate glass. These were made primarily as showpieces for the exhibition and their practical application was limited – not many people would have had the courage to relax on the glass chaise-longue supported by four glass balls, but they were the forerunners of similar furniture realized in lighter plastics.

All-glass exhibit designed by Oliver Hill for Pilkington Bros. for the Dorland Hall Exhibition, 1933

Left Occasional table by Green and Abbott, 1931

Natural bass wood top supported by glass columns.

Right Glass dining table by Dorothy Thorpe, before 1937

Plate glass top supported by illuminated columns of frosted glass.

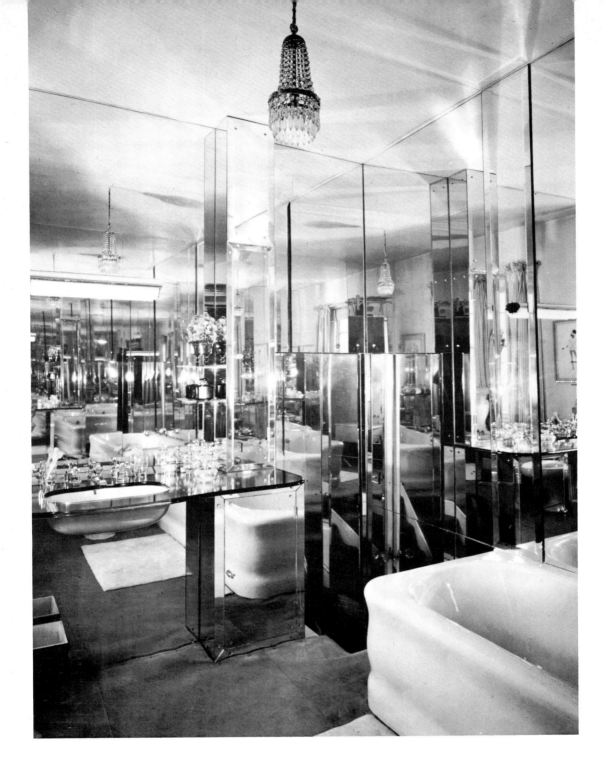

Bathroom, about 1936

With few exceptions, bathrooms in the twenties were purely functional, despite the exotic examples designed for movies featuring Gloria Swanson, Pola Negri and other vamps. Tiled walls and a wooden casing around the bath were often the sole concessions to decoration, while exposed plumbing and a gas heater were common. In the thirties a greater use of central heating and technical improvements both in the function and appearance of plumbing units encouraged the possibilities of decorating the bathroom as carefully as the rest of the house, and a number of bathrooms decorated wholly or partly in mirrors received considerable publicity. Though not so elaborate as those designed by Paul Nash for Mrs Edward James or by Oliver Hill for Lady Mount Temple, this example with its multiplicity of glittering reflections is a far cry from the stark utility of the previous decade.

110

Writing desk by Robert Block, about 1935

Writing desk with three drawers, upper portion covered in mirror glass, the supports of ebonized wood. Robert Block was the director of Studio Athelia at Aux Trois Quartiers. A dressing table of similar design by Block, made by the Société Industrielle d'Art, Paris, for Heal and Son Ltd was illustrated in the *Studio Year Book of Decorative Art* for 1935.

Another form of glass extant in the thirties was Vitrolite, an opaque glass with a smooth face and a back ridged to facilitate fixing with a mastic compound. Vitrolite was made in a number of colours as well as black and white but the insipidity of most of the shades and its rather uninteresting texture limited its general use to restaurants and other places where an easily-cleaned surface was desirable. The black Vitrolite, however, was extremely widely used as a contrast in conjunction with white or peach mirror. (See page 105.)

The wide and varied use of mirror to cover pieces of furniture during the thirties was, like the mirrored rooms, more of a revival than an innovation, though the extended techniques made a greater production possible. During the mid-nineteenth century Baccarat had made for the Sultan Abdul Hamid a suite of furniture entirely covered in engraved mirrors and one piece, a seat, from this ensemble was exhibited by Serge Roche in 1934, undoubtedly proving an inspiration for many other pieces treated in the same fashion but in a more modern idiom. Mirror furniture had a fashionable appeal for the reflective glitter it could lend to an otherwise simple interior and according to its treatment could add to either a starkly modernistic room or a period revival décor.

Used unadorned and in its natural colourless state, mirror covered the top section of the desk designed by Robert Block and made by La Société Industrielle

Table by Dorothy Thorpe, 1937

The plate-glass top was engraved with motifs inspired by the poinsettia flower and was supported on glass rods set in satin-finished silver. Dorothy Thorpe designed a number of tables, plates and silverware for Messrs Gump of Honolulu with motifs inspired by the flora of the Hawaiian islands, such as the 'Poinsettia' illustrated, 'Plomeria and Cornflower', 'Tree Fern', 'Bread Fruit' and 'Cups of Gold'.

d'Art: here the top is supported on two black-lacquered plinths and the only break in the simplicity of the design is made by the flat studs covering the heads of the screws holding the mirror in place. In other cases the fixing screws are covered by small glass-ribbed rosettes. Robert Block also designed the commode illustrated on page 116. Here modernism has given way to period references – the carcass, stripped of its covering of antiqued mirror engraved on the back with gilt lines and arabesques, could be that of a French or Italian commode of the late eighteenth century. Commodes of this type, together with low tables, bedside tables and cigarette boxes covered in mirror, were sold by Fortnum and Mason from 1935 onwards until 1939.

Furniture covered in peach-coloured mirror was extremely popular in England in the mid-thirties, especially the cocktail cabinets which were a necessary furnishing in upper-class homes. The example illustrated on page 117 is covered in peach mirror relieved by two bands of blue mirror, the handles to the upper and lower cupboards being made of sections of peach glass rods. The backs of the upper doors have shaped shelves of sycamore which interlock when the doors are fully opened, providing spaces for bottles and glasses: the lower section has storage space for bottles and a space for an ice container. In this case the glass is fixed to the wooden carcass with a strong adhesive.

Peach mirror also covers the low table (page 117). The problem of covering a curved surface with mirror is solved by the use of Vitroflex, a strong, closely woven fabric upon which were glued small squares or rectangles of thin mirror.

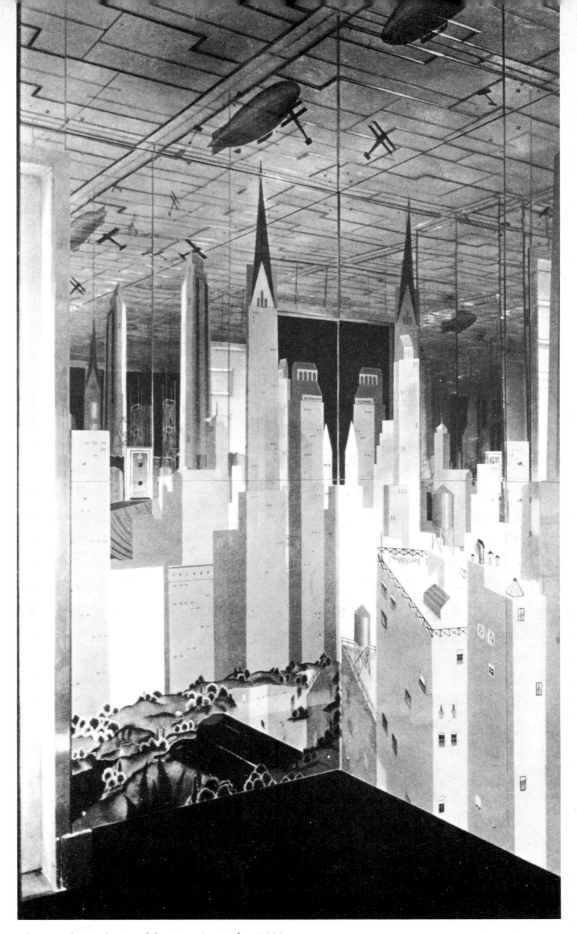

Elevator foyer designed by Kerstin Taube, 1933

The foyer is in a New York apartment building and is painted by Robert Pichenot on black mirror-glass in tones shading from silver to black.

Table with brilliant-cut decorations, by James Clark and Son, 1935

Dining room in a New York apartment, decorated by Inez Croom of Nancy McClelland, Inc., 1935

The walls of this room were painted grey-mauve with a table entirely faced with mirror, which also appeared on the cornice, the surround to the mantel and the door architraves. The modern French screen harmonized with the soft colouring of the carpet and contrasted with the ivory satin of the curtains.

The tendency in the thirties was for the dining room to diminish in size – on occasion to dwindle to a dining alcove off the living room – and, as a writer in the *Studio* commented, few dining tables were designed to seat more than six persons.

Bedhead of peach mirror, 1931

Edward Croghan of Godfrey Giles Ltd designed a bedroom for Mrs Lance Pitman with pale blue-green walls with matching curtains and carpet. The shape of the bedhead in peach mirror – executed by Clark and Son Ltd – was repeated with upholstery round the electric fire. The bedspread was of silver satin.

The flexibility of the supporting fabric enabled Vitroflex to be glued to convex surfaces or even to columns of comparatively small diameter, the small facets of mirror giving a brilliantly glittering effect. The clock (on the table), with a face and frame of peach mirror standing on a black-lacquered base and with the back covered in beige morocco leather, is of French design.

Leslie and Edgar Mendenhall designed for James Clark and Son a number of pieces of mirror furniture using shaped and engraved mirrors, which, to quote from a current advertisement, 'truly reflected the spirit of the new fashion, sophisticatedly modern it is very individual and distinctive.' Cigarette boxes covered in white mirror with a chrome-plated bar handle were on sale at the London firm of Droods in 1935 for 7s 6d (90c).

Serge Roche, a connoisseur with a fastidious appreciation of quality allied to an appreciation of the more fantastic aspects of seventeenth- and eighteenth-century art, in 1934 exhibited a collection of purely decorative objects. Made to his own design, they were deliberately calculated to serve no practical function but simply 'to animate space' and although the exhibition contained a number of pieces of furniture which could be considered functional – commodes, consoles, light fixtures – their treatment was such that they were intended to be regarded as decorative objects to provoke admiration or to stimulate the imagination.

Mirror commode by Robert Block, about 1935

A small commode of three drawers, the mahogany carcass covered with antiqued mirror etched and gilded with lines and ornaments of calligraphic motifs; the handles and feet gilt bronze. A typical decorator's piece combining the form of an eighteenth-century commode with a contemporary surface treatment. Similar commodes with up to six drawers, bedside tables, small occasional tables, clocks, cigarette boxes and decorative obelisks were made in France by SIA and were sold in London by Fortnum and Mason. They were illustrated in numerous advertisements during the mid- and late thirties and a six-drawer commode was featured in *Within Four Walls* by Hayes Marshall. The blackamoor stool was acquired by the present owner in the thirties. This, the white biscuit sphinxes and the blue and white eighteenth-century French *jardinière* are typical of the decorative accessories collected in the later thirties.

116

Cocktail cabinet covered in peach mirror with decorative bands of blue mirror, English; low table of peach mirror probably by James Clark Ltd; clock of peach mirror on black lacquered base, French; all about 1935

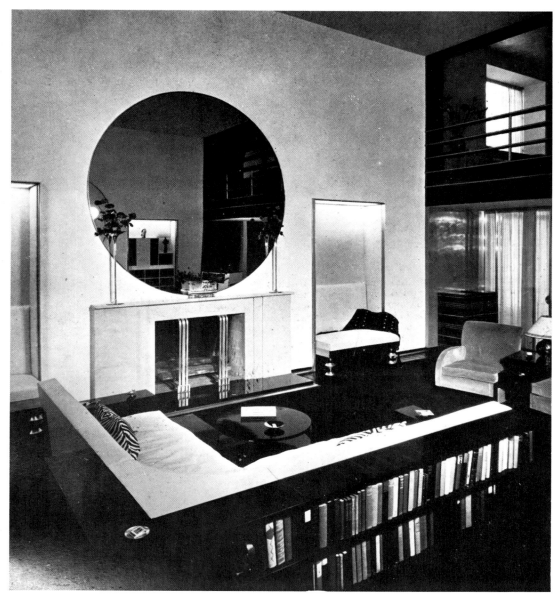

Apartment by Joseph Urban for Miss Katherine Brush, about 1935

Joseph Urban, born in Vienna in 1872, had a distinguished career as an architect – in 1895 he had designed a palace for the Khedive of Egypt – and as a stage designer for major productions of opera. He arrived in America to take charge of the Austrian art exhibit in the St Louis Exhibition and stayed to design for the Boston Opera Company, the Metropolitan Opera and many notable commissions for architectural schemes and interior designs.

Mantelpieces, stools, centrepieces for dining tables with period references to French or Italian baroque were covered with faceted mirrors, as were large and small obelisks – a decorative accessory much in favour during the thirties. The mirror used to ornament these objects was often given an artificial antique effect similar to that caused by age on the mercury-backed mirrors made before the mid-nineteenth century when silver replaced mercury. The mirror illustrated, half sunburst, half sunflower, was designed by Serge Roche in 1936 and shows

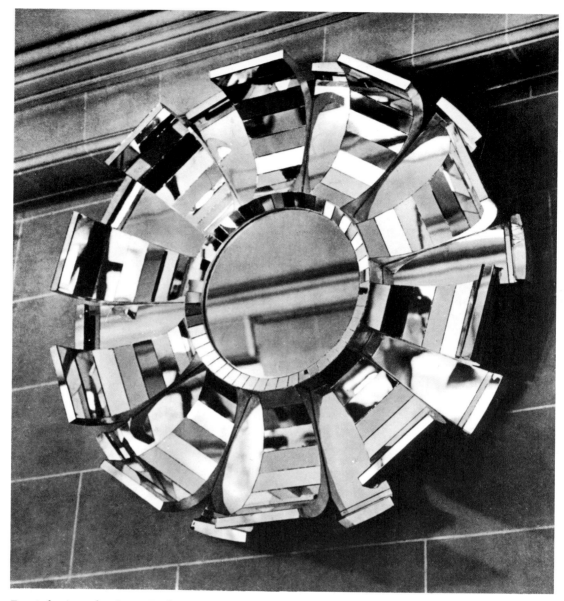

Faceted mirror by Serge Roche, 1936

an ingenious use of small pieces of mirror used to cover a curved surface.

René Lalique was one designer who was unaffected by the enforced austerity. He alone of the French glassmakers maintained his position during the Depression period and was even able to increase his repertory of stock designs. This was probably due to the fact that as most of his products in addition to being beautiful were also practical, they were ideally suited for wedding presents or presentation gifts. Among the gifts made to George VI and Queen Elizabeth on the occasion of

Vase and stopper by Maurice Marinot, 1931

Marinot, unrivalled as a master craftsman in glass, invented a number of techniques including that of imprisoning between two layers of glass another layer evenly interspersed with bubbles. In 1937 he abandoned his work in this field after a career lasting a quarter of a century and returned to his first love, painting.

Left
Vase by W. Clyne Farquharson for Walsh and Walsh, 1939

An unusually elegant example of cut glass which by its comparative simplicity contrasts with the ever-popular variety which earned the scorn of the purists by an over-abundance of faceting applied to poorly designed forms. 'Design still dies the death of a thousand cuts . . . the cocktail has a lot to answer for: much spurious modernism has been inspired by it and most of us have shuddered as we have imbibed from glasses designed in a spirit of squalid gaiety', wrote John Gloag in *Industrial Art Explained*, deploring the fact that examples of restrained design as in this vase and the objects designed by Keith Murray were 'isolated instances'.

Right
Glass sold by Reens-Arta, 1937

A group of flower vases from various sources on sale at Reens-Arta, a London firm specializing in modern furniture.

Opposite
Black and white glass by Steuben, 1932

The glass produced by the Steuben glass division of the old Corning Glass Works in 1932 was greeted with lyrical enthusiasm by Augusta Owen Patterson in *Town and Country*. She found 'in these undecorated shapes a certain likeness to the tall blossoms of the yucca when the moonlight illumines its particle of bloom, giving a translucency to the whiteness which appeals to the emotions and stimulates the imagination', and further described it as 'having the quality of moonlight congratulating a white flower on its perishable attractions'. On a more mundane level, these handmade vases, bowls and candle-holders, some with the opaque white glass outlined with a thread of black glass, were of simple shapes, sometimes reminiscent of those found in Chinese glass, while the urns, finished with black handles were 'of that flexible, all-enduring type which is entirely *en règle* with the Directoire, English Regency and our new fabricated Victorian . . . or it can take its place with the more rebellious Twentieth Century inventions.'

'Monaco' vase with curved handles, 1932; vase with black abstract decorations, 1930; both by René Lalique

Dining table by René Lalique, about 1930

Lalique glass, although never inexpensive, was produced in such quantities as almost to warrant the description of being mass-produced. Large prestige pieces such as this table, however, were made in limited quantities. The top is in one piece of thick glass – there was probably an arrangement for lighting the centre panel from underneath – while the supports and plinth are of cast and acid-etched units held by a framework of chromium-plated metal. A similar technique was used by the rival but less well-known firm of Sabino and an example of a table by each manufacturer can be seen in the *Studio Year Book of Decorative Art* for 1931.

their state visit to Paris was a set of table glass, candelabras and a screen by Lalique, ornamented with motifs of birds. A glass fountain by Lalique was featured in the Main Hall of Olympia during the 1931 *Daily Mail* Ideal Home Exhibition and in the same year a glass chapel was one of the exhibits at the Salon d'Automne in Paris. In June 1933 Lalique was honoured by a retrospective exhibition at the Pavillon de Marsan which embraced the entire scope of his work from the beautiful and fantastic jewelry in the art nouveau style dating from the 1890s to his latest designs for glass.

An article devoted to Lalique's work which appeared in *L'Illustration* for July 1932 and a number of illustrated advertisements by the Brèves Gallery – Lalique's representatives in London – are of some assistance in helping to ascribe dates to the different designs, although the problem is complicated in that a number of models appear to have been in continuous production. As it is extremely rare to find a piece of glass by Lalique dated, the only way to gauge the sequence of design is by comparison of references in periodicals or advertisements and by elimination to establish the earliest date – a method which still leaves room for speculation. An article in the *Studio* for 1931 establishes the fact that the majority of the motor car mascots were designed before that date, though a further complication is added in that the 'Hawk' mascot was also adapted as a decorative handle to a vase in dark brown glass. Of the two vases illustrated, 'Monaco' with its handles of graduated scrolls can be dated prior to 1932 and the unnamed vase decorated with bands of black abstract ornament dates from 1930. A number of vases and other decorative objects with motifs of sparrows or snails can be ascribed to the same year but again the sparrow vases appear to have been in production more recently. From documentary evidence a date no later than 1934 can be applied to the design of the small dining table of engraved glass on a chromium-plated metal framework now in the Brighton Museum. A similar table made by Sabino was illustrated in an advertisement in the *Studio Year Book of Decorative Art* for 1931.

Flint glass bowl and vase by Keith Murray, about 1932

For some years during the thirties Keith Murray designed a number of pieces of glass, decorative and utilitarian, for the firm of Stevens and Williams.

Cube teapot by Wedgwood about 1930

China and ceramics

The *Studio Year Book* for 1931 comments that 'on the Continent dinner services are getting simpler and simpler' and the porcelain designed by Suzanne Lalique, Jean Luce and Marcel Goupy reflects this trend to leave the surface unadorned but for a discreet geometrical ornament or banding in silver combined with a monogram. While the work of these three designers cannot be considered as produced for the popular market, the difference between 'popular' taste in England and Germany is exemplified by the experiment conducted by the Berlin State Porcelain factory in 1930. One hundred and fifty cups of all periods were gathered from museums and collections and visitors to the exhibition were asked to vote as to their preferences for design and ornament as guidance for the development of future designs. By a large majority the favourite was a simple white cup modelled by Wegely for the Berlin factory about 1750, with a classic white cup of the Empire period, equally simple, as second choice. It is safe to say that a similar opinion poll conducted in England would have had a very different result, the taste of the general public, as reflected in trade advertisements, veering more to elaborate shapes over-decorated with ineptly drawn floral motifs.

In the early thirties the jazzing-up process deplored by Paul Nash brought about some eccentric conceptions in the field of commercial ceramics in England. The most fragile of household equipment, pottery and porcelain, absorbed a considerable number of new designs each year, as the manufacturers tempted the public to buy a complete tea or dinner service in an enticing new design rather than replace the broken items of a service in use for some time and consequently over-familiar. Attempting to fit in with the modernistic feeling, manufacturers in France and England experimented with a variety of geometrical shapes which if not as handsome or as practical as the traditional ones were at least different and indicated to the public that the industry was keeping up with the times. For economic reasons the curved shapes inherited or derived from eighteenth-century models still formed the greater part of the production of most potteries but these were decorated with geometrical designs which generally failed to harmonize

Group of Wedgwood ware designed by Keith Murray ARIBA, 1934

Keith Murray designed a considerable number of pieces with matte glazes for Wedgwood. They were hand-thrown and in some cases revived the use of engine-turning. In subdued tones of green, white, grey and buff they were, even for the time, inexpensive, the large vase, for example, selling for 18s 6d ($2.22), the cigarette box for 7s 9d (93c), and the ashtray for 1s 8d (20c).

with the shapes to which they were applied. 'New concepts in tableware', however, appeared in the shape of square, spoutless teapots with recessed handles – an original idea but incurring the disadvantages of scalded knuckles and erratic flow of tea; square cups and saucers – an experiment which died an early death; combined saucer and plate with a depression to take a cup, another concept which failed to attract, and eccentrically designed handles to cups, some solid, some triangular, but all guaranteed to make holding a cup filled with liquid a hazardous venture. One of the more successful of these designs was the 'Vogue' pattern teasets by the Shelley Potteries of whom a writer in the *Pottery Gazette and Glass Trade Review* for March 1931 commented 'Their record for the last few years has provided the dealer with abundant evidence that there is no standing still at the Shelley Potteries', an opinion echoed by the statement in *Woman and Beauty* in the same year that 'The china that is making the tea tray in a smart house as much a matter of fashion as the hostess's gown can be seen in the 1931 shapes and new designs of utter modernity'. In the majority of cases the determined, even frantic, efforts to conform to 'utter modernity' failed to fulfil the hopes of their creators and the public response was cool, preference still being shown for floral designs and conservative shapes. The greater proportion of commercial pottery and porcelain, apart from replicas of traditional patterns, was of a low standard of design ranging from the blatantly ugly to the anaemically refined, and designs similar to those of Suzanne Lalique, Jean Luce and Marcel Rouard in France and Susie Cooper and Keith Murray in England were the exception rather than the rule. The city of Stoke-on-Trent's school of art had departments at Burslem, Hanley, Stoke and Langton, all under the experienced guidance of Gordon Forsyth and all these departments worked in close connection with the pottery manufacturers in the district. The students, after five years tuition, were all absorbed into the industry, an exceptional state of affairs in the economic conditions of the early thirties, but almost without exception they were employed as executants and not as designers. As Josiah Wedgwood pointed out in *Industrial Design* in 1934, 'Movements in pottery design generally start on the Continent, spreading to London five years afterwards, to the provinces three years after that and to the USA still later' – a surprising statement but one which, coming from such an authoritative source, can hardly be doubted. The Wedgwood company entrusted the design of their contemporary production to Keith Murray and his simple and elegant vases, if sometimes rather unmemorable, received considerable publicity and, from the praise accorded them by various writers, seemed to fulfil all the current standards of fitness for purpose. In France, incidentally, Jean Luce was producing a range of vases which bore a close resemblance to those of Keith Murray.

'A few well-chosen pieces of Miss Clarice Cliff's "Bizarre" ware seem just to add the last touch of distinction to a carefully thought out room', ran the text of a 1934 advertisement in the *Illustrated London News*. Clarice Cliff, born in 1900, was trained in all branches of pottery-making, including modelling, at Burslem School of Art before, together with her two sisters, she joined the Burslem firm of A. J. Wilkinson as an apprentice. She was given every encouragement to develop her very original ideas and when she retired in 1939 she was Art Director of Wilkinsons and the subsidiary firm of the Newport Pottery Company. In addition to the 'Bizarre' ware (see p. 130), she originated 'Scarab Blue Inspiration Bizarre' ware, 'Delecia', 'Patina' and a number of patterns like 'Crocus' and 'My Garden', which were executed in on-glaze technique by Clarice Cliff personally or by the assistants she trained. The designs ranged from the fairly conventional 'Crocus' pattern to vases, bowls and large decorative plates boldly ornamented with abstract geometrical designs or arrangements of conventionalized flowers in vivid colourings of orange, blue, yellow and black. Bizarre ware achieved extreme popularity and the pieces were in great favour as wedding presents.

The thirties was not an encouraging period for the studio potters. Too great a dependence on Chinese, Korean or Japanese models as sources of inspiration tended to develop a certain sameness and family resemblance between the products of different potters and the limited clientele for this type of craft diminished during the Depression. The expenditure of time and the outlay on materials beyond the original cost of equipment for throwing and firing the pots was barely compensated by the low prices to be obtained for the finished products, and a further deterrent was that the conventional classic shapes and coloured glazes bore close resemblances to the original Oriental pieces which could be found in considerable numbers at the same or even lower prices. Although it was asserted that studio pottery eventually influenced commercial pottery – a statement which could be accepted with reservations – the commercial designers were on the whole more adventurous in their designs, especially where the basic shape of the vessel was concerned.

The doyen of British potters, Bernard Leach, is recorded as having suffered considerable hardship during the thirties and in 1934 he closed his small pottery in South Devon and together with his Japanese assistant Shoji Hamada returned to Japan, where his reputation was high among connoisseurs and collectors. He returned to England in 1936. Leach's former pupil, Michael Cardew, worked at the Winchcombe pottery which he had acquired in 1926 and William Staite-Murray continued his work, but there are few instances of new talent appearing on the scene. The small demand for studio pottery was more than adequately supplied by the established craftsmen. The Ashstead Potteries, founded after the First World War to give employment to disabled ex-servicemen, extended their range of white glazed ware to include decorative figures of which *Spring* and *Summer*, modelled by Joan Pyman in 1930 and 1931 respectively, are good examples (see page 130).

Plastics

The early thirties saw the production of plastic ware on a commercial scale. Non-inflammable and unaffected by hot water, the tableware produced by Beatl Sales Ltd about 1930 had the added advantage of being almost unbreakable, was without smell and did not alter the taste of the food or drink it contained. Marketed under the name 'Linga-Longa' ware, it was manufactured from a non-phenolic synthetic resin and could be finished in a variety of marbled and mottled effects. Its low cost of production ensured a ready sale in the cheaper markets — it was particularly in demand for picnic baskets — but its rather unattractive colourings and the 'feel' of the material limited its appeal and ensured that it did not become a serious rival to the pottery or porcelain trades. Experiments in the Imperial Chemical Industries Ltd Laboratories resulted in a transparent plastic, white or coloured, which could be moulded under heat into different forms; complete articles could be shaped in steel moulds, flat boards could be pressed and laminated to other materials and plastics could be produced in blocks which could subsequently be shaped by trimming or cutting. Such a material obviously offered new possibilities but nobody seems to have known quite what to do with it, though a certain amount of clear plastic furniture of small dimensions, chairs, coffee tables and so on, was made in the United States, more for exhibition purposes than for practical use. The presses and moulds used for its production were extremely expensive and consequently the material needed to be sold in extremely large quantities to cover the initial costs. Though it was ideal for containers for beauty products, for instance, the cosmetic industry was reluctant to experiment in bulk in case this new and untried material should develop idiosyncracies after a while. It was not until a few years later, during the war, that uses were found for plastics on a large scale.

Decorative painters

Painters as much as anyone were severely affected by the Depression. The dramatic suddenness of the Wall Street Crash brought to an end a boom in Paris where Americans, with the exchange rate very much in their favour, had been lavishly buying contemporary paintings, good and bad. The periodical *L'Amour de l'Art* with its regular feature of critical notices of the many current exhibitions often confined its comments on the work of a painter to one derogatory word, and the paintings illustrated in these articles and in those devoted to the work of an individual painter or sculptor indicate why the reputation of the Ecole de Paris was on the decline. The remark attributed to André Lhote in 1930 that 'Nobody is buying paintings – painting is saved' speaks for itself. Add to the Depression the fashion for bare walls and the prospects for artists in the early thirties were grim, and it is not surprising that many were glad to turn to commissions which in happier times they would have despised, decorative flower paintings, screens or designs for china. In 1934 galleries were selling paintings by Eric Gill, C. W. R. Nevinson, Frank Dobson and Charles Ginner for £10 ($24) or less or, in one case, works by Augustus John and Sickert for £100 ($240) on instalments.

Frank Brangwyn

The decade had opened with a major controversy in the English art world. In February 1930 a Royal Fine Arts Commission inspected five of the eighteen panels destined for the Royal Gallery in the Palace of Westminster, a scheme commissioned from the eminent painter Frank Brangwyn by Lord Iveagh and intended as a memorial to the peers who had lost their lives in the Great War. After deliberation the verdict was given that the panels were unsuitable and the scheme would not be installed. Considerable indignation was expressed in the press about this affront to the artist and to the memory of his patron – who had died three years

Left Blown-glass figure of a dancer in smoky brown and black; *right The Snake-charmer* statuette with inlaid emerald eyes, by Poertzel; both about 1933

Similar blown-glass figures of ballet dancers, acrobats, negro musicians and whimsical animals by Marianne von Allesch of New York, J. Brychta in Czechoslovakia, Guido Balsamo Stella and Venini and Company in Italy, and Fritz Lampl of Vienna were considered suitable ornaments for modernist interiors during the early thirties.

It is surprising to find that the coloured bronze and ivory figures of which Professor Poertzel's *The Snake-charmer* is a typical example had a considerable sale during the thirties. Not by any means inexpensive, they were regarded by many as jokes or suitable only for *nouveaux riches* and were entirely ignored by both the advocates of fitness for purpose and by those experimenting with period revivals for, as far as can be ascertained, not a single example can be found in any of the photographs published in books or periodicals dealing with decoration during the thirties. Yet in spite of this they were sold in sufficient quantities to warrant the distributors, Phillips and MacConnal, taking a stand each year at the Ideal Home Exhibition. The catalogues of the exhibition are the main sources of information as to their creators, for the majority of the pieces were unsigned.

'Continental', generally used as a perjorative adjective, could be applied to these figures with absolute truth, for the sculptors were French, German or Austrian. Professor Poertzel was for many years 'under protection of the Duke of Coburg-Gotha' and the King of Bulgaria purchased his *Bacchanal*. Another statue of Poertzel's was named *Tanz Finale*. Other sculptors were J. Preiss, D. H. Chiparus, Bouraine, Paul Phillipe and Pierre le Faguays 'so well known for his statues seen in the ornate palace cinemas of today'.

Group of china decorated by Clarice Cliff during the 1930s

Demonstrating the various styles of ornament including 'My Garden' (the pitcher with a handle of modelled flowers). The beer mug on the left was designed and painted by Susie Cooper.

Spring and *Summer* china figures with coloured decoration, designed for the Ashstead Potteries in 1930 and 1931 respectively

The fluted draperies echo the bias cut found in women's dresses of the period.

Preliminary study by Frank Brangwyn for the House of Lords murals, submitted to the Royal Fine Art Commission in 1930

before – but it was noticeable that references to the artistic merits of the paintings were guarded and there were few comments to the effect that the members of the Commission were depriving the nation of a great masterpiece. Since 1895 when Brangwyn had painted two large panels, *Music* and *Dancing*, for the entrance of Siegfried Bing's new establishment, L'Art Nouveau, his reputation had always stood higher in Europe, America and Japan than in his own country – though he was born in Bruges his parents were both English – and, particularly in the early 1900s, there were few exhibitions on the Continent which did not feature one or more of his paintings. From about the age of thirty he had led a secluded life, avoiding social intercourse and producing an enormous body of work. The House of Lords panels were to have been both the culmination of his career and a glorification of the riches, the natural beauties and the magnificence of the British Empire, symbolizing the heritage for which so many had died in the First World War, rather than the fact of their death. Since the work was commissioned in 1925 Brangwyn had worked unceasingly on the seventeen large panels, after

131

preliminary work on quarter-size cartoons and innumerable studies in different media for figures, birds, animals and plants. Brangwyn was a superb draughtsman in a tradition already beginning to be discredited in the late twenties. The drawings in red, blue and black crayon of animals and plants are masterly in execution and in quality superior to the finished panels. These were treated in the manner of verdure tapestries, the colouring clear and bright, the subjects depicted with the minimum of shadows and sparely modelled in colour. The difference in scale of the various elements – figures peering through thickets of brightly coloured flowers nearly as large as themselves – gives some of the panels a curious and obviously unintended resemblance to Richard Dadd's *The Fairy Feller's Master Stroke*, where the tiny fantastic figures are similarly dwarfed by the surrounding vegetation. This riot of bright colour and the occasional illogicalities in the design probably influenced the Commission in their decision when they saw five of the panels erected in the gallery for which they were intended – a gallery noted for the gloomy melancholy of its decorations. Another factor which may have influenced them is that there was hardly any sky to be seen in any of the panels and, as any art dealer will witness, it is almost impossible to dispose of a landscape painting, no matter how exquisitely painted, which does not show at least a third of the canvas area as sky – an illogical reaction on the part of the picture-buying public which keeps many restorers busy rearranging old paintings of views.

Brangwyn was not allowed to suffer financially by the rejection, for the commission was honoured by Lord Iveagh's heir, and he finished the remaining panels, though with an inevitable sense of discouragement and the knowledge that, at the time, there was no home for them. An offer of £40,000 ($96,000) for the finished panels from an American admirer of Brangwyn was not his to refuse. It is recorded that Brangwyn never saw the panels as an ensemble, though they were exhibited at the *Daily Mail* Ideal Home Exhibition in 1933. Eventually they were used as decorations for the new Guildhall at Swansea in Wales, and were unveiled by Prince George in 1934.

Possibly as a relaxation from his work on these panels, Brangwyn had found time to design a number of furnished rooms for an exhibition at Pollard and Sons which was opened by a fellow Academician, the portrait painter Sir John Lavery, in October 1930. The furniture was made to his designs by Pollards', the pottery, glass and carpets by Doulton, Powell, and Templeton respectively. Again the reception by the critics was lukewarm – even embarrassed – and that of a writer in the *Architectural Review* confirms the memories of the present writer: 'Now quaint, now just a little art nouveau, now faintly reminiscent of this period or that, now "modern" yet somehow not "modern".' Obviously out of sympathy with the starkness of modernism, Brangwyn seems to have attempted to establish a style with no affinities with any period, rather in the way that a designer faced with the problem of creating a setting for a play in, say, Atlantis or some other mythical milieu invents an idiom of decoration which he hopes has an air of authority but is nevertheless unconsciously flavoured by references to known periods.

His murals painted on silver leaf for the dining room of the *Empress of Britain* sank into the obscurity which usually seems to overwhelm the decorations on liners, while his murals in the Great Hall of the RCA Building in the Rockefeller Centre, New York, dating from 1934, were overshadowed by those of José-Maria Sert and of Diego Rivera.*

* Diego Rivera was described by a contemporary as 'the Raphael of Communism'.

Rex Whistler

Rex Whistler was twenty and fresh from the Slade School, where he had studied under Henry Tonks, when he was commissioned by Lord Duveen to decorate with mural paintings the restaurant of the Tate Gallery, a work which occupied him for two years. These paintings – still in the sketch state in one or two places, notably in the areas around the windows – were on the theme of 'In Pursuit of Rare Meats' and demonstrate Whistler's admiration for the architecture of Inigo Jones and his eighteenth-century followers. A guide to the events depicted in the murals was written by Rex Whistler and Edith Olivier and later published as a pamphlet by the Trustees of the Tate Gallery: in this various people and places depicted are referred to with anagrammatic titles, Tonks as Dr Knots, Pugin as Ugpin, and Bernard Shaw, who opened the room in 1927, appears as Count Brendar Wahs, 'the Palace Librarian and Public Orator'. These murals established the reputation of Whistler as a decorative artist and his wittily elegant designs were in great demand until his untimely death in 1944 at the age of thirty-nine.

Rex Whistler's art was sometimes dismissed as pastiche and nothing more, but this is less than the truth. There was no element intended to deceive, no deliberate imitation of the work of any one artist but rather a synthesis of all the eighteenth-century draughtsmen – most of his work incorporated decorative motifs from the late seventeenth and eighteenth centuries, though he was equally adept at conveying the precise atmosphere of the Regency, Victorian and Edwardian periods – and he drew in the mannered fashion because it came naturally and expressed his ideas as no other way could. The contemporary scene he avoided, with few exceptions – a small number of fashion drawings for *Vogue* and, at the time of the coronation of George VI and Queen Elizabeth, some portrait drawings of the King and Queen and princesses in their robes – and these, though skilled, give the impression of a certain lack of interest.

Whistler's many patrons were drawn from those whose tastes were more traditional than *avant-garde*. Living mainly in eighteenth-century houses, either inherited or acquired from choice, and surrounded by furniture and objects of the same date, they had cultivated, literary tastes. They might understand and even admire the latest developments in the decorative arts but preferred for their own surroundings the more serene products of the past. For them he tirelessly painted murals, drew bookplates, illustrated novels and volumes of poems. Through their patronage his work was brought to the attention of theatrical impresarios who had connections with this circle and as a result theatregoers were given the benefit of some of the most beautiful productions of the thirties. Posters for the London Museum, the Tate Gallery and the London underground enlivened the streets with his elegant wit.

Whistler's most important commission was for the dining room at Plas Newydd, the residence of Lord Anglesey. The long room, perhaps too long for its width, was transformed into a baroque loggia, the ceiling coffered in *trompe l'œil*, the smaller walls at each end treated architecturally with pilasters enclosing the chimney piece, *œil de bœuf* grilles over the doors and false perspectives, while the long wall facing the windows was transformed into a romantic idealized landscape of a harbour surrounded by mountain ranges – a harbour dotted with islands reminiscent of Isola Bella, and crowded with sailing vessels anchored in safety behind moles and jetties from the storm hinted at by the high-piled threatening clouds. Separating this landscape from the room and acting as a link between the real and the imaginary are low walls and a jetty littered with fishing tackle,

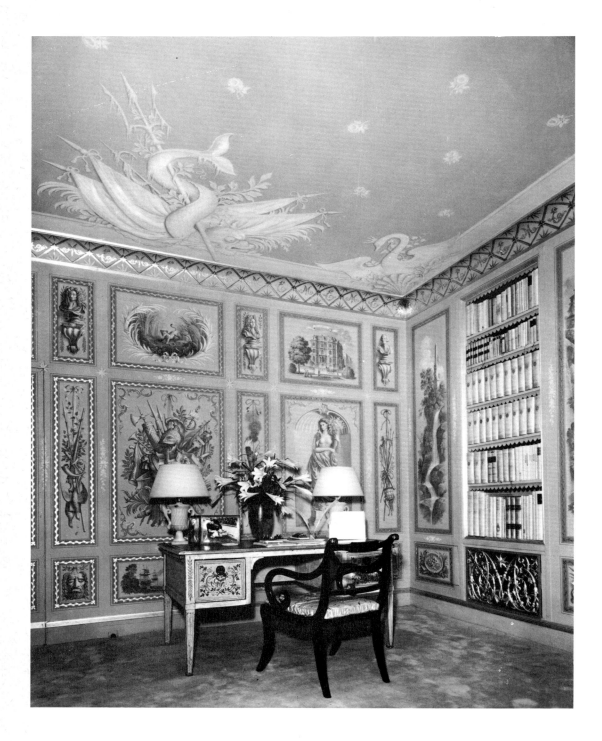

Mural decoration by Rex Whistler for Lord and Lady Louis Mountbatten, in the penthouse, Brook House, London, 1937

Each panel in this decoration has a personal reference and the carved gilt grille concealing the radiator and the decoration on the writing desk incorporate the initials of Lady Mountbatten, EM.

anchors, chains and objects emblematic of the sea, while the painter's sense of humour, never for long absent, shows itself in a trident, wreathed in seaweed, propped against a classical urn, and a wet footprint on the pavement, with the implication that Neptune had risen from the sea and was exploring this house which encroached on his domain. The treatment of the architectural details is masterly enough to satisfy the most scholarly enthusiast of the eighteenth century.

Rather different in treatment were the mural decorations at Brook House executed for Lord and Lady Louis Mountbatten. These were in the sitting room of the penthouse apartment of the block erected on the site of the former Brook House in Park Lane, and in this case the walls were treated as panels in three tiers, each panel enclosing a painted landscape, a trophy, a *trompe l'oeil* alcove with a statue or an allegorical composition. The criticism might be made that the over-all effect is crowded and restless, that there are too many vignettes, but the *grisaille* colouring and the quality of the paintings go far to mitigate this possible fault. The murals at Mottisfont Abbey, an essay in the eighteenth-century Gothic manner, are perhaps a trifle mechanical and betray the effect of numerous rejections of proposed designs – much of the repeated architectural detail was done by an assistant under the artist's supervision.

In 1930 the Cresset Press published an edition of *Gulliver's Travels* in a two-volume edition with illustrations by Rex Whistler, an edition which has become a collector's item as only 195 copies on handmade paper were produced. A surviving proof with Whistler's corrections shows the painstaking care he took to ensure that his illustrations were reproduced with complete fidelity and here again is demonstrated that passion for eighteenth-century architecture which was so characteristic. At first sight some of the architectural fantasies appear improbable, but on closer examination they prove to be entirely practical and could in fact be realized in stone and brick. The success of this edition led to Whistler's work being in demand for other illustrations, notably for *The Lord Fish* by Walter de la Mare, *Fairy Tales and Legends* by Hans Andersen, *The Next Volume* by Edward James and for the volume of poems *Armed October* by his brother Laurence Whistler; and for dustjackets – Isaak Dinesen's *Seven Gothic Tales*, Constance Wright's *Silver Collar Boy*, Vincent Sheean's *San Felice* and for Laurence Whistler's definitive volume *Sir John Vanbrugh*, a study of an architect with whom, in versatility, Rex Whistler had much in common.

However, it was in his work for the theatre that Rex Whistler's work reached the widest public. Charles B. Cochran, always ready to encourage new talent, gave him his first opportunity, a small scene in Cochran's 1931 revue at the old London Pavilion Theatre in Piccadilly Circus. The Cochran revues and other productions which were so much a part of theatrical life in the 1930s were always mounted with taste and style and among the many decorative artists who were given an opportunity by Cochran was Christian Bérard, then unknown in England, again in the 1931 revue. From 1933 Whistler designed one or more productions for the theatre or the ballet practically every year. *Ballerina* in 1933, settings for *Fidelio* at Covent Garden in 1934 – settings worthy of revival – a *Marriage of Figaro* at Sadlers Wells and in 1935 the costumes and settings for the ballet *The Rake's Progress* inspired by Hogarth's engravings with the addition of a drop curtain representing a street in eighteenth-century London.

Nobody in the audience at Sadlers Wells witnessing the first performance of *The Wise Virgins*, a ballet with Whistler's designs, could possibly have imagined that the scenery and costumes would be destroyed through enemy action in

Holland five years later in 1940 and that some of the dancers would barely escape with their lives. The backcloth depicted the baroque gates to heaven and the costumes of the frivolous foolish virgins left one breast bare or seemingly so, for in the less permissive thirties what appeared to be bare flesh was actually chiffon with a rosy nipple painted on.

In 1935 *Victoria Regina* by Laurence Housman was presented at the Broadhurst Theatre in New York with Rex Whistler's explorations into the nineteenth-century styles. This play was presented with designs by Roger Furse in London at the tiny Gate Theatre – as there were regulations regarding the portrayal of royalty it was not possible to admit the public so that the London showing was limited to this club theatre. These regulations did not apply to New York, of course, and the Whistler designs, especially the scene in the tartan tent erected in the grounds of Balmoral, were widely admired, being in the opinion of many influential in furthering the popular revival of interest in Victoriana. In 1936 London saw a never-to-be-forgotten production of *Pride and Prejudice* with Whistler's charming scenery and costumes as a setting for the performance of Celia Johnson, the perfect embodiment of Elizabeth Bennett.

Almost archaeological in their attention to period detail but at the same time composed into beautiful stage pictures, Whistler's settings avoided any garish extravagance and his costumes were always exactly right for the character, without any eccentric and bizarre exaggerations of period characteristics.

The neo-romantics

Christian Bérard, Pavel Tchelitchev, the brothers Eugène and Léonid Berman, Thérèse Desbaines and Kristians Tonny, formed the group known as the 'neo-romantics' when they first exhibited at the Galerie Druet. There is a curious lack of agreement as to the date of this exhibition. Waldemar George, writing in 1934 and giving the group an alternative title of 'neo-humanists', gives a date of 1924, Julien Levy places it in 1925 while Lincoln Kirstein in his monograph on the drawings of Pavel Tchelitchev gives yet another date, that of 1926, a date confirmed by Parker Tyler in his recent biography of Pavel Tchelitchev. Even the spelling of the name of the gallery varies between Druet and Drouot. All the members of the group had studied at the Académie Ranson where they had been influenced by Maurice Denis, Vuillard, Bonnard and Valloton. Desbaines, of whom little was heard after that first exhibition, and Bérard were French, and Tonny was Danish. The others were Russian, and all three had spent years since their leaving Russia during the Revolution wandering from one country to another, studying under different masters, before settling in Paris. These years, with their different influences, left their mark in characteristics which were to become more pronounced in time, though at the point when their ways coincided and for a brief period, they could be collectively designated as neo-romantics. All of them were under the spell of Picasso's Blue Period with, in the opinion of Waldemar George, traces of cubism, expressionism, surrealism and the imagery of popular art.

Eugène Berman's sojourns in Rome and Venice had imbued him with an enthusiasm for Palladian, mannerist and baroque architecture which became the predominating factor in his paintings, murals and stage designs. The melancholy of ruined architecture took precedence over the human condition as subject-matter in his compositions and he coupled this with an absorption in the ingenuities of *trompe l'œil*. Figures, when incorporated into the compositions of ruined, crumbling architecture, invariably represented beggars or gipsies, dispossessed and wandering, introduced less as individuals than as devices to give scale to the architecture or to accentuate the desolate melancholy of the scene. The bizarre landscape of Les Baux with its weather-worn rocks tortured into freakish shapes appears many times as a setting for decayed architectural vistas under skies filled with perspectives of fleecy clouds – vistas depicting the aftermath of a titanic struggle between rocks, trees and buildings.

Berman's paintings earned him the patronage of a number of distinguished collectors during the 1930s. Already the owner of a number of canvases by Chirico, whose use of architectural perspectives to give a surreal effect of a disturbing sense of strangeness had been an early influence on Berman, Arthur Jeffress became an enthusiastic collector of Berman's paintings, creating a setting for them, in collaboration with John Hill of Green and Abbott, of Empire furniture and sombre walls and curtains in shades of tobacco brown and spinach green in the dining room of his country house near Winchester. Edward James acquired a number of paintings and drawings (at the time of writing, 1971, on loan to Brighton Museum). A trip to America in 1935 enlarged Berman's circle of admirers and the scope of his activities. For Julian Levy he executed a series of mural paintings in *trompe l'œil*, depicting empty wooden picture frames inlaid in a chevron design of differently coloured woods enclosing, in lieu of pictures, painted representations of tattered scraps of canvas, some depicting scenes of gipsy encampments – criss-crossed with random loops of cord. (See page 140.)

In the same year, 1936, he completed a series of painted panels of beggars and their makeshift tents of tattered draperies for the dining room of James Thrall Sobey and in 1938 Berman, in a room for Wright Ludington, experimented further in illusionistic techniques. Here the wrinkled and torn canvas with scenes of desolate landscapes with figures is apparently carefully pinned to the wall, framed by and superimposed upon still more ragged fabric.

Berman's poetic obsession with fantastic architecture and its treatment in perspective combined with his faculty for conveying a disturbing atmosphere of still, magical desolation, rendered him particularly eligible for designing for the theatre and, in particular, for ballet, but, apart from a number of projects which never came to fruition, his only work of note during the thirties consisted of settings and costumes for the ballet *The Devil's Holiday* presented in 1939 by the Ballets Russes de Monte Carlo with choreography by Frederick Ashton to music by Niccolo Paganini. Berman designed several covers for the periodical *Town and Country* before the war but his most frequent contributions in this field, as in ballet, were executed after 1940.

The painted wardrobe (page 141) exhibited at the Galerie Drouin a month or so before the outbreak of war shows what Eugène Berman might have accomplished if given the opportunities to realize his architectural fantasies in three dimensions. In this piece of decorative furniture (whose whereabouts are now unknown) he achieved, by forcing illusionistic techniques of painting to their utmost limit, the effect of a ruined stone framework – built perversely as a ruin, opening on to the limpid sky with no horizon and punctuated by bronze rings which serve no purpose, nails and odd pieces of wood and rags, which by the simplest means contribute to as great a feeling of strangeness as all of the sometimes strained imagery of Salvador Dali.

The years of the Depression had not allowed many opportunities for elegance or gaiety. By 1934 however there were signs of recovery which coincided with

Painted screen by Etienne Drian, about 1938

Drian's fashion drawings appeared in *Le Gazette du Bon Ton* in 1913 and during the twenties and thirties he drew in charcoal or sanguine most of the elegant women of the day. In addition to his portrait drawings, which were somewhat in the tradition of Boldini, he executed many decorative paintings and screens such as the one illustrated.

Versailles and its gardens had a particular appeal for him; the Cent Pas appear in the panels he executed for Elsie de Wolfe in the Villa Trianon at Versailles and again in the *trompe-l'œil* murals in an apartment decorated by Nasenta. Here views of Versailles in late-eighteenth-century frames appear to be held up by assymetrical arrangements of cords and are partially obscured by swags and draperies – equally simulated. The simple Louis XVI furniture was upholstered in satin.

138

Sketch for *Aquarius* by Jean Dupas, 1934

One of a series illustrating the signs of the Zodiac.

Decorative panel by Duncan Grant, 1933

Decorative panel consisting of an octagonal centre painting of flowers in a vase against a background of sky and sea, enclosed in a larger panel with swags of drapery treated in a pseudo-*trompe l'oeil* manner and surmounted by a circular mirror with a frame painted in a design of circles, the whole mounted on plywood. Together with a companion panel with a different flower painting, this formed part of the decoration of a music room designed by Duncan Grant and Vanessa Bell exhibited at Alex Reid and Lefevre Ltd in 1933. An illustration in colour of part of the room can be seen in *Colour Schemes for the Modern Home* by Derek Patmore and shows the carpets, fabrics, ornaments and tiled hearth decorated by Vanessa Bell and Duncan Grant in their characteristic calligraphic style. The fabrics by Duncan Grant were printed by Allan Walton and incorporated a swagged border design which was used as a pelmet and on the upholstered settee and chairs.

Duncan Grant was active during the thirties as a mural painter, often in conjunction with Vanessa Bell, as a designer of textiles, and as a designer of ceramics.

Panel by Eugène Berman for Julian Levy, 1936

One of a series of panels painted in *trompe l'oeil* by Eugène Berman for Julian Levy, the author of a volume devoted to Berman's work from the early exhibitions in Paris during the twenties until the mid-forties. The meticulously detailed empty picture frames, apparently riddled with age and worm-holes, enclose simulated fragments of pictures, scraps of drapery, pebbles or sprouting bulbs criss-crossed and, as it were, trapped in a fragile cage of knotted strings which cast their painted shadows on the objects behind them. The walls of the room itself were painted in exactly the same colour as that of the backgrounds of the panels in order to accentuate the deception.

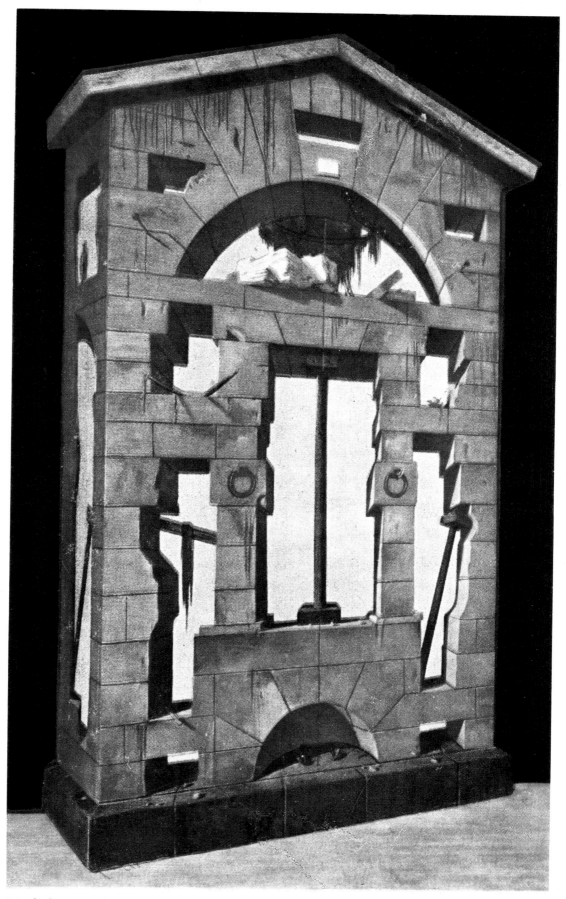

Wardrobe painted in *trompe l'œil* by Eugène Berman, exhibited at the Galerie Drouin, Paris, 1939

Design for mural painting in a London department store by Clement Cowles, before 1934

The rebuilding of many department stores, originally an inconvenient huddle of small shops added to as neighbouring premises became available, into large and often imposing modern buildings started at the beginning of the century and continued, despite the Depression, into the thirties. The large wall spaces began to be used for mural decorations as prestige attractions and those by Cowles – a regular exhibitor at the Royal Academy – reflect the growing interest in Victoriana. It is recorded that 'while the work was in progress, groups of people were always to be found watching the painting, and criticism was flattering, idiotic or vitriolic, but always lively, which pleased the store gods by producing a ''happening'' atmosphere.'

Decorative panels by Léonor Fini, exhibited at the Galerie Drouin, Paris, 1939

The Galerie Drouin, specializing in the work of leading surrealist and neo-romantic painters was opened in the Place Vendôme. Everything seemed favourable for its success, the decorations were lavish, the site excellent (next to the Schiaparelli boutique), the painters exhibiting had considerable reputations – only the opening date in the summer of 1939 was ill-omened. The decorations of the three main rooms were remarkable for each was devoted to a single colour, grey, sapphire blue and red. The walls including the mouldings were covered in velvet with the carpet exactly matching, the early-eighteenth-century ceilings being painted white. Each room took on the semblance of a precious casket enshrining the paintings displayed and the sole exhibit in the red room was a large and sinister canvas by Max Ernst. Among the other exhibits was a *trompe l'œil* cupboard by Eugène Berman (see illustration page 141) and another painted by Léonor Fini with winged seraphim.

An early exhibition of Léonor Fini's paintings in 1934 had attracted the favourable notice of the critic Germain Bazin and although the painter's name was misspelt as 'Chini' the terms used to describe her – 'elle a presque un air de suffragette' – and her work – 'hermaphroditism, auto-eroticism, sapphism . . . equivocal' – were enough to intrigue a new circle of admirers.

Entrance Hall designed by Allan Walton for Fortnum and Mason, London, about 1935

The walls are lightly marbleized in ivory and pale olive green as a setting for the large panel painted on glass and intended to give an illusion of space. The floor is of rubber inlaid in tones of beige and pink while the furniture – described by a contemporary writer as 'Empire' – is English of the Regency period.

the appearance in the pages of *Vogue* of drawings by an artist new to the majority of the magazine readers, though his reputation had been steadily growing among the *cognoscenti* of Paris since the Galerie Druet exhibition ten years before. This artist, Christian Bérard, was to wield a growing influence on taste in the theatre, fashion, and decoration – he was in many ways to occupy the position formerly held by Paul Poiret.

Christian Bérard's work had attracted the favourable attention of the influential critic Gustave Geffroy some time before the Galerie Druet exhibition which added so considerably to his reputation as a painter. Waldemar George, the artistic editor of *L'Amour de l'Art*, became another enthusiastic supporter, writing articles on Bérard's work and giving high praise in particular to his portraits which he considered reflected the painter's admiration for Fayum funerary portraits. Other critics praised Bérard's 'désir d'exprimer la vie intérieure' and drew flattering parallels with Degas – no small compliment to a painter still in his twenties. Waldemar George's support was unfailing. When a series of panels painted by Bérard with reminiscences of Le Nain were commissioned by the architect Pierre Barbe and refused by the client, George rushed to the painter's defence, declaring in print that such a refusal was nothing but an honour for Bérard.

Bérard was criticized during his lifetime for neglecting his more serious painting in favour of fashionable but less permanent pursuits. It is possible that he found a greater outlet for his fertile imagination in magazine covers and fashion drawings and in designs for the theatre and in particular for the ballet. Certainly as a result of them he became the virtual arbiter of taste in Paris during the second half of the thirties. Few designers have had so many opportunities of disseminating their work. Hardly an issue of *Vogue* appeared without a contribution from him in some form or another, whether a cover, a series of fashion drawings in colour, or illustrations to a feature article on fashion or decoration, and his décors and costumes for the Ballets Russes were seen by audiences in the United States and South America as the company went on their lengthy tours. Yet of this enormous body of work little remains to record the achievement of perhaps the most influential designer of the thirties. None of the ballets he designed are still in the repertory of any company, while copies of *Vogue* or of any periodical to which he contributed, either during the thirties or in the postwar years, are extremely scarce. The setting and the lovely clothes for *Cotillon* (see over page), for *Symphonie Fantastique* (page 151) or *Seventh Symphony*, for the plays *La Voix Humaine* and *La Machine Infernale* by Jean Cocteau, for *La Reine Margot* and *Cyrano de Bergerac* – all of these survive only in memories or in photographs which fail to convey the magic of the originals. Bérard's draughtsmanship, apparently effortless and at times reminiscent of Japanese drawings, was combined with a highly personal use of colours associated with the fairgrounds and circuses which he depicted so often and with such sympathy – the brilliant pastel shades of clowns' costumes, candy floss and cheap sweets, the deep rich crimson of velvet theatre-curtains or the violets and deep greens of grapes, moss and ivy. With a few strokes of a brush he could draw on his knowledge of architecture to suggest a period, and his fashion drawings, economical to the point of leaving out the faces entirely, transmute the models into a timeless elegance, however typical of the style of a certain year. It is difficult to overestimate Bérard's influence on taste in Paris and elsewhere, for his advice and approval were sought by dress-makers, interior decorators and leaders of fashion.

Bérard's costume designs, like his fashion drawings in *Vogue*, were evocative

'The Hand of Fate' dance from *Cotillon*, danced by Lubov Rostova and David Lichine, setting and costumes by Christian Bérard, 1932

Sketch design by Christian Bérard for a detail of the drop curtain for *Mozartiana*, 1933

rather than explicit and, in the hands of an ordinary dressmaker, their magic could have been blunted. Together with other painters working in the theatre he was fortunate in having his sketches interpreted with great sensitivity by Madame Karinska who with creative artistry of a high degree was able to translate Bérard's calligraphic doodles into practical clothes that worked in a feasible manner and, at the same time, retained the intangible feeling of the original drawing. Her unorthodox dressmaking could transform a scarf or sash rendered in an apparently hurried and careless manner by Bérard with a brushstroke or two of Chinese white into a drapery which was a replica of the original in movement and in repose. Madame Karinska's methods of interpretation were as unconventional as her life prior to her first theatrical commission, the making of Derain's costumes for the ballet *Concurrence* in 1932. No one at the ecstatic première of Massine's ballet *Symphonie Fantastique* would have found it easy to believe that the creator of Bérard's lovely costumes in the ballroom scene (see page 151) had been, not so long before, the editor of a socialist newspaper in Russia. She and her first husband (Karinsky was her second husband) were extremely politically minded before and during the Bolshevik Revolution, but with the changing temperature of political thought in Russia, she judged it expedient on being offered an important museum appointment to declare it necessary to study museum techniques in Germany and on being given official permission to do so left Russia never to return. Her artistic inclinations had led her to apply to Sovely Sorine for tuition in painting, meeting with a cold refusal, though Sorine later admitted that he had been wrong in rebuffing her. Her introduction to the theatre came about, it was reported, as a result of repairing the ballet dress of a dancer, a fellow exile from Russia, a task which she did with so much skill that, much to her relief as she was extremely hard up, more important tasks were entrusted to her talents. Apart from her collaboration with Bérard, she and the couturier Agnes made the costumes for a production of *The Cenci* starring the beautiful Ilya Abdy and, surprisingly, designed by Balthus: as a result the Renaissance berets and doublets featured in the play had a considerable influence on the Paris collections of 1935. She realized the designs of Raoul Dufy for *Beach*, a charming lightweight ballet which failed to survive more than a season or two after its première in 1933. Also in 1935, she worked with Jean Hugo on the designs for *Les Cent Baisers*, an underrated ballet with music by Jean Françaix and choreography by Bronislava Nijinska. Hugo's witty illusions to the lithographic illustrations in nineteenth-century books of fairy tales failed to gain the appreciation the designs deserved and objections were made to the

Setting for *Les Valses de Beethoven* by Emilio Terry, 1933

Terry, one of the most imaginative architect/designers of the thirties, collaborated with George Balanchine in the scenario for this ballet, which was part of the repertory of Les Ballets 1933. The story, a version of the myth of Apollo and Daphne, was less remarkable than the décor and settings. Terry later worked with Carlos de Bestigui in creating with exquisite taste a series of interior decorations and follies.

heroine, danced by Irina Baronova, being dressed in black. Karinska also worked with Cassandre, who by a coincidence was born of French parents in Karkov, the town where she and her first husband had pursued their editorial careers.

Pavel Tchelitchev, like Berman and Bérard, was drawn into the milieu of the ballet soon after the exhibition at the Galerie Druet and was the only one to work in direct contact with Serge Diaghilev. *Ode*, designed in 1928, was Massine's last ballet for Diaghilev and, despite the latter's straining after novelty to keep the attention of the public, he seems to have taken little interest in the production. Tchelitchev in his décors indicated the preoccupations with metaphysics and hermetic mysteries which were later to confuse and even alienate his admirers and the complications of the settings, with rows of dolls in perspective suspended on a network of cords, film projections and illuminated costumes were too much of a novelty even for Diaghilev. Edward James's enthusiasm for the neo-romantics embraced the work of Tchelitchev as much as that of Berman and Bérard and in addition to collecting some of the painter's best early drawings and canvases, he commissioned Tchelitchev to design the ballet *Errante* for the Ballets de 1933 organized by James to further the career of his wife Tilly Losch. Tchelitchev was at the time working on the theme of draperies in metamorphic compositions and for the ballet he devised a setting composed of white draperies. Arnold Haskell, already assuming the mantle of high priest of the ballet, described the scenery as 'a big white sale' and made scathing comments about Tilly Losch's dress with its thirty-foot-long train. One of the rooms in Edward James's London house was strongly reminiscent of the setting for this ballet. Several important paintings by Tchelitchev were hung in a décor of festooned draperies supported by marble columns and a marble Renaissance mantelpiece which had come from Lord Rosebery's collection. And the décors of *Errante* were possibly the original inspiration for the plaster draperies used by a number of decorators in London and Paris during the thirties.*

Two years later Tchelitchev designed *Nobilissime Visione*, a ballet based on the life of St Francis of Assisi, choreographed by Massine for the Ballets de Monte Carlo.

The surrealist influence on decoration

For many people the Surrealist Exhibition which opened in June 1936 at the New Burlington Galleries in London was the first opportunity of seeing the work of a movement which had its inception before the Great War.

A few painters, poets and writers in England were familiar with the somewhat vague philosophies behind the surrealist movement, which was regarded in some quarters with suspicion because of its shifting political associations – and a few patrons, Edward James for instance, wisely purchased some of the best early work of Dali, Magritte, Picabia, and other painters who were attempting to realize Rimbaud's philosophy that life must be changed by depicting the workings of the subconscious mind. Films made by Salvador Dali and Luis Buñuel, *Le Chien Andalou* and *L'Age d'Or*, had had an extremely limited showing in private cinema clubs since they were made in 1929 and 1930 respectively, but the circuit managers would not have allowed either of them, even if the local authorities permitted their being shown, to disturb or alienate a public accustomed to Al Jolson or Shirley Temple. Similarly, the periodical *Minotaure*, founded in 1933 and enlivened with cover designs by Picasso, Derain, Miró, Max Ernst, Magritte, Dali and

---

* The process of making these plaster draperies was both difficult and messy as the required pieces of fabric had to be soaked in liquid plaster and placed in position in a matter of moments before the plaster set hard. No second thoughts or alterations were possible so that in most cases it served as a simple form of tenting – it was useful for disguising awkward corners – or in simple swags draped over a pole for the pelmets in a Regency scheme. Usually the effect desired was in the romantic baroque vein but no attempts were made to emulate the fantasy of the baroque ceiling of the ballroom in the Palazzo Albrizzi in Venice, dating from 1712, with its elaborate agitated draperies upheld by flying cherubs.

Duchamp, was obtainable only in one or two bookshops in London, where its high price and French text ensured the smallest circulation. The general public were unprepared for the impact of this, the first international exhibition of surrealism. The press, delighted to have an opportunity of being facetious at the expense of other artists besides Jacob Epstein and Pablo Picasso, their usual targets, seized every occasion to express horror and indignation at the many exhibits and one in particular, the tea-cup, saucer and spoon made of squirrel fur by Meret Oppenheim, became almost a symbol of the whole exhibition. Every day for the two weeks the show lasted the galleries were crowded with visitors, most of whom came to jeer or to be shocked. Many, however, were won over by the gaiety and impudent wit of certain of the exhibits — not all of them of uniform quality, it must be admitted — and the more perceptive realized the sincerity and importance of the movement.

The organizer of the exhibition was the English painter and collector Roland Penrose and through his initiative the work of more than sixty artists from fourteen countries was shown collectively for the first time. In addition there were surrealist *objets trouvés*, drawings by children and the mentally disturbed, sculpture and objects from Africa, Oceania and America — such a diverse collection of apparently unrelated artefacts that some members of the public began to feel uneasy at the thought of so much 'surrealism' having been in their lives without their realizing it. The following December an even larger exhibition was organized by Alfred Barr in New York under the title 'Fantastic Art, Dada and Surrealism'. In this case the boundaries of surrealism, already extensive, were enlarged to include the work of artists and designers of the past, Dürer, Bosch, Arcimboldo, Piranesi, Hogarth and many others — the catalogue ran to 250 pages. Again the press and the critics alternated between abuse and praise. Before the exhibition left for a tour of a number of cities in America attempts were made to impose a censorship by removing some exhibits which were considered too shocking — the fur tea-cup and saucer was one — but this move was defeated and the exhibition toured in its entirety.

Both these exhibitions could be regarded as dress rehearsals for that held in Paris early in 1938. Far more ambitiously conceived and with the purpose of avoiding any atmosphere of taking place in a museum or gallery, this took the form of tableaux and theatrical set pieces. Salvador Dali's *Taxi Pluvieux* with its snail-encrusted occupant continually drenched in rain, the *Rue Surréaliste* inhabited by mannequins designed by Man Ray, Max Ernst, Dali, Tanguy, Duchamp and others, an enormous room with beds, pools of water, ferns and a ceiling hung with hundreds of sacks of coal by Marcel Duchamp — these were only a few of the fantasies assembled to shock and delight.

It is obvious that these exhibitions contributed enormously to the general taste for fantasy which was current from the mid-thirties until the outbreak of war. Designers, decorators, commercial artists, dressmakers, jewellers and photographers strained their imaginations to the utmost to produce fantasies in the surrealist vein. The more decorative aspects of the movement were cultivated and the sinister, violent and macabre avoided or at least only alluded to obliquely.

The exhibitions, particularly those in New York and Paris, had shown that elements of surrealism could be found in most periods of the past from the sixteenth century onwards and the strong flavour of the nineteenth century which could be seen in many contemporary surrealist creations — for example Max Ernst's collages of Victorian prints in which illustrations of that period were

Sketch design by Christian Bérard for the ballroom scene in the ballet *Symphonie Fantastique*, choreographed by Leonide Massine to the music of Berlioz, 1936

The blood-red arcades giving on to a view of a desert with a brooding winged sphinx provided a perfect setting for the feverish mood of the second movement of the Berlioz symphony and set in relief the whirling figures of the dancers in their romantic dresses – though at the Covent Garden première one or two of the dancers' white dresses showed a slight tendency to fall apart.

Drawing by Charles Martin for *Harper's Bazaar* August 1931

Jewelry by Maubousson

Le Corbusier's bedroom designed by himself, prior to 1935

In an article in the *Architectural Review* P. Morton Shand points out 'the relationship established "accidentally" between the exposed plumbing, the painting, the wall and the basket chair (the tip of which is reflected – with what art – in the dressing table mirror) is typical of the "poet" in Corbusier and his uncanny gift of extracting ever fresh aesthetic values from old and new materials alike.' Few readers of the *Architectural Review* can have agreed with Mr Shand's eulogy of this example of Le Corbusier's talents as an interior decorator, considering the inconvenience of the height of the bed, the lack of privacy in the sanitary arrangements – the bidet as a toilet adjunct was almost unknown in England in the thirties – and the general air of clinical discomfort.

rearranged with malevolent results – provided a link with the current revival of Victoriana.

Among the most fantastic examples of surrealism in the decorative arts were Schiaparelli's creations, discussed in the chapter on fashion (pages 185–96). Schiaparelli had sought the advice of Jean-Michel Frank concerning the decoration of her various apartments and it was for him that Dali designed the pink satin

Drawing room in Paris apartment of Carlos de Bestigui, before 1936

settee in the shape of Mae West's lips, derived from several drawings representing the actress as a room, her nostrils forming a fireplace, her eyes two framed pictures and her hair the swirling looped draperies or *portières*.

In 1936 the *Architectural Review* featured an apartment in Paris which combined a certain surrealist perverseness with extreme luxury – all the more surprising as the austere surroundings designed by Le Corbusier were a setting for nineteenth-century mock-baroque of an exuberance completely alien to the ideals of an architect who maintained that a house was a machine for living in. The explanation of this anomaly was given a year or two later by Jean-Michel Frank. Between the time that the work on the structure of the penthouse had finished and the moment when it was necessary to decide on the furnishings, modernism had

Drawing room in Paris apartment of Carlos de Bestigui, before 1936

The framed mirrors with their superimposed candle sconces slid to one side at the touch of a button to reveal cinema projectors.

become as 'démodé as art nouveau' and consequently a more exuberant and decorative style was imposed upon Le Corbusier's austerity.

Carlos de Bestigui was then on the threshold of a career as one of the great patrons of the decorative arts in this century. A privately printed volume of his own poems, *Songeries*, illustrated with coloured reproductions of his drawings, very much in the Paul Poiret-George Barbier manner, had marked his début as a patron as far back as 1914, but the decorations of the penthouse overlooking the Etoile were very different from the derivative 'Persian' of his earlier enthusiasm. Le Corbusier's structure was simplicity itself, an arrangement of stark, unornamented boxes with huge plate-glass windows, terraces and roof gardens on several levels. Consisting of a salon, dining room, bedroom, bathroom and kitchen it was a machine for entertaining. At a touch of a button, entire walls appeared or disappeared, windows slid back to incorporate terrace into room, chandeliers slid along hidden rails in the ceiling to allow uninterrupted screening of movies projected from apertures ordinarily concealed behind ormulu wall brackets superimposed on framed mirrors. The use of electricity was confined to the elaborate mechanical tricks in the apartment, for the only illumination was from

Roof garden of Carlos de Bestigui's Paris apartment, before 1936

candles whose flattering light was reflected from the white walls and ceiling of the salon to shine softly on the glass chairs, the white and gold rococo commode and the ice blue velvet of the curtains and upholstery of the Second Empire white and gold settees and on the *pièce de résistance* of the décor – an over-life-size figure of a blackamoor dressed in ostrich feathers and standing on a white and gold rococo pedestal. This had been specially made to the order of M. Bestigui in Dresden porcelain and was inspired by the smaller eighteenth-century porcelain figures which decorated the dining table and were reflected in the panelled mirror doors.

But the ultimate fantasy was to be found in the roof garden where a magnificent eighteenth-century portrait was casually hung on an outside wall, where entire box hedges slid apart to reveal views of Paris, and where one finally arrived at an open-air room, the floor carpeted with a daisy-strewn lawn, a real fireplace with a clock, candlesticks surmounted by a circular picture which was actually a view of the Arc de Triomphe and a marble 'commode' supporting a birdcage with a mechanical songster.

Edward James in his novel *The Gardener who saw God*, published in 1937,

Two plates decorated by Jean Cocteau for Christofle, Paris; plate decorated by Marie-Laure (the Vicomtesse Marie-Laure de Noailles) for Christofle, Paris.

Pieces such as the plates decorated by Jean Cocteau and Marie-Laure de Noailles for Christofle reflect the surrealist influence of the latter years of the decade.

The Vicomte and Vicomtesse de Noailles were ardent patrons of painters, poets and musicians and their salon decorated by Jean-Michel Frank was the meeting place of fashion and the arts. They had financed the making of the *avant-garde* films *L'Age d'Or* and *Le Sang d'un Poète*. The Vicomtesse, under the name 'Marie-Laure', had exhibitions as a painter and is often mentioned in publications of the thirties as an exponent of surrealism.

Bedroom for Mrs Constance Spry, about 1936

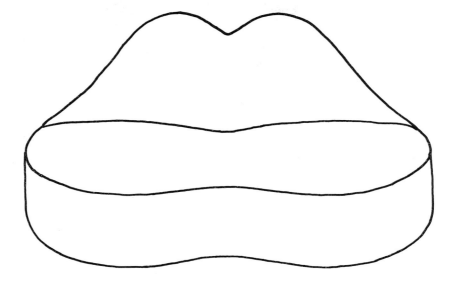

Settee in the shape of Mae West's lips, by Salvador Dali, 1936

depicted an English nobleman of great fortune whose passion for surrealism finally ruined him. Always conventionally dressed, with the exception of a gold and enamel tiepin made to represent a tiny poached egg, such was his passion for the work of the surrealists in general and Salvador Dali in particular that his Gothic castle in Berkshire was surrounded by marble grand pianos hoisted into trees, colossal poached eggs of painted alabaster apparently floating in the pools, dovecotes made of sponges, a hen roost of cheese while 'two large Elizabethan yews which had formerly been chipped into the likeness of a lion and a unicorn . . . [were] now retrimmed into the shape of that pair of half-bowed, half-stooping figures of a French peasant and his wife at evening prayer taken from the well-known picture by Millet called "The Angelus" '. A loaf of real bread thirty-five yards in length was placed on the lawn, thousands of painted porcelain imitations of ants and grasshoppers were spread under the beeches, sewing machines and umbrellas carved from granite served as garden seats. 'The good, mad lord' finally ruined himself by these extravagant follies, the finishing touch being the construction of two gigantic ears which he built on to the north and south wings of his home, ears large enough to contain sitting rooms, electric organs and a Turkish bath.

Almost as strange were the decorations of Edward James's own house in London – which included the telephones designed by Salvador Dali in the shape of lobsters (see page 200).

Dali's 'mouth' settee and Schiaparelli's bizarre buttons of red galalith representing lips (page 200) were in the surrealist tradition of Man Ray's celebrated painting eight feet long, *A l'Heure de L'Observatoire – Les Amoureux*, in which 'red lips floated in a blueish-grey sky over a twilight landscape with an observatory and its two domes like breasts dimly indicated on the horizon'. Equally surrealist was

L'ultra-meuble' by Kurt Seligmann, exhibited at the Paris Surrealist Exhibition, 1938

Kurt Seligmann's 'L'ultra-meuble', a stool made of four realistic legs wearing high-heeled shoes joined above the bent knees to form a stool – a combined piece of furniture and *objet fabriqué* exhibited in the Paris Surrealist Exhibition. Raoh Schorr, a Swiss sculptor working in London, had created a number of glass-topped tables supported by realistically modelled human legs for display purposes a year or two previously and Costa's table in the form of an over-scaled hand equally antedates 'L'ultra-meuble' by at least three years. This absorption during the thirties with portions of human anatomy as decorative objects concentrated even more upon the hand, and in this the trends of surrealism and Victoriana found a motif in common. Man Ray, Max Ernst and Joyen had all at one time or another used the human hand, divorced from the body, as an element in their paintings or sculptures, as had the group of Herold, Breton, Tanguy and Brauner in their joint 'exquisite corpse' drawings. In their case the hand was used to give a shock effect, unlike the more sentimental and purely decorative treatment in the nineteenth century. In 1931 the American edition of *Harper's Bazaar* showed a photograph of a group of hand-ornaments dating from 1850 and later which were described in the caption as 'Pale hands you'll love! They are seventeenth-, eighteenth-, nineteenth-century but all of them as Victorian in feeling as anti-macassars and hassocks'. Similar hand-ornaments of the white alabaster-like porcelain invented by Bennington in 1852, made at the Copeland and Minton factories, and called 'Parian' ware, or of the Irish Belleek ware originated about 1860 and covered with an iridescent glaze, were eagerly sought in junk shops or street markets and could be had for a few shillings. Hands holding shells, detachable trumpet vases or vases in the shape of buds or flowers were ideal containers for the small posies of mixed flowers which Constance Spry had brought once more into fashion. The life-size carved marble hands resting on realistically rendered books or cushions fashionable as keepsakes – Queen Victoria had all

Right
Table by Costa-Achillopulo, about 1935

The hand-shaped support is of carved wood and plaster, the top glass.

Left
Wall lamp by Nicolas de Molas, about 1935

De Molas, a nephew of the composer Rimsky-Korsakoff, enjoyed a considerable vogue in the thirties. He was dubbed by a journalist 'the Noel Coward of Art'. A painter of moderate talent he had a usefully acceptable style which could create a mock Tiepolo ceiling for the drawing room of Mrs Woolley Hart's London house, decorated by the Marchesa Malacrida in 1931 and illustrated in the *Studio Year Book of Decorative Art*; *faux naif* murals of Italian scenes somewhat reminiscent of Jean Hugo for Fortnum and Mason's showrooms; scenic wallpapers for Katzenbach and Warren, Inc., and a design for a painted ceiling for Paul Louis Weiler. In the theatre he designed the setting and costumes for Noel Coward's song 'Mad Dogs and Englishmen' in the short-lived 1931 revue at the London Pavilion, productions in Paris for Sacha Guitry and for the opera *The Italian Girl in Algiers* at Covent Garden.

her children's hands reproduced in white statuary marble – were brought out of obscurity to grace papier-mâché tables. Blue or white glass cornucopia vases terminating in gilt bronze hands, with ornamented cuffs and rings, were more sought after than similar examples with stags' heads or conventional scrolls, though the stags' heads in particular were also popular. Victorian pinchbeck sets of brooches and earrings representing hands – 'Pinchbeck star rises again', declared *Vogue* in 1935 – were reproduced as costume jewelry and their popularity inspired the Cartier hand-brooches illustrated.

The basis of many surrealist paintings was the juxtaposition of disparate objects to induce in the spectator a sense of unease. To accentuate the incongruity of such an alliance the objects concerned were delineated with a meticulous technique which left the beholder in no doubt as to their identity and all the devices used by the *trompe l'œil* painters of the seventeenth and eighteenth centuries were once more brought into use. This in turn led to a reawakening of interest in the work of artists long neglected, even despised, but now found to have the same hallucinatory and often sinister qualities to be found in canvases by Salvador Dali,

Left
Pas de deux from *Jeu d'Enfants* danced by Roland Guérard and Lubov Rostova, setting and costumes by Joan Miró, 1932

Right
Publicity photograph by Peter Rose Pulham, about 1937

The painter Peter Rose Pulham created a series of photographs in a vein of romantic surrealism which were used as advertisements in fashion magazines by the distinguished couturier Victor Stiebel. This example of his work has, with hindsight, a prophetic quality in its symbolism.

160

Dress clip in the shape of a hand holding a rose, by Cartier, about 1937

This was produced in several versions with the hand of ebony or red or white coral, the rose either golden or carved coral.

René Magritte or Pierre Roy, whose paintings were used for a number of covers for *Vogue*. The tortured landscapes of Salvator Rosa, the feverish portraits of demented clerics and gipsies by Alessandro Magnasco, the fantastic architecture dissolving into a livid light against black skies painted by the mysterious Monsu Desiderio – these were all described by William Gaunt in *Bandits in a Landscape* published in 1936. Discriminating collectors with a taste for the bizarre were searching for examples of their work and, like Arthur Jeffress, putting them in places of honour in rooms furnished with silver-lacquered Venetian or Charles X furniture. Canvases by Guiseppe Arcimboldo representing the four seasons, the four elements or the senses and composed of personages constructed from flowers, vegetable shells or books and paintings which had originally graced the cabinets of curiosities of sixteenth-century Hapsburgs, now re-emerged from obscurity as decorative accompaniments to carved wood blackamoors or Victorian papier-mâché furniture.

Throughout the thirties American collectors had been increasingly interested in the paintings and artefacts of the early years of the United States. These 'primitives', who were sometimes skilled in execution but more often painted with more enthusiasm than technique, had an appealing quality of freshness combined with intensity of feeling. In 1935, by chance, the work of a hitherto forgotten painter emerged from the shadows. Alfred Frankenstein tells the story in *After the Hunt*. Edith Halpert, the director of the Downtown Gallery in New York, was offered a painting called *The Faithful Colt* which in addition to its masterly handling of *trompe l'œil* technique had the quality of suggesting hidden implications, of arousing speculations. William Hartnett, the creator of this painting (now in the Wadsworth Atheneum in Hartford, Connecticut) had emerged from an obscurity which though brief in terms of time – he died in 1892 – was profound. Other examples of Hartnett's work were discovered, and by patient scholarship the facts of his life established. The work of a number of imitators also came to light, in fact it was revealed in time that there had been a school of painters in *trompe l'œil*, highly individual and intent on creating more and more convincing illusions. These in turn influenced many young painters, decorative artists and illustrators.

Mayor Gallery

There are certain galleries whose closing leaves a gap that can never be quite filled. Usually the reflection of the individual taste of one or two people either indifferent to or independent of commercial stresses, they generate a quality of excitement, freshness and originality which sets them apart from the average commercial gallery with less interest in the current exhibitions than in the more profitable sale of paintings by established artists which are in the regular stock. Curtis Moffat's shop and gallery must have been one such, as was the Arthur Jeffress gallery at a more recent date – both, incidentally, Americans. Another was the Mayor Gallery in Cork Street, London, whose proprietors, Frederick Mayor and Douglas Cooper, introduced the work of many Continental artists to the British public – work which was met too often by a cool indifference. The gallery opened in April 1933, the frontage in a then shocking colour scheme of white, orange and vermilion. The interior was designed by Brian O'Rorke in a fashionably modernist scheme, the simplicity of which offered no competition to the exhibits, which was enhanced by pale-blue walls and indirect lighting hidden by false hanging ceilings. Arundell Clarke designed the furniture. Here Paul Klee had his first exhibition in London (with extremely poor sales) and in the following year George Grosz was introduced to the British public. Max Ernst, Joan Miró, Edward Wadsworth, Marie Laurençin's flower paintings framed in wide bands of antique mirror (commissioned by Lady Cunard for her dining room in Grosvenor Square and presented with a catalogue foreword by Somerset Maugham), George Rouault, Aristide Maillol, Max Jacob, Christian Bérard, portrait drawings by Jean Cocteau (at 12 guineas, about $30, each), Curtis Moffat photographs and Allan Walton fabrics, all these were among the exhibits at the Mayor Gallery between its inception and the outbreak of war. An early show in 1933 was that of Unit One, a group exhibition with works by Paul Nash, Ben Nicholson, Edward Wadsworth, Frances Hodgkins, Henry Moore and Barbara Hepworth, the first exhibition to be gathered to illustrate an art book – *Art Now* by Herbert Read.

German decorative pictures

Significant of the times and the prevailing influence in Germany is the type of painting or decorative picture to be found in the rooms featured in decorating magazines during the 1930s and particularly after 1933. A careful examination of a periodical such as *Innen Dekoration* will show that, in photographs of interiors, the paintings are such that there could be no possibility of the owner being accused of harbouring decadent art. Possibly anyone owning a picture by a proscribed artist would have discreetly removed it and replaced it with a harmless substitute before the photograph was taken, knowing that the magazine was likely to be scrutinized closely and any offender denounced – though it is more likely that to avoid denunciation, even by a member of the family, any controversial painting would have been disposed of in any case. A necessarily anonymous correspondent to the *Studio* gives a revealing picture of the state of affairs in artistic circles in Germany in 1935, two years after the seizure of power by Adolf Hitler. An annual exhibition in Munich totalling 820 paintings, drawings and etchings, closed with a total of 182 having been sold, of which just over half were acquired by the state. The cash value of the exhibits sold was considerably lower than in previous years. This was the first exhibition fully to show the effects of the new compulsory registration by every artist at the Chamber of Culture, a body with leaders appointed by Dr Goebbels. Included in the exhibits were five bronze busts of Hitler 'in the familiar defiant posture' – for none of which had he posed – a painting of two Hitler youths learning to play the flute from an old village musician, bought by Baldur von Shirach, the head of the Hitler Youth Organization, and a view of a village decorated for the elections of 1933 which was purchased by the Ministry of Propaganda, giving rise to the comment in the article that 'it is fairly safe to assert that such a picture with the words "Wir wollen den Frieden" flaunted on bunting in the foreground would not have met with the aesthetic approval of a pre-Hitler jury.'

Posters and publicity

As the force of the Depression gathered strength in a series of financial crises, the need for more systematic and adroit publicity schemes on the part of manufacturers and retailers became intensified. In the face of dwindling markets the need grew for more direct and compulsive advertising and the change of title of the periodical *Posters and Publicity* to *Modern Publicity* in 1930 may be interpreted as indicative of the changing circumstances and the necessity of advertising organized and adapted to meet the prevailing difficult trade circumstances. The poster became too costly as a means of drawing attention to a particular product, especially if it were printed in colours and commissioned from a well-known artist, and business concerns allocated a greater proportion of their necessarily limited budget for advertising to space in newspapers and periodicals where it reached a wider public. The tendency was for the poster to become more of a prestige symbol than a direct means of salesmanship and 'to represent a relatively small part of the business of calling attention to various goods and services', as John Gloag wrote in 1934. In spite of the enlightened policies of such organizations as Shell Petrol, the London underground and the various branches of the railways in England, the tendency was to patronize the designers already flourishing in the twenties, Tom Purvis, Frank Newbould, Austin Cooper, Norman Wilkinson and E. McKnight Kauffer. In their different styles they had all mastered the technique of presenting a message with an immediate urgency and an economy of means comparable to the masterpieces of poster design produced by Cassandre in France. A new development influencing the design of posters was the repetition of a theme or slogan in various forms – 'That's Shell, that was', 'Guinness is Good for you', the 'Mr Therm' designed by Eric Fraser for the Gas Light and Coke Company or the Dubonnet posters by Cassandre which became so much a part of the Paris scene.

The situation in the United States in 1930 was a grim one for the manufacturer and national advertiser. The prevailing buyers' market was forcing prices down and the limited money available for advertising necessitated its being disposed in such a way as to provide the best results. It is recorded that almost no manufacturers of national standing stopped advertising in 1930, but equally the standard of design was mediocre. In spite of the increasing number of commercial artists, the Art Directors' Guild had difficulty in finding enough works out of the thousands submitted to fill the quota of 1350 exhibits for their annual exhibition and in consequence it is understandable that French artists should have been commissioned by American firms to provide style and elegance for their publicity. Saks Fifth Avenue, for instance, commissioned a series of drawings by Jean Dupas, though it is noticeable that the exaggerated elongation of the female figure and the bizarre costumes characteristic of his work were modified almost

Painted room at 'Eleven Arches' near Tucson, Arizona, about 1938

Designed by Joseph Joesler and decorated by Miss Marckwald of Smyth, Urquhart and Marckwald Inc., New York, this large house in the Arizona desert was constructed of adobe and the murals in the living room were painted by the owner, Louise M. Grace. They depict the mountains and the flora and fauna of the surrounding countryside in winter and summer and were executed in tones of grey-green, rust brown, blue, black and white.

to the point of conventionality. Marie Laurençin and Pierre Roy were introduced to a wider public in America through their drawings for shipping lines and wines and mention must be made of the enterprise shown by the fashion magazines in commissioning covers drawn by Chirico, Dali, Berman, Marie Laurençin (*Vogue* had two covers by her in one year), Pierre Roy (a number of his mysterious and magical still lifes also appeared on *Vogue* covers during the thirties) and, of course, the omnipresent Christian Bérard. Cassandre was commissioned to design a series of twelve covers for *Harper's Bazaar* (as a replacement for Erté with whom the publication had parted company after a long association) and in 1936 he created the setting for the Balanchine version of the ballet *Aubade* – first produced in 1929 with choreography by Nijinska and settings by Jean-Michel Frank.

Modern Publicity records that the only good posters to be found in Germany were those produced in Munich and Dresden and here again recourse was made to French commercial artists for fashion drawings, with the added factor that as there were no German specialists in this type of drawing the 'sweet' drawings of pretty girls came from England.

As the decade advanced the techniques of reproduction improved until the point was reached when it was no longer necessary for a poster designer to think in simplified masses of flat colour. Richard Lindner's three posters for Barnes Pianos, conceived in a neo-Victorian style in the current trend, were printed by photolitho in twelve colours in 1939 and created such a stir that Barnes were inundated by requests from the public for copies. (See page 179.)

A poster by Anna Zinkeisen for the Southern Railway, of a rather lower artistic standard, necessitated no less than seventeen printings – a costly process reflecting the importance attached to prestige posters at a time when the English railway system was divided into regional services, each competing to entice the holiday-going public of foreign tourists to visit the resorts and beauty spots in each region.

164

Period revivalism

Evelyn Gardner, in an article entitled 'Forward to Neo-Victorianism' published in a 1937 issue of *Harper's Bazaar*, reflects on the increasing tendency to collect the artefacts of the nineteenth century, commenting that 'there is one important thing to bear in mind when you decide to follow the fashion and furnish your flat in the neo-Victorian manner and that is *now* is the time to buy these Victorian objects . . . soon prices will soar and those with slender incomes will find that neo-Victorianism is not for them.' The trend was not, in the opinion of the writer, a wholesale return to the modes or manners of the Victorian period but rather, in fashion and in furnishing, a judicious mingling of old and new. 'The modern young women . . . has not turned herself into a Victorian, she has decided to become more feminine', and being 'bold and adventurous and having filled her flat with glass and steel furniture, she realizes that it will make an excellent setting for the Victorian decorative objects which she was taught in her childhood to despise. There, amongst the straight lines and simplicity of the furniture, the shell flowers which have lingered so long in dark corners or have been covered by the dirt and dust of the lumber room will look their best.' Among 'the many beautiful and amusing Victorian objects for us to choose from', the author cites glass ships; embroidered cushions – 'definitely amusing' – which as they are 'all exceedingly funny and their colours being strong and determined are particularly suited to the modern room'; Victorian glass pictures and wool pictures which 'should always be massed together' – a suggestion which in itself is an indication of the changing tastes – and papier-mâché boxes, trays and desks which have 'an air of determined usefulness . . . they look out of place as mere ornaments . . . they must be used.'

It has come to be accepted that the first signs of a new interest in Victoriana were the results of Lytton Strachey's two biographies *Eminent Victorians* (1918) and *Queen Victoria* (1921). Strachey's original approach to his subjects and his imaginative renderings of the atmosphere of the nineteenth century made him a celebrity overnight and, incidentally, drew the attention of young intellectuals with artistic leanings to the background details of Strachey's subjects. Harold Acton, later to become an eminent biographer of more bizarre personalities, gives an account of his *Confessions of an Aesthete* of the cult of Victoriana which infiltrated Oxford in the early twenties as a reaction against the cult of the 1890s which was still a 'faint but flickering tradition'. The wan ghosts of Beardsley and Wilde and the echoes of the Grosvenor Gallery received their intimations of oblivion when Harold Acton painted his rooms in Meadow Buildings lemon-yellow and filled them with Victorian bric-à-brac, artificial flowers and fruit, and a collection of paperweights 'imprisoning bubbles that never broke and flowers that never faded'. Evelyn Waugh remembers Harold Acton collecting Victoriana when Mr Betjeman was still a schoolboy rubbing brasses, but does not mention the Acton wardrobe of Victorian-style clothes or the broad trousers which were the originators of the 'Oxford bags' of the twenties. The Hypocrites Club was closed as a result of a fancy-dress party at which Robert Byron appeared too realistically as

Queen Victoria, an occurrence which led to the banning of a proposed 'Early Victorian Exhibition' organized by Harold Acton and with an illustrated catalogue by Lytton Strachey. Banned too was a Queen Victoria ballet. This new enthusiasm for the nineteenth century was not, of course, confined to a coterie of undergraduates at Oxford. Harold Acton on another occasion mentions the mingled baroque and Victorian decorations of Osbert Sitwell's house in Carlyle Square when he visited it soon after the first performance of *Façade* in 1931.

This tentative revival of the Victorian style might have flickered out as the result of being confined to a comparatively small circle whose interests would have transferred to some other exoticism when its appeal had begun to fall. It so happened, however, that in the early thirties two circumstances combined to spread and to strengthen it. One was the financial effect of the Depression, the other the paucity of contemporary idioms of ornamentation.

For in certain circles the tendency to ornamentation was apparent even in the early thirties. There were many who emphatically disagreed with the statement of H. S. Goodhart-Rendel, the vice-president of the British Art and Industry Exhibition, that 'a fondness for ornament is no more readily acknowledged by refined persons than a fondness for gin, and the natural appetite of the unrefined for pretty patterns is represented as a weakness requiring drastic methods of cure.' They were as unashamed in their preference for ornament as in their fondness for gin and in the absence of a popular contemporary ornamented style their only recourse was to that of a past period. Antiques of the sixteenth and seventeenth centuries were beyond the means of most people wanting an original and even slightly outrageous décor. In a period of financial stress it was necessary for interior decorators, artists and anyone even remotely connected with the arts to stand out as possessing adventurous taste and to own an apartment which would be talked about and possibly even photographed for one of the magazines specializing in interior decoration or society gossip. At the same time the elements of such a décor had to be cheap and to certain extent it became permissible to boast of how little one had paid for a chair or an ornament. For such people the rediscovery of the artefacts of the nineteenth century, and in particular the Victorian period, came as a godsend.

It was most welcome also to those decorators, and there were a number of them, who quite early in the decade had begun to realize that it was not altogether in their own interests to encourage their clients to indulge in the fashion for modernist rooms. The return to a period style produced not only more spectacular results but, more importantly, greater profits. For while Regency and Victorian furniture was very cheap and the decorator could both acquire and install it with the minimum of effort, either period, once installed, called for harmonizing wallpapers, elaborate window treatments and a plethora of ornaments and pictures – and a bigger profit margin.

The earlier Regency had its adherents, especially among those whose aim was an atmosphere of elegance combined with novelty. Particularly popular was wallpaper and fabric with a 'Regency Stripe', a decorative motif of dubious authenticity which after the Second World War was to become a hackneyed cliché. As early as 1932 and even in the relentless modernism of Broadcasting House, London, there could be found an essay in the Regency manner. Designed by Dorothy Warren Trotter, the basement studio was given an intimate atmosphere by means of a false window screened by pale green curtains with a swagged pelmet, white-painted bookcases, pale terracotta pink walls and Regency furniture, including an armchair formerly in Arnold Bennett's collection. The colour illustration of this room featured in the *Architectural Review* showed the contrast between this decorative scheme and the functional austerity of the other studios with their steel furniture and modernistic carpets by Marion Dorn.

Victorian furniture and ornaments, however, could be found at even lower prices than their Regency counterparts and the full-blooded exuberance characteristic of the artefacts of the mid-nineteenth century was in sufficient contrast to the monotone sleekness of modernism to have a degree of shock value which gave an added zest to the sensation of being able to appreciate a style still out of favour with the majority.

Junk shops and street markets were crammed with the artefacts manufactured in vast quantities in the mid-nineteenth century. Since the end of the war the big houses of the middle classes, formerly inhabited by one family, had been sold or split into several apartments – an increasing trend as money grew scarcer and domestic help beyond most people's means – and their contents dispersed. Those with 'more taste than money' (to quote a description appearing in *Vogue* during the thirties) discovered the Caledonian Market and the Marché aux Puces to be full of nineteenth-century treasures at derisory prices. The Caledonian Market, or to give it its proper name The Islington Cattle Market, was open on Tuesday and Friday for the sale of second-hand objects, the dealers occupying the enclosures reserved for livestock on the other days. A certain number of stalls were under cover but these were mostly occupied by silver dealers whose stocks were, it was said, of dubious origin. The real bargains were to be found on the cobblestones – the market was affectionately known as 'the Stones' – and there, for a few shillings or even pence, could be found an assortment of good and bad articles from all periods and countries. Victoriana was particularly abundant, ranging from original Worth dresses, jet and pinchbeck jewelry to complete suites of parlour furniture in rosewood or papier-mâché, often with the original Berlin woolwork coverings embroidered with lush pink roses or beadwork lilies.

Support for the neo-Victorian trend came also from another direction. Throughout the twenties the majority of picture dealers in London and Paris had thrived on the export of old masters to the United States and particularly on the sale of eighteenth-century portraits by Romney, Gainsborough and Reynolds, for which there was an insatiable demand. Many dealers relied entirely on this export trade and did not consider it necessary to hold exhibitions of contemporary painters, which in many cases entailed considerable work with little material profit either to the gallery or the artist. The gain from the sale of one old master could amount to more than that from a year's showings of even established living artists. This flourishing state of affairs was suddenly ended in December 1929 and many dealers found themselves in the position of having a number of valuable paintings in the United States which had not been paid for and which the clients were in no position ever to pay for. In addition the majority of their clients, if not actually ruined, were in no mood to invest any further in unnecessary luxuries. Thus many galleries found themselves facing ruin and bankruptcy.

The Leicester Gallery, however, had for a long time pursued the policy of holding regular exhibitions of contemporary English and French painters, and by maintaining high standards of quality in their shows had built up a faithful clientele. As they were not so dependent on the export of old masters, the gallery was in a better position than most to weather the dreary years of depression which lay ahead, although the chances of selling expensive paintings remained small.

'Victorian' sitting room, about 1938

The Victorian needlework which is a feature of this interior was both inexpensive and plentiful between the wars and the carpet, the cushion in beadwork and the long footstool cover were typical of the many thousands of pieces of embroidery which could be found with the Berlin wool in its original brilliant and still unfaded colours. Equally easy to find and as inexpensive were buttoned armchairs – often to be bought for a few shillings – settees and gilt gesso console tables similar to those in this room. The glass vases in the shape of cornucopias with terminals of gilt bronze stags' heads resting on black marble bases were eagerly collected, as were the bouquets of artificial flowers under glass shades. The wallpaper, the glazed chintz of the curtains with their elaborately swagged pelmet and the chintz roller blind printed to simulate Venetian blinds were modern.

Sensing that the interest in Victoriana might attract his clients, who could not resist the appeal of an attractive painting provided that the price was reasonable, Oliver Brown, a director of the Leicester Gallery, collected together examples of the work of a number of painters who flourished in the Victorian period, whose names had been almost forgotten, about whom little was known and, in consequence, whose paintings and drawings could be found at a very small price. An exhibition of drawings by Constantin Guys, a French artist with many connections with England, was extremely successful and every drawing was sold. This was followed in 1933 by the work of James Tissot, another French painter working in England in the 1870s. The immaculate finish of his canvases depicting elegantly dressed women in the charming fashions of the day posed on the decks of yachts were a popular success and were much reproduced in the press. For those who could not afford a Tissot or a Guys there were thousands of Victorian fashion plates available for as little as a few pence each. The paintings of Richard Dadd, whose acute mental disturbance was reflected in the sinister stare common to all his characters and in the fantastic imagery which is seen at its best in *The Fairy Feller's Master Stroke*, Gustave Doré's engravings and illustrations, the paintings of John Martin and those of other minor but fascinating artists helped to swell the interest in Victoriana.

Interest naturally turned to the Victorian narrative paintings and to scenes of everyday life. By the thirties Victorian women's costume was no longer considered hideous or funny and had begun to acquire a period charm. The solid comfort depicted in so many narrative paintings and the crowded clutter of furniture and ornaments, which like the women's dresses was beginning to be looked at with admiration, was a reminder, at a period of depression and uncertainty, of the security and expansion of middle-class life in England. The fact that underlying the surface of prosperity and cosy warmth depicted in Victorian narrative painting there was an almost limitless area of misery and degradation was as yet unexplored, though hinted at in many paintings. It is possibly too extreme to find an explanation for the Victorian revival of the 1930s in a desire to escape from uncertainty into a past which seemed in retrospect more secure: what is certain is that the elaboration of Victoriana came as a reaction against the starkness of modernism.

'The Victorian Age Returns' was the heading of an article in *Vogue* in 1931. In *Vogue* circles it had returned already. In another three or four years the fashion had become general, and by the time that Evelyn Gardner wrote the Victorian revival was in full swing. However, the reappraisal of Victorian decorative arts was not, of course, endorsed by the advocates of simplicity, and John Milne, a member of the executive committee of the British Art in Industry Exhibition gave voice to a typical view that 'to us the Victorian age stands out as a conspicuous example of a period of retrogression' and that 'the Great Exhibition of 1851 was the high-water mark of assertive bad taste'. As late as 1945, Hayes Marshall, Director of the Decorative Furniture Department at Fortnum and Mason, was of the opinion that 'there may be a flashback to "Victoriana" for a little while, but I do not view this seriously and suggest you restrain your thoughts in this direction. Little furniture of the period is worth a second thought and beyond this reference I wish to forget it.' Nevertheless, during the 1930s Mr Marshall's department had stocked numerous pieces of Victorian furniture and ornaments made into lamps.

Settee by Hayes-Marshall for Fortnum and Mason, 1933

'Tenway' settee by Hayes Marshall for Fortnum and Mason, 1935

As a general rule the *Architectural Review* gave prominence to examples of modernistic interior decoration, but occasionally space was devoted to illustrating a scheme which was of exceptional interest from a decorative aspect. Three of these were the apartments, in Paris, of Carlos de Bestigui, Helena Rubinstein and Nicholas de Plantier. The Bestigui apartment has already been discussed (pages 153–5) in relation to the surrealist influence on decoration.

Nicholas de Plantier's apartment featured in 1934 was a portent of the craze for elegant fantasy which conquered Paris during the latter years of the decade, mounting to a climax in 1938. The text accompanying the illustrations was careful to point out that the decorations were an example of 'period revivalism' – a very different matter from furnishing in period style, something which would not have merited recognition from the *Architectural Review* with its policy of presenting the best of modern furniture and decoration.

Period revivalism – a clumsy title which failed to gain currency – was, in fact, not quite so different from furnishing in a period style as the article suggested, but gave the decorator more freedom to indulge in rather theatrical flights of fancy or to combine genuine antiques with modern pastiches of the same style. Perhaps the most noticeable characteristic was a partiality for the neglected periods, for the more decorative furniture of the Biedermeier, Victorian baroque or eighteenth- or nineteenth-century gothic revival or even ancient Greek styles. The salon of the De Plantier apartment was planned to give an atmospheric setting for a collection of Etruscan pottery, a Greek marble torso and a classic sculptured head. The obvious clichés of classic columns or key patterns were avoided and the walls and ceiling were painted in a shade of 'clouded terracotta'. The chairs of oak were of simplified Greek shapes, more a reference to than a copy of those depicted in Greek vase paintings, and the upholstery in rough wool fabric was complemented by the thick white fur rugs. In complete contrast was the bedroom where the walls, equally plain, were painted rose cyclamen and draped with white transparent fabric. Two Second Empire chairs, one of black papier-mâché inlaid with mother-of-pearl flowers, the other upholstered and deep-buttoned in satin, formed a contrast with the long, low dressing table, square and modern in design and covered with mirror.

In marked contrast is the room designed by J. H. Robsjohn-Gibbings to serve as a showroom. This aroused considerable interest when it opened in 1936. Its

Robsjohn-Gibbings showroom, 1936

A decorative scheme intended to break with both the contemporary concepts of modernism and the accepted 'period' associations. The 'klismos' chairs were of waxed birch and the mosaic floor was inspired by the fourth century BC example in the House of Good Fortune at Olynthos near Salonika.

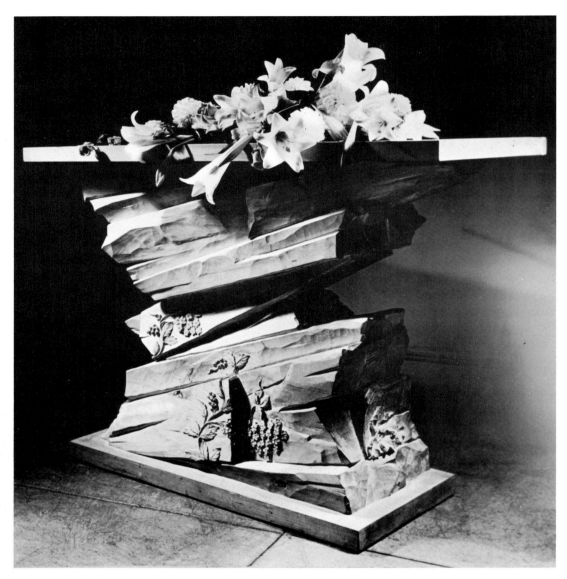

Console table by Robsjohn-Gibbings, 1939

Console table in waxed birch carved with rocks and mountain flowers: a handsome piece of decorative furniture conceived in a quasi-surrealist manner by one of America's leading designers. The lily still holds sway as the photographer's favourite accessory.

creator had first arrived from England in 1929 to assist Joseph Duveen in his vast enterprise of transferring eighteenth-century England across the Atlantic – an undertaking which suffered a severe check after the Wall Street Crash. The rich diet of period reconstruction imposed upon anyone connected with the Duveen firm came to be antipathetic to Robsjohn-Gibbings – as can be seen in his book, *Goodbye Mr Chippendale* – and it was towards the combined simplicity and elegance of classical Greek furniture and ornament that he turned for inspiration. The so-called timelessness of the majority of modernist designs was in his view a fallacy – time has proved the accuracy of this opinion – and the doctrinaire adherence to stark, straight outlines and unornamented surfaces a retrograde step.

Louvred drawer invented by Robsjohn-Gibbings, 1938   Chair by Robsjohn-Gibbings, 1936

The search for beauty could encompass a graceful curve or a subtly moulded outline to a support. The form of his 1936 chair still in production owes more than a little to Greek prototypes, but the elegant simplicity of its lines makes it one of the classics of modern chair design.

Few decorative schemes received more publicity in France, England and the United States than that for the residence of Helena Rubinstein in Paris. Situated on the Ile St Louis, the seventeenth-century house at 26 Quai de Bethune had been modernized by the distinguished architect Louis Sue, one of the leading exponents of the art déco manner. Madame Rubinstein was an inveterate collector with a wide appreciation of different styles and being a 'princess of industry' had the means to gratify her taste and knowledge. Very little seems to have remained of the interior structure of the house after its adaptation to form a setting for Madame Rubinstein's collection, and certainly it is doubtful if without extensive alterations the ancient structure could have supported the weight of the pool with illuminated fountains containing over four thousand gallons of water which was placed on the roof, alongside a small dining room with walls of mirror brick and a glass ceiling.

The task facing Louis Sue, that of creating settings for collections of antique furniture and contemporary works of art, was no easy one, but there were few who could have solved it more satisfactorily. As early as 1911 Madame Rubinstein had demonstrated her prowess as a collector when she entered Paterson's Gallery in Bond Street and unhesitatingly purchased the entire exhibition of sculpture by her Polish compatriot Elie Nadelman, a protégé of Leo and Gertrude Stein and according to some critics the original creator of cubism. Since then her collection of sculpture had been enlarged with works by Brancusi – his *Bird in Space* was given a special place before a window where it was silhouetted against the Church of St Louis-en-l'Ile – Picasso and 'anonymous negro and Egyptian artists of primitive persuasion'. Selected pieces from this collection were arranged in the entrance hall in company with paintings by Picasso, Dufy and Marie Laurençin: the rugs and upholstery were woven under the direction of Madame Cuttoli and the simple vellum-covered stools and low tables were by Jean-Michel Frank. All

Bedroom by Louis Sue for Helena Rubinstein's house in Paris, about 1938

the curtains throughout the apartment were designed and woven by Madame Paule Marrot. The dining room was decorated with a set of antique hand-blocked wallpaper by Dufour representing views of Lyons and furnished with Charles X furniture. The most spectacular room, however, was undoubtedly Madame Rubinstein's bedroom, in which all the furniture was veneered in mother-of-pearl, a conception which if not unique – Misia Sert had a number of pieces of similarly treated furniture of the same period, the Second Empire – was more memorable than the occasion for which it was originally created, the marriage of the Duc de Montpensier, fifth son of Louis Philippe, and the sister of Queen Isabella II of Spain. To set off this furniture Louis Sue had created a décor of yellow walls and white padded satin decorated with gold cord in diamond patterns.

Madame Rubinstein's apartment was possibly the climax of 'une offensive de goût baroque', as it was described by René Charance.

The baroque revival with its emphasis on the decorative rather than the historically accurate brought back into popularity the carved wood figures collectively known as blackamoors. Long out of fashion, these had gathered dust in storerooms, attics or the basements of antique shops where the hopelessly unsaleable objects were banished. The smaller porcelain figures of negroes and Moors, sometimes forming parts of sets representing the four continents, had

174

Room by Louis Sue for Helena Rubinstein's house in Paris, about 1938

Even at a time when fantasy was in vogue, Madame Rubinstein was considered to have reached the limit in this scheme. Such disparate elements as the near life-size painted and gilded negress, the tortured and fretted Indian chair and table, the silver-leaf-finished Italian shell-settee combined with African sculpture and Pavel Tchelitchev's portrait encrusted with sequins to create an appropriate setting for one of the more flamboyant personalities of the time.

Entrance hall by Louis Sue for Helena Rubinstein's house in Paris, about 1938

Here modern and African art are mingled in a setting composed of furniture by Jean-Michel Frank and carpets and fabrics by Madame Cuttoli. The paintings include examples of the work of Picasso, Dufy and Marie Laurençin and sculptures by Brancusi find affinities with the work of unknown African and Egyptian craftsmen.

Interior by Elsie de Wolfe, before 1938

The theatrical element characteristic of many interiors of the later thirties can be seen in this drawing room with its baroque details silhouetted against 'antiqued' mirror and the alcove lined with velvet and displaying a ruin painting. The modern furniture, loosely based on Italian eighteenth-century originals, shows the feeling for elaboration prevalent at the time.

always been sought after by china collectors, but the larger wooden figures, even if serving a practical purpose, could find no room in art nouveau, art déco or modernist schemes.

This new fashion was undoubtedly of Parisian origin and appears to have begun about 1933. Before long a number of exclusive Paris decorators, including Jean-Michel Frank and Serge Roche, were displaying blackamoors in their different postures. Carlos de Bestigui's Dresden copy of a blackamoor figure (see page 153) was one of the most spectacular. A few of the blackamoors, mainly in the form of *torchères*, dated from the eighteenth century but the majority had been made in the 1860s and 1870s, thought these too were generally attributed to the earlier period. These painted and gilded wooden figures, often life-size, were of Italian origin and depicted negroes male and female, though a less popular type had bearded Moorish features. Half-concealed under carved wooden draperies they

Interior by Elsie de Wolfe (Lady Mendl) before 1938

Lady Mendl, who had declared in an interview reported in the *Studio* in 1933 'I don't consider a room complete until it has a fine parquet floor and a painted ceiling', was credited with the revival of baroque about 1937/8, but a number of decorators, including Serge Roche, had already been experimenting in this idiom for some years.

One of a set of three posters by Richard Lindner
for Barnes Pianos, 1939

Printed in twelve colours by photolithography.

Opposite
Poster by Cassandre for Cooks' Wagon Lit, 1933

A prestige advertisement by the most distinguished
French poster designer. His work was as well
known in the thirties as it had been in the
twenties.

Design by Erté for set of *Rio*, Scala theatre, Berlin,
production 1936/7

supported console tables; dressed in gilded and painted costumes they held small trays for visiting cards; small figures supported stools while there was a type much sought after which represented acrobats, standing on their hands and supporting a tray on the soles of their feet or crouched in an uncomfortable posture holding up the upholstered seat of a stool on their feet.

This fashion, which quickly spread to England and America, inevitably led to the appearance of many more or less convincing fakes – a trade which still exists though, in the present climate of opinion, the fashion has more or less passed and the figures are less controversially referred to as 'Nubians'. Cases were known of carved wood figures of angels from Italian baroque churches which were recarved and painted to simulate negroes to meet the demand and one collector proudly installed a pair of life-size negro acrobats as supports in the inglenook of the dining

A corner of a Parisian drawing room decorated in one of the idioms current in the two or three years prior to the outbreak of war

The curtains of a heavy satin quilted in a design of squares, the divan covered in the same fabric and bearing large cushions, the low painted chair based on a Louis XV model and covered in buttoned satin and, above all, the carved and painted figures of kneeling blackamoors holding sprays of exotic fruit or flowers – all these elements add up to the opulent neo-baroque look fashionable in France, England and the United States.

The traditional craft of quilting was given a new lease of life during the thirties. The humble cotton or calico which had been used for over a hundred years by miners' wives in Durham and South Wales was replaced by gleaming satin or taffeta in beige, cream, oyster, white or tête-de-nègre tones and quilted borders to curtains, quilted bedspreads and cushions as well as quilted dressing gowns and bedjackets became fashionable in England – and incidentally did much to relieve the poverty in the distressed coal-mining areas.

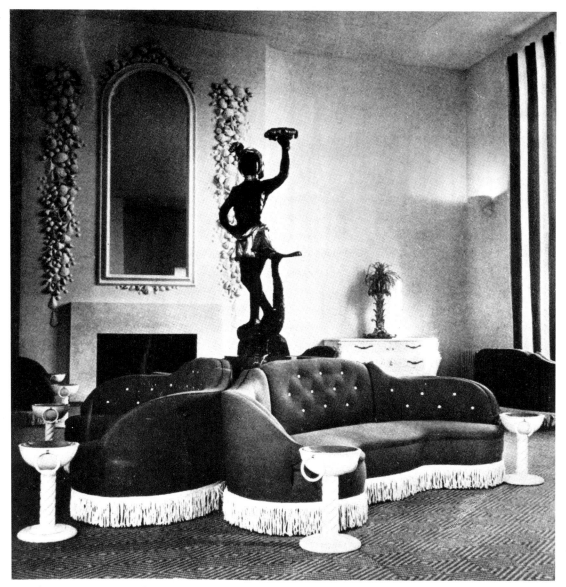

Neo-baroque interior, about 1937

An assemblage of the favourite motifs used in this type of slightly theatrical decoration – the carved and painted wood figure of a blackamoor, the buttoned settees covered in felt and trimmed with cotton fringe, the white-painted commode with its palm-tree ornament, the boldly striped curtains and the decoration of real shells surrounding the mirror, applied to the walls and painted in the same colour. The simplicity of the mantel surround and the absence of mouldings suggest that before the neo-baroque fashion the room may have had a starker appearance.

room in a fake Tudor cottage – ignorant of the fact that his carved wood eighteenth-century blackamoors were in fact plaster and had been made less than a year previously for a window display in a department store. The blackamoor theme was continued in jewelry. In the eighteenth century a favourite negro slave would wear a collar with the name of his owner engraved upon it – the pathetic story of such a slave was told by Constance Wright in her novel *Silver Collar Boy*,

181

published in 1934 with Rex Whistler's illustrations. Now the position was reversed – a fashionable woman would wear at her neck Cartier's gold, onyx and enamel clip of a negro's turbanned head.

Among the exhibits shown by Serge Roche in 1934 was a decorative plaster lamp standard modelled as a conventionalized palm tree – the indirect lighting concealed in the spreading leaves at the apex. In design it resembled eighteenth-century prototypes by Delafosse, Roubo and Blonde among others, and may have been directly cast from an architectural fragment of the period. A complete table, also of plaster, with a top supported by two truncated palm sprays, bore a close family resemblance to Roche's lamp standard and appeared in a number of drawing rooms in France and England, where it was incorporated into schemes of decoration by Syrie Maugham.

Another eighteenth-century motif to come back into fashion was the sea-shell, the curves and convolutions of which were among the basic ingredients of the rococo style. In a number of cases the derivation from eighteenth-century sources was obvious, for instance in the carved and painted dining table and chairs illustrated. The groups of three over-scaled shells forming the table supports were conceived with a gusto which an earlier period might have found excessive but the chairs are more conventional in design, the shell motif being confined to the carved wooden back. Eighteenth-century Venetian chairs of silvered wood with seats and backs carved as flat shells and the legs representing mollusc-encrusted stalactites were once again sought after as decorative pieces and about 1938 Arthur Jeffress decorated a bedroom in his country house with a collection of silvered furniture in this style, combined with mural paintings in sanguine monotone by the author.

Dress clip by Cartier, about 1937

The design of the clips or brooches was reputed to have been based on an original eighteenth-century Venetian model. A passable imitation of the blackamoor head was mass-produced in gilded metal with the face painted black and the turban white, with smaller versions as ear clips.

Dining table and chairs, American, about 1936

Console, possibly by Serge Roche, date unknown
Made of plaster, with supports in the form of palm trees.

Dining room, American, about 1938

A dramatic scheme of decoration demonstrating the theatrical manner commented on by contemporary writers as coming to the fore in the United States. The indirect lighting fitment in the form of a plaster palm tree probably owed its inspiration to those designed by Serge Roche; the chairs of a not particularly striking design are transformed by the upholstery in simulated zebra skin, one of the typical motifs of the thirties, while the dark walls, reverting to those of the early twenties, accentuate the various decorative accessories such as the mirror-covered moulding to the fireplace and the patterned border to the carpet.

184

Fashion

The trends in interior decoration were closely paralleled through the thirties by women's clothes, especially in the case of the models designed in Paris. In the same way that the Depression influenced interior design, so the luxury trades in which Paris, in the thirties as much as the twenties, was the undisputed arbiter of taste, reflected the economic stresses of the early years of the decade. Fabrics hitherto regarded as unsuitable were used for evening dresses and models in cotton in its various forms were shown by the younger designers like Chanel and Schiaparelli. Similarly, cotton ticking or the blue and white striped fabric used for butchers' aprons was made into curtains or used for upholstery as a substitute for silk or damask – a false economy in actual fact as the cost of labour involved in making up the curtains remained the same whatever the material, and clients were often disconcerted to find that their new curtains made from a fabric costing a mere two shillings or so a yard did not after all work out at a tenth of the price of a more expensive fabric.

The fashion for frankly artificial jewelry which Chanel had been instrumental in launching during the twenties became a necessity rather than a diverting whim. The Colonial Exhibition held in Paris in 1931 led to a spate of barbaric heavy jewelry made of gilded or silvered metal combined with enamelling, carved from horn – a favourite material of Colette Guedon, the designer for Au Printemps – tortoiseshell or artificial substances like galalith and catalin, the forms and decorations being drawn from negro prototypes and blended with cubism. The *avant-garde* obsession with machinery could be seen in such an example as the Jean Fouquet bracelet of ebonite rings enclosing chromium-plated ball-bearings, the heads of the connecting screws being left unconcealed.

On a more sumptuous scale, Maubousson and Van Cleef and Arpels were designing jewelry influenced by 'ornaments strange and exotic from darkest Africa', to quote from a feature article with coloured drawings by Charles Martin in *Harper's Bazaar* for August 1931. Here yellow, red and white gold, ivory and carved coral were combined in a necklace, earrings and clip while Maubousson

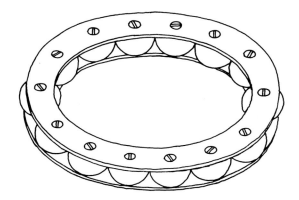

Bracelet by Jean Fouquet, 1932

created an even richer effect by the use of gold, platinum, blue enamel, black enamel and brilliants in a parure of a brooch and necklace. (See cover and page 151.)

The number of clients rich enough to indulge in such elaborate jewelry was strictly limited, however, and even these were cautious about spending money at a time when the general financial stability was in such a precarious condition. The simplicity of the fashions of 1930 reflect not only the trend to elimination of ornament but also the need for economy. The boyish look of the mid-twenties with its short, straight dresses was already on the wane by the end of the decade – skirt lengths had dropped by 1930 to a generally accepted level of fourteen inches off the ground for day wear, twelve inches for afternoon wear and ankle-length for evening. 'We have finished with angularity and hardness', declared a fashion writer in 1930. The new soft yet streamlined look was achieved by intri-cate bias-cutting around the hips and thighs, the waistline, where marked, being either in the natural position or lower according to taste and the bust unemphasized in the evening, while the bodices of day dresses had 'scarfs, jabots, revers, girdles and bows, all of these frequently merging softly one into the other'. Hair was set close to the head, covered in daytime by small hats of draped felt or worked straw, no longer worn down to the eyebrows as in the twenties but revealing the fore-head on one side and caught by a jewelled clip. These clips, either single or in pairs which could be combined to make a brooch, were absolutely essential as an ornament to any well-dressed women during the thirties, and innumerable models were designed – many, Depression or no Depression, in real diamonds set in the newly fashionable platinum or white gold, and of course even more in paste.

Dress clips by Cartier 1935–8

Intended to be used either as a single brooch when linked together or as a pair of clips to catch in the neckline of a dress, these jewels, which are representative of those made between 1935 and 1938, give an idea of the thousands of dress clips which were made in materials ranging from rubies, emeralds, sapphires and – most commonly – diamonds to paste and various forms of plastic. They were by far the most common piece of jewelry during the thirties, being followed by flexible bracelets, earrings of pendant type or in a smaller version of the clips, and cocktail rings.

One can only admire the ingenuity of designers in contriving endless variations upon the same theme.

Furs were of the short-haired variety and breitschwanz, shaved caracal, lamb, beaver and astrakhan were treated to be supple enough to be used as knots on collars or bows on coats and capes.

The sleek look considered desirable in 1930, entailing the use of smooth fabrics – crêpe, satin or facecloth – and the lack of any ornamental detail beyond the often intricate cutting of the fabric, was not for the majority of women an easy fashion to follow. The clinging evening dresses shaped to the figure by bias-cutting were mercilessly revealing and required a perfect Junoesque figure and a minimum of underwear, unless the lines of the dress were to be spoiled by bulges and too many shoulder straps. In the following year a more accommodating look began to appear and the first signs of the direction in which fashion was to develop during the next ten years can be detected. 'Women will, at last, wear clothes worthy of the name', was the relieved comment of a journalist in this year, forecasting the more individual approach to fashion design characteristic of the decade. This was owing to a variety of reasons: the economic conditions, the gathering momentum towards period revivalism and the fiercer competition for an entirely different clientele. The days when Paul Poiret could snub a rich client whom he considered not to have been sufficiently appreciative of his creations had vanished and, although there were still patrons able to order a new wardrobe every season, the wholesale buyers from abroad and the editors of fashion magazines were becoming more necessary to the career of any couturier and particularly important to the new couturiers. Maggy Rouff, daughter of Drécoll, opened her salon in 1929, as did Bruyère, who had worked with Jeanne Lanvin, Mainbocher opened in 1930, Nina Ricci in 1931, and Alix, a former sculptress and pupil of Premet, two years later. Chanel, of course, had been well established for some considerable time, while Schiaparelli had opened her doors at 21 Place Vendôme, the former house of Cheruit, in 1929. Chanel's ascendancy as a designer for the young was unchallenged, though Schiaparelli's flair for publicity and exploitation of novelty had led her to be considered by many contemporary journalists as more in tune with the period.

The smaller collections shown in Paris in 1932 were a sign of the times and equally significant were the individual efforts of the couturiers to express their ideas of the development of fashion. While Molyneux dropped the waistline to the hips and Schiaparelli raised it to just under the bust, Worth and Lanvin left it in its natural position. Mainbocher made tentative efforts to emphasize the bust, Worth plunged with enthusiasm into military effects of epaulettes, brass buttons and small peaked caps, and Patou designed variations on the diagonal line. Striped fabrics and elaborate buttons were prevalent but the most marked feature of the year was the preponderance of white, from evening dress to beachware.

In 1933 a fashion correspondent made the observation that the chic new word was 'amusing . . . no longer is anything a "bore" '. It was too early for this to be taken as a significant pointer to the lessening of the Depression, which was in fact to linger for nearly two years more, but as a word it was useful to describe the vagaries of fashion. Another word constantly used by caption writers until 1939 was 'romantic' – increasingly popular as the neo-Victorian trend gathered momentum. It was applied to the 'Empress Eugènie' hat popular in 1931-2, a small hat resembling a flat bowler, decorated with a sweeping ostrich feather and worn

Suits by Chanel, 1930   *Left* evening dress by Patou;   Cotton evening dress
                                     right evening dress by P⸱quin; both 1930   by Schiaparelli, 1932

tilted over one eye. Originally of hatters' velvet with a thick luxuriant feather, it was copied in cheaper versions until it finally became a skimpy travesty of the original and then suddenly disappeared as a fashion.

Small hats continued to be worn in 1933, generally on the side of the head, and as many variations on the fez, the beret and the stocking cap were devised as there were on the diamond clip. Schiaparelli's stocking cap proved so popular that the design was pirated in America and in her autobiography she describes how tired she became of seeing it everywhere 'until one day it winked at her from the bald head of a baby in a pram. That day she gave the order to her salesgirls to destroy every single one in stock, to refuse to sell it and never to mention it again.'

Shoulders began to be accentuated, raglan sleeves were revived, particularly by Charles James, an inspired master of the intricate cut. Three-quarter length 'swagger' coats and tunics for dresses were introduced – the mid-calf skirt length and natural waist remaining standard through all the collections. Silver fox – another thirties motif – appeared both as trimming for coats or jackets or more often as a separate fur used singly or doubly. Black monkey-fur was also used and reappeared in collections throughout the thirties, but somehow it never caught on and its decorative possibilities found little response.

It is perhaps an oversimplification to select one evening dress out of the thousands designed in Paris in 1934 as being particularly significant but in retrospect the Marcel Rochas model, full-skirted, its minimal bodice decorated with a whole stuffed seagull, stands out as a portent of the quasi-surrealist fantasy which was to become increasingly noticeable until 1939. The clinging bias-cut

Silver *minaudière* by Cartier, about 1937

dresses of three or four years before were giving way to fuller skirts with the waistline clearly defined and the silhouette of day and evening clothes was becoming increasingly diversified. The trend of accentuation of the shoulders was even more marked in coats and dresses, either by padding or decorative motifs such as the cartridge-pleating favoured by Schiaparelli, and hats grew larger to balance the often excessive width of the shoulders.

Much publicity was given in this and the following year to a new fashionable accessory – the *minaudière*. At a time when a long dress was still considered essential for the theatre, dances or dinner parties, the well-dressed woman had to have several evening dresses in her wardrobe. To solve the problem of finding an evening bag that would harmonize with all these, Van Cleef and Arpels invented a rigid

On pages 190–1

The Ballroom of the Dorchester Hotel by Fortunio Matania, 1931

The Dorchester Hotel, built on the site of the former Dorchester House, was started in 1930 and completed at the rate of one floor a week. The opening was celebrated by the publication of a volume which included a short story by Michael Arlen, 'A Young Man Comes to London', and articles illustrated by folding colour plates, describing the demolition of the mansion designed by Vulliamy and the construction of the new hotel.

Fortunio Matania was extremely popular as an illustrator during the twenties and thirties and his historical reconstruction, rendered with great accuracy of detail, were much in demand by popular magazines. His statuesque women, bursting with vitality, were immediately recognizable whether dressed as ancient Romans participating in an orgy or in the contemporary evening dress of 1931.

Left evening coat in white satin with sable cuffs, by Augusta Bernard, 1933; *right* evening gown by Molyneux, 1933

Left 'Romaine' afternoon coat; *right* white swagger coat; both by Schiaparelli, 1933

metal box with compartments for cigarettes, powder, lipstick, money, etc., the exterior finished in lacquer, engine-turned gold or silver and even chromium plate. This was oddly named after a French adjective meaning simpering, affected or lackadaisical, though the compact planning of the interiors of these boxes should have earned the praise in England of the disciples of 'fitness of purpose'. The *minaudière* was sold exclusively in England by Asprey's at prices around £70 ($168), but was soon copied in different versions by other jewellers.

1935 saw the opening of the first 'boutique' by Schiaparelli in her new premises in the Place Vendôme and 'it became instantly famous because of the formula of "ready to take away immediately". There were useful and amusing gadgets afire with youth. There were evening sweaters, skirts, blouses and accessories previously scorned by the *haute couture*.' As she remarks in her autobiography, 'the year 1935 was such a busy one for Schiaparelli that she wonders how she got through it'. Schiaparelli numbered among her friends all the *avant-garde* designers, including Dali, Jean-Michel Frank, Fini and Bérard. Frank was entrusted with the decoration of the boutique, which he transformed into a gilded bamboo birdcage as a setting for displays of the new scent 'Shocking' in its bottle (in the shape of a Victorian dress dummy) designed by Léonor Fini, for the house-mascot Pascal, a life-size artists' layfigure in wood, and for an enormous stuffed bear given by Edward James to Salvador Dali, who dyed it shocking pink and put drawers in its stomach.

'Shoe' hat by Schiaparelli, 1936

Left 'Lobster' dress by Schiaparelli;
right 'Romantic' dress by Charles James; both 1936

It was Dali who inspired Schiaparelli most. 'Schiaparelli went up into the rarified skies of her most fantastic imagination and set off cascades of fireworks. Fantasy and ingenuity broke forth, with complete indifference not merely to what people would say but even to what was practical. She sought only an absolute freedom of expression . . .' and in so doing Schiaparelli set a pace of hectic invention which not only reflected the mood of the time but also influenced other couturiers, who might have eyed askance her more exotic flights of fancy but had perforce to provide their clients with something of the excitement she engendered. To elegance she added the attraction of the surrealistic, the bizarre or the incongruous. In 1932 she had included in her collections a number of dresses with painted decorations by Jean Dunand, but in 1936 a collaboration with Dali, a creator of far more feverish imagination, led to the appearance of an evening dress with the skirt printed with a life-size red lobster with a few green motifs scattered on the bodice to represent parsley. Dali's wish to spatter the dress with real mayonnaise was thwarted, to his intense regret. This dress, in fact extremely pretty, received much publicity in the fashion magazines, as did another Schiaparelli-Dali creation, a black felt hat in the form of a shoe, with a shocking-pink velvet heel, a reversal of function which was entirely in the surrealist manner. 1936 was the year when Dali drew *The City of Drawers*, representing an agonized nude female with a torso composed of a series of half-open drawers and *The Venus de Milo of the Drawers*, a plaster cast of the famous statue treated in a

Afternoon dress by Victor Stiebel, 1935

Sanforized shrunk cotton coat and two-piece
by Digby Morton, 1937

similar fashion. Schiaparelli records in her autobiography that 'We devised together the coat with many drawers from one of his famous pictures' – much to the pleasure of the fashion writers who approved rather less of another collaborative effort, a hat 'resembling a lamb cutlet with white frill on the bone'. The fruits of this collaboration with Dali more than anything else contributed to Schiap's fame for eccentricity, but almost as extraordinary were the embroidered reproductions of Jean Cocteau drawings on evening coats, her scarves and hats of fabric printed by Colcombet with news articles about herself, her use of the hitherto neglected zipper as a decorative feature, her buttons designed by Jean Clement* in wood, metal and plastics, buttons representing padlocks, mouths, butterflies, mermaids, fox-heads and inevitably hands – these creations were guaranteed to ensure a constant stream of publicity in the fashion magazines.

If she did not inaugurate the practice of basing a collection upon a theme, then she was one of the first to do so. Christian Bérard enthusiastically recorded for *Vogue* her 'circus' collection with its motifs of sequinned clown hats and short evening coats embroidered with prancing, plumed white horses. A 'pagan' collection of simple, clinging classical gowns embroidered with 'wreaths and leaves of delicate flowers' and an 'astrological' collection with horoscopes, the stars, the moon and the sun glittering at every step, did not, as might have been expected, shock her more conservative clients – who responded with enthusiasm – but also

---

* Schiaparelli refers to Clement in *Shocking Life* as 'a genius in his way, a real French artisan, who would work with such burning love that he was almost a fanatic. He would arrive at the moment when we had given up all hope of having anything to fasten our clothes. There would be a smirk of triumph on his face while he emptied his pockets into my lap, waiting anxiously for a word of praise.'

194

gained her many new ones. These collections based on motifs were a boon to the fashion writers who were released from the tedium of discovering trends in the diversity of fashions in the years between 1935 and 1939. Christian Bérard's designs for *La Reine Margot* in 1935, a Winterhalter of a Constantin Guys exhibition, the Balthus designs for *The Cenci* – anything new served as an inspiration for a collection.

Mainbocher's new collection in 1938 was actually a preview of the postwar New Look, with its full skirts over petticoats. A writer in *Harper's Bazaar* described the collection as 'significant and prophetic' – a prophecy which in fact was realized only after the Occupation – and while the French found them reminiscent of the illustrations in the Bibliothèque Rose volume of children's stories *Les Malheurs de Sophie*, the American buyers chauvinistically decided they had been inspired by *Little Women*.

The prevailing bias towards period revivalism to be found in interior decorating during the late thirties was reflected in high fashion. The Edwardian period inspired the upswept hair, full skirts and soft pastel colours, but in this case a corresponding influence was absent from the décor of the house – art nouveau was still a sleeping beauty despite Evelyn Waugh's efforts to interest the readers of the *Architectural Review* in the work of Gaudi. Balenciaga, newly arrived in Paris as a refugee from the Spanish Civil War, had opened a salon (after a brief unsuccessful sojourn in London) and was reminding Parisiennes of the paintings

Black satin evening gown by Mainbocher, 1938   'Malheurs de Sophie' dress by Mainbocher, 1938

Day suit by Molyneux, 1938   Dyed kid evening coat by Schiaparelli, 1938

of Velasquez, using a typically Spanish palette of rich dark colours and a determination to awaken a realization of the elegance of black combined with brown. Patou's collection influenced by Egyptian mummy wrappings brought about a charming series of drawings by Bérard but little else, and in London the highly successful and talented theatrical designers working under the name of Motley opened a *salon de couture*, but their first collection, inspired by medieval sources, was considered to adhere too closely to the originals to be chic and came more into the category of fancy dress than fashion. It was, in fact, thirty years ahead of its time.

Opposite

Top
Group of dresses, May 1935

Left to right black tulle evening dress by Worth; parma violet crêpe evening dress with parma violet sequin jacket by Hartnell; peach and silver lamé dress and cape by Enos
Bottom
Group of dresses, summer 1931

Left to right 'Antilles' designed by Jeanne Lanvin – a morning dress of fancy woollen with piqué collar and a waistband of ciré satin, the sleeves being detachable at the elbow; 'No. 19', a shantung sports dress by Molyneux with a matching coat; 'Les Vagues' by Worth, a three-piece of trousers, pullover and blazer.

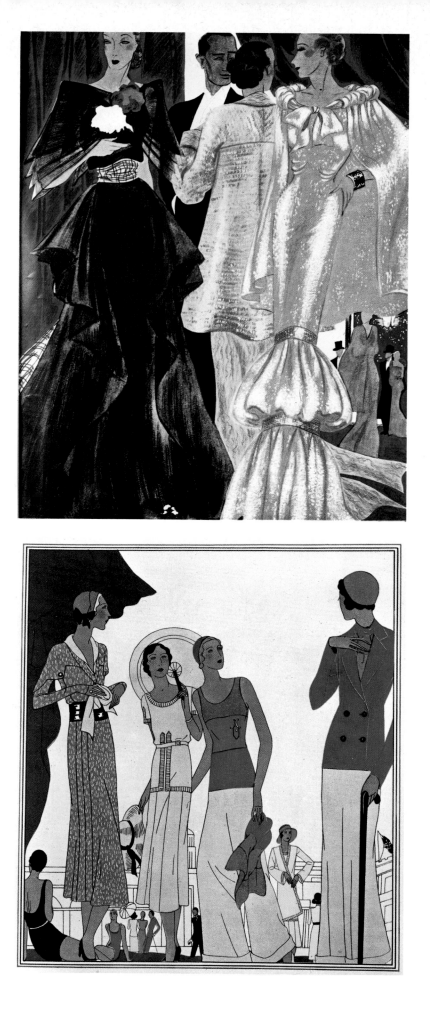

Hollywood style

Cinemas were the dream palaces of the thirties where moviegoers could find momentary escape from the worries and irritations of everyday life. These dream palaces with their exotic decoration, multicoloured lighting and soothing music were a prelude to the moment when a warm, comforting darkness enveloped the audience and the gleaming satin curtains swept aside to display the titles of another movie where wrong triumphed over right, true love conquered all and the final embrace of hero and heroine was a guarantee of a lifetime of perfect bliss. For the female members of the audience there was the possibility that even if their lives could never begin to approximate that of their favourite stars as shown on the screen or written about in the movie magazines, they could at least wear a frock or a hat similar to that of their idol and by doing so perhaps acquire a morsel of the cool elegance of Myrna Loy, Katherine Hepburn or Norma Shearer. For during the thirties Hollywood and its dress designers began seriously to rival Paris.

The advent of the talkies had brought a new element into Hollywood, an influx of talent from the legitimate theatre. Actors, playwrights and directors were lured from New York and London to translate successful plays into the new medium and although the many musicals produced in the late twenties and early thirties continued the Hollywood tradition of decorative fantasy, the domestic dramas or drawing-room comedies demanded a more restrained and naturalistic idiom of dress design once the human voice was added. At the same time 'certain actresses of great personal chic in private life refused to be dressed like Christmas trees on the films'. The talents of new designers, such as Adrian and Howard Greer, were engaged by the major companies to enhance and accentuate the different personalities of the movie stars. It was not an easy assignment. Between the designing of the clothes and the release of the film a period of anything up to a year might elapse, during which time Paris might have dictated a sudden change in silhouette or length. In addition a successful film might be shown for a couple of years or more and it was essential that the leading players should not appear old-fashioned. Thus the influence of Paris came to be disregarded and attempts were made to evolve a style of designing which would appear fashionable but would be at the same time dateless. Yet, by strange coincidence, Paris and Hollywood often appeared to have the same ideas at the same time. Garbo's clothes designed by Adrian for Mata-Hari had the same accent on broad shoulders as those shown in Paris collections at the time the film was released, and similarly, small pill-box hats appeared at the same time in the French collections and in the movies. To cut down costs of photography some women's magazines, in particular *Woman and Beauty*, used publicity stills from the Hollywood studios to illustrate the articles on fashion, carefully choosing those which most nearly approximated the latest Paris models, with the added glamour of being able to use the names of currently popular stars. Wholesale manufacturers were quick to exploit the influence of Hollywood fashions and as soon as a film was released the ready-made dress shops were flooded with copies or inexpensive versions of the outfits worn by the star. One London hat shop during the thirties had the idea of placing small cards bearing the names of the current film favourites on each hat displayed, with the result that an extravagant creation might one day be labelled Myrna Loy, the next day Joan Crawford, and on subsequent days Carole Lombard, Greta Garbo, Rosalind Russell, until it was finally sold.

On the other hand, Hollywood's influence on interior decoration was negligible if, in fact, there was any at all. The number of movies with settings in a modern idiom was surprisingly small considering the enormous output from the Hollywood studios. The sets created for musicals like the series starring Fred Astaire and Ginger Rogers, for instance, were so lavishly unrealistic as to be impractical as a source of inspiration. Of the more naturalistic films many were on historical themes set in various periods – these included, of course, the many Westerns – and while the dresses and particularly the hairstyles of the actresses often made few concessions to historical veracity (many an eighteenth-century character or saloon-bar girl in a Western turned her back to the camera to reveal a very obvious zip-fastener), the settings usually showed a considerable degree of period accuracy. Even when it was necessary to provide a modern background suggesting wealth or elegance, the set designers, possibly for the same reasons that the costume designer had to design clothes that avoided any sudden changes of fashion in the world of reality, invariably tended to think in terms of pseudo-eighteenth-century rooms with anonymous period furniture. This furniture came from the studio storerooms and could be used over and over again suitably re-covered in different materials to avoid being recognized – though there were a number of decorative pieces which inevitably became familiar to ardent filmgoers. Strictly contemporary furniture of extreme design was seldom, if ever, used as its practical life would be confined to one film of importance.

This adherence to period décors even in movies set in modern times, was to a certain extent reflected in the homes of the stars themselves. An article by Geoffrey Boumphrey in the *Architectural Review* reflected the somewhat patronizing attitude adopted by many in pseudo-intellectual circles toward Hollywood and its products. In this case the homes of some of the leading actresses, whose hospitality presumably Mr Boumphrey had enjoyed, were described with some acidity in an article entitled 'Hollywood Party'. The Louis IV dining room of 'the world's most famous blonde', admittedly no masterpiece of period reconstruction, earned the comment 'Hollywood has Mae West and Mae West has Louis and what has Louis to do with life as lived by Mae West except that it costs a lot of money.' The home of Miriam Hopkins, described as a 'Ye Olde Worlde Interior', was faintly praised as 'on the whole not a bad room – I have seen far worse in the homes of our own artistic intelligentsia', but Ida Lupino's living room was found to be 'horridly Victorian – I had thought in my simplicity, that except for the Sitwells, rooms like this one only occurred as accidents in these days.' Silvia Sydney committed the unforgiveable sin – that is, presumably, unforgiveable by the purist contributors to the *Architectural Review* with their passion for plain surfaces – of putting a chintz pattern on the walls of her living room and a different pattern on the chairs and settees, earning the sarcastic comment that she had missed the opportunity for more and different designs on the carpet and lampshades. Another room in Miss Sydney's house, innocuously decorated with an oak dresser and windsor chairs, was dismissed as 'Babes in the Wood' decoration. Mr Boumphrey's scathing comments were directed towards the houses of several other film stars and he concluded 'we have discovered nothing definable or even comprehensible – no

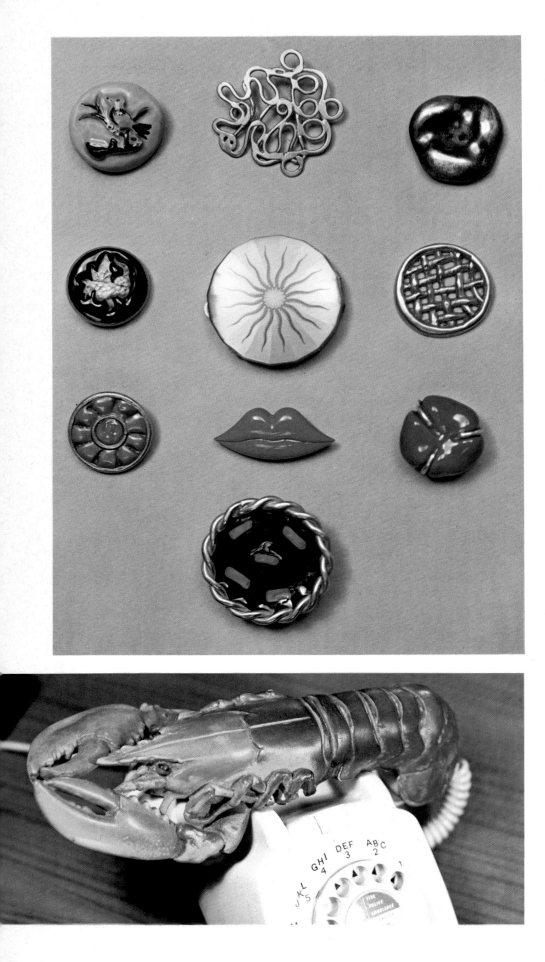

one style, that is, nor set of principles on which a style might be based.'

Probably he was not invited to the newly decorated house of Gary Cooper designed by Mrs Ernshaw of Else de Wolfe, Inc. Elegantly spacious and uncluttered, the rooms were white throughout with touches of pastel tones of pink and yellow and considerable use was made of mirrors, the faceted mirror consoles and plaster palm tree light fittings designed by Serge Roche of Paris, and of zebra skins. The fireplaces were surrounded by cast-glass bolection mouldings – a motif sometimes used to frame pictures.

Group of buttons made for the leading Paris dressmakers during the thirties; powder compact designed by Reco Capey for Yardley, 1934

The 'mouth' button is of plastic and was designed for Schiaparelli. The other buttons were made by François Hugo.

'Lobster' telephone receiver by Salvador Dali, about 1933

Designed by Salvador Dali, these composition lobsters were intended to cover the handpiece of the telephone and were commissioned by Edward James for his house in Wimpole Street, London.

Envoi

There is a tendency to treat the thirties as a forgotten period – an interlude between the frenetic gaieties and excitements of the twenties and the grim realities of the forties and the Second World War. Those who have written on the period have been mainly political writers preoccupied with the growing rise to power of the dictators and the inevitability (in hindsight) of world conflict. But for the majority of people, and perhaps more especially artists and craftsmen, and for the greater part of the decade, the main concern was with the hazards of earning a living during the Depression. Thoughts of war began to take on an aspect of fearful reality only in the last year or two before the actual outbreak of hostilities. Ironically enough it was during those same two or three years before 1939 that the careless extravagance of the twenties briefly reappeared, and with it some of the fantasy and imaginative creativity of the earlier decade.

It is almost impossible to distil the essential flavour of the thirties in the way that one could have done in the twenties – to cite a room, a dress or a decorative object which, despite the changes in fashion, seems to sum up the whole decade. As we have seen, a 'typical' thirties room could be strikingly functional and streamlined, an essay in neo-baroque, weirdly surrealist, a modernized version of Victoriana, Regency or even classical Greek. It is this diversity of styles that makes the period original and exciting. In the words of the Cole Porter song of the period, 'Anything goes'.

Interior of the New Victoria Cinema designed by Trent and Lewis, 1930

The New Victoria Cinema, described as 'a dream-like palace under the sea' was an imaginative concept which received the dubious distinction of being used by a specialist in abnormal mentality as a text-book example for his students of 'folie de grandeur', alongside the architectural projects of Adolf Hitler.

Bibliography

Abercrombie, Patrick (ed) *The Book of the Modern House*. London: Hodder and Stoughton, 1939

Acton, Harold *Memoirs of an Aesthete*. London: Methuen & Co. Ltd, 1948

Alexandrian, Sarane *Surrealist Art*. London: Thames and Hudson; New York: Frederick A. Praeger, Inc., 1970

Arlen, Michael *A Young Man Comes to London*. London: The Marshalsea Press, 1931

Bernard, Oliver P. *Cock Sparrow*. London: Jonathan Cape, 1936

Binder, Joseph *Colour in Advertising*. London: The Studio, 1934

Brown, Oliver *Exhibition*. London: Evelyn Adams and Mackay, 1968

Carrington, Noel (ed) *Design in the Home*. London: Country Life Ltd, 1933

Chase, Edna Woolman, and Ilka Chase *Always in Vogue*. London: Victor Gollancz Ltd; New York: Doubleday and Company, Inc., 1954

Doesburg, Theo van *Principles of Neo-plastic Art*. London: Lund Humphries, 1969; Greenwich, Conn.: New York Graphic Society, 1968

Dowling, Henry G., RRSA *A Survey of British Industrial Arts*. Benfleet, Essex: F. Lewis, 1935

Eberlein, H. D. and C. van Dyke Hubbard *Glass in Modern Construction*. New York: Charles Scribner's Sons, 1937

Frankenstein, Alfred *After the Hunt*. University of California Press, 1953

Frankl, Paul T. *New Dimensions*. London: Payson and Clarke Ltd; New York: Harcourt Brace, Inc., 1928

Gaunt, William *Bandits in a Landscape.* London: The Studio, 1937

Gloag, John (ed) *Design in Modern Life*. London: George Allen and Unwin Ltd, 1934

Hayes Marshall, H. G. *British Textile Designers Today*. Leigh-on-Sea, Essex: F. Lewis, 1939
　　　Within Four Walls. Leigh-on-Sea, Essex: F. Lewis, 1948

Holme, Geoffrey *Industrial Design and the Future*. London: The Studio, 1934

H.M.S.O. *Art and Industry*. London, 1932

James, Edward *The Gardener who saw God*. London: Duckworth; New York: Charles Scribner's Sons, 1937

Jean, Marcel *Histoire de la Peinture Surréaliste*. Paris: Editions du Seuil, 1959

Joel, David *The Adventure of British Furniture*. London: Ernest Benn Ltd, 1953

Kirstein, Lincoln (ed) *Pavel Tchelitchev Drawings*. New York: H. Bittner and Co., 1947

Levy, Julien (ed) *Eugène Berman*. London and New York: American Studio Books, 1946

Lurçat, Jean *Designing Tapestry*. London: Rockcliff, 1950; New York: The Macmillan Company, 1951

Meller, S., F. Lewis and E. Entwistle *A Century of British Fabrics*. Leigh-on-Sea, Essex: F. Lewis, 1955

Miller, Duncan *More Colour Schemes for the Modern Home*. London: The Studio, 1938

Nash, Paul *Room and Book*. New York: Charles Scribner's Sons, 1932

Naylor, Gillian *The Bauhaus*. London: Studio Vista; New York: E. P. Dutton and Co., Inc., 1968

Olivier, Edith *In Pursuit of Rare Meats*. H.M.S.O., n.d.

Patmore, Derek *Colour Schemes for the Modern Home*. London: The Studio, 1933

'Plastes' *Plastics in Industry*. London: Chapman and Hall Ltd, 1940; New York: Chemical Publishing Company, 1941

Ray, Man *Self Portrait*. London: Andre Deutsch Ltd; Boston: Little Brown and Co., 1963

Read, Herbert *Art and Industry*. London: Faber and Faber, 1934; New York: Harcourt Brace, Inc., 1935

Roche, Serge *Mirrors*. London: Duckworth, 1956

Rose, Muriel *Artist Potters in England*. London: Faber and Faber; New York: Pitman Publishing Corp., 1955

Schiaparelli, Elsa *Shocking Life*. London: J. M. Dent and Sons Ltd; New York: E. P. Dutton and Co., Inc., 1954

Spry, Constance *Flowers in House and Garden*. London: J. M. Dent and Sons Ltd, 1937; New York: G. P. Putnam's Sons, 1938

Valette, John de la *The Conquest of Ugliness*. London: Methuen and Co. Ltd, 1935

Waldberg, Patrick *Surrealism*. London: Thames and Hudson, 1965; New York: McGraw-Hill Book Co., 1966

Wolfe, Elsie de *After All*. London: William Heinemann Ltd; New York: Harper and Brothers, 1935

Magazines and exhibition catalogues

L'Amour de l'Art. Paris

The Architectural Review. London

Art and Decoration. New York

Art, Goût et Beauté. Paris

The Bournville Works Magazine. Birmingham

British Art in Industry. Illustrated catalogue of the exhibition at Burlington House, London, 1935

L'Exposition de Paris. Introduction by Albert Laprade. Paris: Librairie des Arts Décoratifs, 1937

Harper's Bazaar. London, New York

House and Garden. London, New York

Ideal Home Exhibition catalogues. London

Modern Publicity. London

Photography Year Book. London

The Sculpture of Elie Nadelman. New York: Museum of Modern Art, 1948

The Studio. London

The Studio Year Book of Decorative Art. London

Town and Country. New York

Vogue. London, New York, Paris

Woman and Beauty. London

Index

Page numbers in italics refer to
illustrations on those pages

Aalto, Alvar *48*
Abdul Hamid, Sultan 111
Abdy, Ilya 147
Académie Ranson 136
Acton, Harold 165–6
Adam, Robert & James 20
Adrian 198
*The Adventure of British
  Furniture* 94
After the Hunt 161
L'Age d'Or 149, 156
Agnes 147
Albi 106
Alhambra Theatre, London 44
Alix 187
Allan Walton Fabrics *103*
L'Amour de l'Art 15, 67, 129,
  145
Amours 30
Andersen, Hans Christian 135
Anglesey, Lord 133
Antiques 17, 18, 67, 81
The Apocalypse of Angers 104
Après le Cubisme 12
Aquarius 139
Arabian Nights 12
Arbus, André 74
Architectural Review 18, 39, 48,
  56, 59, 62–3, 71, 78, 86, 91,
  132, 152, 153, 167, 170, 195,
  199
Arcimboldo, Giuseppe 161
Arlen, Michael 189
Armed October 135
Armstrong, John *43*, 50, 91
Arts and crafts movement 17
Art and Industry 18
Art déco 10–11, 12, 15, 32,
  176
Art Direction 84
Art Directors' Guild 163
Art in industry 48–61
Art nouveau 10, 11, 12, 15, 176
L'Art Nouveau 131
Art Now 162
Ashbee, Charles Robert 68
Ashstead Potteries 127, *130*
Ashton, Frederick 137
Asprey's 192
Astaire, Fred 199
Atelier Martine 11
Atelier Pomone 11
Au Printemps, Paris 11, 185
Aubade 164
Aubusson workshops 81, 99,
  101, *102*, 104–5, 106
Australia 30
Austria 11
Avinoff 90
Azema, Edrei and Hardy 15, *16*

Baccarat 111
Bacon, Francis 63–4, 65
Bakst, Léon 11
Balanchine, Georges 164
Balenciaga 195
Ballerina 135
Ballets Russes 11, 39, 145
Ballets Russes de Monte Carlo
  30, 137, 149
Balthus 147, 195
Bandits in a Landscape 161
Barbe, Pierre 145
Barbier, Georges 11, *154*
Barnes Pianos 164, *179*
Baronova, Irina 148
Barr, Alfred 150
Barron, Phyllis 68, 103
Bauhaus 14–15, 18, 23

Bawden, Edward 63
Bayes, Alexander 65
Bazin, G.R.M. 143
Beach 27, 147
Beardsley, Aubrey 165
Beatl Sales Ltd 127
Beauvais tapestry works 104
Bell, Vanessa 50, 63, 64–5, 139
La Belle Hélène 78, *78*
Belleek Ware 159
Bemelmans, Ludwig 25
Benedictus, Edouard 52
Bennett, Arnold 167
Bérard, Christian 81, 84, 135,
  136, 145–8, *146*, *147*, 149,
  151, 162, 164, 192, 194–5,
  196
Berlin 167
Berlin State Porcelain Factory
  124
Berlioz, Hector 151
Berman, Eugène 136–7, *138*,
  140, 143, 148, 149, 164
Berman, Léonid 136
Bernard, Oliver 45, 46, 47,
  91–2
Berners, Lord 81
Best and Lloyd 60
Bestigui, Carlos de 148, *153*,
  154–5, *154*, *155*, 170, 176
Betjeman, John 165
Betty Joel Ltd *54*, 55
Biedermeier furniture 170
Bignou Galleries, New York
  106
Bing, Siegfried 131
Bird in Space 173
Block, Robert 111–12, *111*,
  116
Blonde 182
Blount, Anthony 57
Bon Marché, Paris 11
Bonnard, Pierre 136
Boston Opera House 45, 118
Boumphrey, Geoffrey 199
Boucher, François 104
Bournville 49
Braddell, Darcy 39, *40*
Braddell, Mrs Darcy 96
Brancusi, Constantin 173, 175
Brandt, Edgar 51
Brangwyn, Frank 45, 50,
  129–32, *131*
Braque, Georges 106
Brauner, Victor 159
Breton, André 159
Breuer, Marcel 15, 56, 91
Brighton Museum 70, 71, 123,
  137
British Art in Industry
  Exhibition 53–9, 166, 169
British Empire Exhibition, 1924
  45
British Industries Fair 94
British Vitrolite Company 104,
  105
Broadcasting House, London
  38, 166
Broadhurst Theatre, New York
  136
Brook House, London *134*, 135
Brown, Oliver 169
Bruhns, Ivan Da Silva 51, *102*
Brush, Katherine 118
Brussels 106
Buñuel, Luis 149
Burslem 126
Butt, Baseden 91
Byron, Robert 165

Cadbury family 49
Caledonian Market 167
Cambridge 33
Cambridge Theatre, London 41
Campbell Fabrics *101*
Capey, Reco 43, 70, 71, *71*, *72*,
  201
Cardew, Michael 127
Carpentras 106
Carpets 99–104
Cartier 24, 160, *160*, 182, *182*,
  186, *189*
Casa Maury, Marquis de 89
Casino de Paris 45
Cassandre 148, 163, *178*
The Cenci 147, 195
Les Cent Baisers 147
Ceramics 124–7
Chanel 25, 84, 185, 187, *188*
Charance, René 174, *175*
Charles X furniture 161, 174
Charreau, Pierre 15
La Chatte 12
Cheesman, Kenneth *105*
Chelsea 69, 74, 78
Cherbourg 24
Chermayeff, Serge 44, 65
Cheruit 187
Chevill 104
Chicago 106
Le Chien Andalou 149
China 53, 124–7
Chinese furniture 16
Chinese pottery 126
Chippendale style 16, 20
Christine 70
Christofle, Paris 156
Cinema 198–202
The City of Drawers 193
Claridges Hotel, London
  34–5, *35*
Clarke, Arundell 69, 162
Clement, Jean 194
Cliff, Clarice 50, 126, *130*
Cochran, Charles B. 78, 135
Cocteau, Jean 145, *156*, 162
Cogniat, Raymond 10, 67
Colcombet 194
Colefax, Lady *82*
Colonial Exhibition, Paris 1931
  185
Colour and Interior Decoration
  72, 75
*Colour Schemes for the Modern
  Home* 76, 89, 139
Comédie Française, Paris 70
Concurrence 147
Confessions of an Aesthete 165
Connard, Philip 49
The Conquest of Ugliness 30–1
Constructivism 12
Cook's Wagon Lit *178*
Cooper, Austin 163
Cooper, Douglas 162
Cooper, Gary 201
Cooper, Susie 126, *130*
Copeland 159
Copenhagen 22
Corner House, Tottenham Court
  Road 45
Costa-Achillopulo 158, *159*
Cotillon 84, 145, *146*
Coutaud 106
Covanna, Paris 15, *16*
Covent Garden Opera House
  45, 135, 151, 159
Cowles, Clement *142*
Coypel 104
Cox & Co. 97

Craftsmen 31–2
Crawford, Joan 199
Cresset Press 135
Criaerd 79
Crofts, Mary 50
Crofts, Stella 68
Croghan, Edward 114
Croom, Inez *114*
Crowther, Pollard 74
Cubism 12
Cummings, Rose 90
Cunard, Lady 162
Cuttoli, Madame 106, *107*, 173,
  175
Cyrano de Bergerac 145
Czechoslovakia 97

Dadd, Richard 132, 169
Daily Mail 54, 90, 123, 132
Dali, Salvador 84, 137, 149,
  150, 152–3, 157, *157*, 160,
  164, 192, 193, *200*
Deane, Humphrey 39, *40*
De Andrada, Madame 52
De Chirico, Giorgio 137, 164
Décoration Intérieure Moderne
  39, 85
Degas, Edgar 145
Dejean 26
Delafosse 182
De la Mare, Walter 135
De Lanux, Eyre 86
De la Tour d'Auvergne,
  Princesse *73*
Delaunay, Sonia 16
De la Valette, John 30–1
Délices 30
De Meyer, Baron 74
De Molas, Nicolas *159*
De Monval, Bernard Boutet 21
Denis, Maurice 136
De Noailles, Vicomte 84, 156
De Noailles, Vicomtesse
  Marie-Laure *156*
Dent, Olive 90
De Pisis 84
De Plantier, Nicholas 170
Depression 21, 23, 24–32, 39,
  45, 48, 61, 70, 88, 90, 126,
  129, 137, 163, 166, 185, 186,
  187, 203
Derain, André 106, 147, 149
Desbaines, Thérèse 136
Desiderio, Monsu 161
Design and Industries Associa-
  tion 18, 59–60, 88
Design in Industry Exhibition,
  1935 39
Design in Modern Life 48
Deskey, Donald 96, 108
Desny 86, *87*
Dessau 14
De Stijl 12, 64
De Vilmorin, Madame 27
The Devil's Holiday 137
De Wolfe, Elsie 20, 138, *176*,
  177
Diaghilev, Serge 12, 148–9
Le Dieu Bleu 12
DIM 39, 85
Dinesen, Isaak 135
Dior, Christian 30
Dobson, Frank 129
Dorchester Hotel, London
  190, *191*
Doré, Gustave 169
Dorland Hall Exhibition, 1933
  88, 108
Dorn, Marion 35, 75, 99, *102*,

167
Doulton 53, 132
Downtown Gallery, New York
  161
Drécoll 187
Dresden 155, 164
Drian, Etienne *138*
Droods 115
Dubonnet 163
Duchamp, Marcel 150
Dufour 174
Dufrêne, Maurice 11
Dufy, Raoul 27, 30, *100*, 106
  147, 173, 175
Dulac, Edmund 49
Dunand, Jean 25, 26–7, *28*,
  42, 84, 193
Dunlop, Sybil 68
Dupas, Jean 163
Durham 180
Duveen, Joseph 20, 172
Duveen, Lord 133

Ecole de Paris 25, 129
Edinburgh Weavers 53, 103
Edward VIII, King of England
  31, 48–9, 50
Elden (London) Ltd 75
Elizabeth, Consort of George VI
  119, 133
Elsie de Wolfe Inc. 201
Elwes, Guy 36
Elwes Ltd 35–6
Eminent Victorians 165
Empire style 21
Empress of Britain 132
L'Epoque 74
Epstein, Jacob 150
Ernshaw, Mrs 201
Ernst, Max 143, 149, 150, 158,
  162
Erté 164, *179*
Etchells, Frederick 84
Everard, Frederick 23
Errante 149
Exhibition of Applied Art, 1910
  11
Exhibition of Industrial Art,
  1917 61
Exposition des Arts Décoratifs
  et Industriel, 1925 10–11, 12

Fabrics, industrial design
  99–106
Façade 166
*The Fairy Feller's Master
  Stroke* 132, 169
Fairy Tales and Legends 135
The Faithful Colt 161
'Fantastic Art, Dada and
  Surrealism' 1937 150
Farquharson, W. Clyne
  121
Fashion 185–96
La Ferronerie 51
Fidelio 135
Fini, Léonor 143, *143*, 192
Fitzroy Square, London
  52, 85, 86
Flaxman, John 50
Foley Potteries *43*, 50
Folies Bergère, Paris 45
Follot, Paul 11
Fortnum and Mason 81, 112,
  116, *114*, 159, 169, *170*
Fortune 23
Forum Cinema, Bath 51
Fouquet, Jean 185
Fox, Charles 51

Françaix, Jean 147
Frank, Jean-Michel 72, 76, 83–4, *83, 84*, 152, 153, 156, 164, 173, 175, 176, 192
Frankenstein, Alfred 161
Frankl, Paul 19–20, *19*, 23
Frankl Galleries 108
Fraser, Eric 163
French, Leslie 38
Fund for The Preservation of Ancient Cottages 59
Furse, Roger 136

Gabo, Naum 12
Gainsborough, Thomas 167
Galerie Drouin, Paris 137, *141*, 143, *143*
Galerie Druet, Paris 136, 145, 148
Galeries Lafayette, Paris 11
Ganymede and the Eagle 22
Garbo, Greta 198, 199
The Gardener who saw God 155
Gardiner & Sons 51
Gardner, Evelyn 165, 169
Gas Light and Coke Co. 163
Gate Theatre, London 136
Gaudi, Antonio 195
Gaunt, William 161
Gayfere House 35, *36*, 37
Le Gazette du Bon Ton 138
Geddes, Norman Bel 21, 23
Geffroy, Gustave 104, 145
George VI, King of England 119, 132, 133
George, Waldemar 136, 145
Georgian houses 16
Geraldy, Paul 70
Germany 11, 14, 15, 103, 162–3, 164
Gertler, Mark 49
Giacometti, Alberto *83*
Giacometti, Diego 84, *84*
Gilbert, W.S. 39
Gilbert Scott, Crewe and Masey 44
Gill, Eric *38*, 39, 129
Ginner, Charles 129
Girault, Paris 15, *16*
Glass, interior design 107–23
Gloag, John 59, 60, 75, 121, 163
Gobelins tapestry works 104
Godfrey Giles Ltd 115
Goebbels, Paul Joseph 163
Goodbye Mr Chippendale 172
Goodhart-Rendel, H.S. 59, 166
Gorell, Lord 49
Gorell Report 49, 88
Goupy, Marcel 124
Grace, Louise M. 164
Grant, Duncan *43*, 50, 63, 64–5, 103, *103*, 139
Great Exhibition, 1851 169
Green and Abbott 87, 137
Greer, Howard 198
Grierson, Ronald 57, *101*
Gromaire 106
Gropius, Walter 14, 15, 18
Grosvenor Gallery, London 165
Grosz, George 162
Groult, André 11
Guedon, Colette 185
Guérard, Roland *160*
Guinness, Mrs Ernest *75*
Guitry, Sacha 159
Gulliver's Travels 135
Gump, Messrs, of Honolulu 112
Guys, Constantin 169, 195

Hackett, Walker 41
Halpert, Edith 161
Hamada, Shoji 127
Hanley 126
Hapsburgs 161
Harlow, Jean 78
Harper's Bazaar 74, 86, 151, 159, 165, 185, 195
Hart, Mrs Woolley 159
Hartnett, William 161

Haskell, Arnold 149
Hatry, Clarence 24
Heal, Sir Ambrose 56
Heal and Son Ltd 111
Healthy Wealthy and Wise 87
Helen! 78
Henderson, Ian 69
Hepburn, Katherine 198
Hepworth, Barbara 50, 162
Herold, Jacques 159
Herbert, A.P. 78
Herbst, René 15
Herman Miller Clock Co. *21*
Herman, A., Ltd *94*
Hill, John 137
Hill, Oliver 33, 35, *36*, 37–9, *37, 38*, 58, 108, 110
Hitler, Adolf 162, 163, 203
Hodgkins, Frances 162
Hoffmann, Josef 11
Hogarth, William 135
Holland 14
Hollywood style 198–202
Hope, Thomas 63
House and Garden 94
House of Good Fortune, Olynthos 171
House of Lords 129–31
Housman, Laurence 136
Hugo, François *201*
Hugo, Jean 147, 159
Hypocrites Club 165

ICI *see* Imperial Chemical Industries
Ideal Home Exhibition, 1930 69, 90, 91
Ideal Home Exhibition, 1931 123
Ideal Home Exhibition, 1933 132
Ideal Home Exhibition, 1935 54, 57
Ile de France 25
Illustrated London News 126
L'Illustration 90, 123
Immigration 30
Imperial Chemical Industries 127
Industrial art 48–61
Industrial Art Explained 59, 121
Industrial design 23
Industrial Design 126
Ingrand, Max 108
Inison, Byron 35
Innen Dekoration 69, 162
Interior decoration 62–91
Ionides, Basil 36, 39, *41*, 72
Iribe, Paul 11
Iron, wrought 15
Isabella II, Queen of Spain 174
Islington Cattle Market 167
Italy 97
Iveagh, Lord 129, 132

Jacob 70
Jacob, Max 162
Jacobean style 18
James, Charles 188, *193*
James, Edward 135, 137, 149, 155–7, 192, *201*
James, Mrs. Edward 108, 110, 149
James Clark & Son *114*, 115, *116*
Janneau, Guillaume 15, 73, 104
Japanese pottery 126
Jeanneret, Pierre 15
Jeffress, Arthur 137, 161, 162, 182
Jensen, Georg 48
Jeu d'Enfants 160
Joel, Betty *54*, 55, 57, 58, *58*
Joel, David 94
Joesler, Joseph *164*
John, Augustus 87–8, 129
John Crossley & Sons 51
Johnson, Celia 136
Jolson, Al 149
Jones, Inigo 133

Jourdain, Francis 15, *101*
Journal of the RIBA 18
Joyen 158
Junge, Alfred 58
Juta, Jans 21

Karasz, Ilonka 96
Karinska, Madame 147–8
Katzenbach and Warren Inc. 96, 159
Kauffer, E. MacKnight 63, 67, 85, *85*, 86, 87, 99, 163
Kelso 96
Kirk, Eve 87–8
Kirstein, Lincoln 136
Klee, Paul 14, 162
Klotz, Madame 27
Knight, Dame Laura 49, 50
Koch, Alexander 69
Kohlmann, Madame 11
Komisarjevsky, Théodore 44
Korean pottery 126

Lalique, René 26, *26*, 35, 37, 58, 97, 108, 119, *122*, 123
Lalique, Suzanne 124, 126
Lallemand, Robert 86
Lambert, Maurice 63
Lamps 96–9
Langley 126
Lanvin, Jeanne 11, 187, *196*
Larcher, Dorothy 68
Laurencin, Marie 86, 96, 162, 164, 173, 175
Laurent 70
Lavery, Sir John 132
Leach, Bernard 126–7
Le Corbusier 12, 15, 18, 60, 107, *152*, 153–5
Leedsware 72
Léger, Fernand 106
Leicester Galleries, London 49, 167
Lelong, Lucien 84
Le Touquet 78
Levy, Sir Albert 37
Levy, Julian 136, 137, 140
Lewis, Wyndham 18, 86
Lhote, André 129
Lichine, David 146
Lighting, interior design 96–9
Lindner, Richard 164, *179*
Liners 25–30
Little Women 195
Llewellyn, Sir William 53
Loewy, Raymond 23
Lombard, Carole 199
London 14, 24, 31, 36, 49, 55, 106, 167, 195, 196, 198
London Museum 133
London Pavilion Theatre 135, 159
Lord Benbow competition 62–3, *64*
The Lord Fish 135
Lorne, Marion 41
Losch, Miss Tilly 108, 110, 149
Louis XIII furniture 106
Louis XIV style 199
Louis XV furniture 75, 81, 106, 180
Louis XVI furniture 11, 81, 138
Love and Let Love 58
Lovet-Lorski, Boris 21
Loy, Myrna 198, 199
Luce, Jean 124, 126
Ludington, Wright 137
Lupino, Ida 199
Lurçat, Jean 104, 106
Lusitania 45
Lutyens, Robert 59
Lutyens, Symonds 36

Macy 20
McGrath, Raymond 33–4, *34*, 35, 39, 63
Machines, as source of design 23
La Machine Infernale 145
Mackintosh, Charles Rennie 11,

62, 63
Maclaren, Denham 63
McMillen Inc. 20, 21
Magasins du Louvre 11
Magnasco, Alessandro 161
Magritte, René 149, 161
Maillol, Aristide 162
Mainbocher 187, 195, *195*
Maison de l'Art Nouveau 70
La Maison Moderne 11
La Maîtrise, Galeries Lafayette 11
Malacrida, Marchesa 159
Les Malheurs de Sophie 195
Marckvald, Miss *164*
Marcoussis 106
Mare, André 11
Marie-Laure (Vicomtesse de Noailles) *156*
Marinot, Maurice 120
Marriage of Figaro 135
Marrot, Paule 174
Marshall, Hayes 116, 169, *170*
Martin, Charles *151*, 185
Martin, John 169
Marx, Enid 68
Mass production 14, 59
Massine, Leonide 30, 78, 147, 148, 149, 151
Matania, Fortunio *190–1*
Matisse, Henri 106
Maubousson *151*, 185–6
Maugham, Somerset 162
Maugham, Syrie 72–81, 76, 77, 80, 104, 182
Maufe, Edward 36
Maynard, Alistair 54, *54*, 55
Mayor, Frederick 162
Mayor Gallery, London 162
Medici Society, London 53, 80
Medley, Robert 63
Medwin, R. Gardner 94
Meissen ware 68
Mendenhall, Edgar 115
Mendenhall, Leslie 115
Mendl, Lady *see* De Wolfe, Elsie
Messel, Oliver 78, *78*
Metropolis 60
Metropolitan Museum of Art, New York 19, 61
Metropolitan Opera, New York 118
Mies van der Rohe, Ludwig 14, *14*, 107
Mignard 104
Miller, John Duncan 88, *88, 89*
Millet, Jean François 157
Milne, John 53
Milne, Oswald 34–5, *35*
Minotaure 149
Minton 159
Miró, Joan *102*, 106, 149, *160*, 162
Mirrors 108–19
Modern Publicity 163, 164
'Modern Ware for the Table' exhibition 1934 50
Modernism 12, 15, 19, 20, 21, 32, 176
Moffat, Curtis 52, 53, 60, 85–90, *86, 87*, 162
Moholy-Nagy, László 14,
Molyneux 187, *192, 196*
Mond, Henry 39
Monro, Mieda 25
Montpensier, Duc de 174
Monza Exhibition, 1930 52
Moore, Henry 162
More Colour Schemes for the Modern Home 89
Morinère, Comtesse Hervé de la 78
Morton, Digby 17, *194*
Motley 196
Mottisfont Abbey 135
Moutbatten, Lady *134*, 135
Mountbatten, Lord Louis *134*, 135

Mount Temple, Lady *36*, 37 110
Mozartiana 147
Mulberry House, London *40*
Munich 11, 162, 164
Murray, Keith 121, *123, 125*, 126
Mussolini, Benito 52, 53

Nadelman, Elie 173
Le Nain 145
Nancy McClelland, Inc. 114
Nasenta 138
Nash, Paul 17–18, *19*, 50, 51, 63, *64*, 67, 68, *100*, 108, 124, 162
Nazi régime 23
Negri, Pola 108
Negro art 12, 85, 86, 90, 175
Neo-Georgian style 16, 18, 62
Neo-Regency style 22
Neo-romanticism 136–49
Nevinson, C.R.W. 49, 129
New Burlington Galleries, London 149
New Dimensions 19
New Victorian Cinema, London *202*
New York 10, 24, 84, 106, 132, 136, 150, 198
Newbould, Frank 163
Newcomb, Mary 87
Newport Pottery Co. 126
The Next Volume 135
Nicholson, Ben 50, 162
Nicolson, Harold 82
Nieuwe Amsterdam 29
Nijinska, Bronislava 147, 164
Nobilissime Visione 149
Normandie 25–30, *26–8*
Normandy 106
North House, Westiminster 37, 38
Nossiter, Dorrie 68
Nozze di Figaro 135

Ode 148
Odeon Cinema, Leicester Square *44*
Olivier, Edith 133
Olynthos 171
Omega Workshop 63, 86
Oppenheim, Meret 150
Orgues 30
Oriental motifs 11
Orion 29
O'Rorke, Brian *29*, 162
Oudry, Jean-Baptiste 104
Oxford 165, 166
Ozenfant 12

PLAN *48*
Packaging 49
Paganini, Niccolo 137
Palace of Westminster, London 129–31
Palazzo Albrizzi, Venice 149
Papéete 106
Paquin 188
Paramount Theatre, Newcastle upon Tyne 51
Paris 10, 11, 12, 14, 15, 24, 25, 53, 78, 84, 123, 129, 136, 145, 150, 167, 170, 173, 176, 185, 187, 188, 195, 198, 201
Paris Exhibition, 1925 51, *51*, 53, 58, 59, 61, 70
Paris Exhibition, 1937 37, 74
Paris International Exhibition 103
Paris Surrealist Exhibition 158
Paterson's Gallery, London 173
Patmore, Derek 76, 85, 89, 139
Patou 188, 196
Patout 15–16, *16*
Patronage 10, 14, 20, 133, 137
Paul, Bruno 11
Pavillon de Marsan, Paris 123
Peche, Dagobert 11

PEL 91–2, *91*, *92*
Penrose, Roland 150
Period revivalism 165–84
Perriand, Charlotte 15
Persia 53
Petit, Nicolas 79
Pevsner, Anton 12
Philadelphia 106
Phoenix Theatre, London 44
Picabia, Francis 149
Picasso, Pablo 106, 136, 149, 150, 173, 175
Pichenot, Robert 113
Pickford, Mary 221
Pilkington Bros. 108
Pitman, Mrs Lance 115
Plas Newydd 133
Plastics 127
Pleydell-Bouverie, David 65, *66*
Poertzel, Professor *128*, 129
Poiret, Paul 11, 30, 145, 154
Pollard & Sons 132
Pollitzer, Sigmund *105*, 108
Polunin 44
Porter, Cole 203
Posters 163–4
Posters and Publicity 163
Pottery Gazette and Glass Trade Review 125
Practical Equipment Ltd *see* PEL
Premet 187
Pride and Prejudice 136
Printz, Eugène *73*
Pritchard, J.C. *52*
Proctor, Dod 49, 50
Proctor, Ernest 49
Publicity 163–4
Pugin, Augustus Welby Northmore 96, 133
Pulham, Peter Rose *160*
Purvis, Tom 163
Pyman, Joan 127, *130*

Queen Anne style 16, 18, 89
Queen Elizabeth 29
Queen Mary 29
Queen Victoria 165

Rackham, Arthur 49
Rading, Adolf *13*
The Rake's Progress 135
Ray, Man 150, 157, 158
Read, A.B. 96
Read, Herbert 18, 56, 162
Redon, Odilon 104
Reens-Arta *121*
Regency style 21, 144, 166–7
La Reine Margot 145, 195
Reinhardt, Max 78
Reisener, J.H. 70
Reproduction furniture 17, 18, 32, 67
Reynolds, Joshua 167
Reynolds' Illustrated News 57
Ricci, Nina 187
Richard Thibaut Inc 96
Rimbaud 149
Rimsky-Korsakoff, Nicholas Andreievich 159
Rio 179
Le Rire 104

Rivera, Diego 132
Riviera 78
Robertson, Doris Howard *17*
Robsjohn-Gibbings, J.H. 171–3, *171*, *172*, *173*
Rochas, Marcel 188
Roche, Serge 14, 115, 118, *119*, 176, 182, *183*, 184, 201
Rockefeller Centre, New York 132
Rockefeller, Nelson 84
Rodier, Paul 70
Rodocanacchi, Jean 84
Rogers, Ginger 199
Rohde, Gilbert *21*, 96, 108
Roland de l'Epée, Baron de 84
Rome 136
Romney, George 167
Room and Book 17–18, 51
Rosa, Salvator 161
Rosebery, Lord 149
Rostova, Lubov *146*, *160*
Rothenstein, Sir William 50
Rouard, Marcel 126
Rouault, Georges 106, 162
Roubo 182
Rouff, Maggy 187
Rowley Gallery 53
Roy, Pierre 161, 164
Royal Academy 53, 59
Royal Academy Exhibition, 1935 53
Royal Fine Arts Commission 129
Royal Pavilion, Brighton 44
Royal Society of Arts 49, 53, 59
Royal Staffordshire Pottery 50
Royal Wilton Carpet Co. *102*
Royère, Jean 69
Rubinstein, Helena 170, 173–174, *174*, *175*
Rue Surréaliste 150
Ruhlmann, Emile-Jacques 12, 27, 70–2, *72*, 83
Ruhlmann, Madame Emile-Jacques 70
Russell, Gordon 53
Russell, Rosalind 199
Russia 12, 14, 147
Russian Ballet 11, 39, 145
Rutherston, Albert 50

Sabino 97, 108, 122, 123
Sadler's Wells Theatre 135
Saks Fifth Avenue, New York 163
Salon d'Automne, Paris 70, 123
Salon des Décorateurs, Paris 15, 73
San Felice 135
San Francisco 84, 106
Le Sang d'un Poète 156
Savoy Theatre, London 39–41, *41*
Scala Theatre, Berlin 179
Scandinavia 21
Scheherazade 11, 12
Schiaparelli 25, 84, 152, 157, 185, 187, 188, *188*, 189, *192*, 192–4, *193*, *196*, 201
Schlemmer, Oskar *13*, 14
Shoolbred 33

Schorr, Raoh 158
Schrijver, Herman *75*
Schumacher, Hans 107
Seale, Gilbert 41
Segonzac 106
Seligmann, Kurt 158, *158*
Sert, José-Maria 132
Sert, Misia 174
Seven Gothic Tales 135
Seventh Symphony 145
Shand, P. Morton 152
Shaw, George Bernard 133
Sheean, Vincent 135
Shearer, Norma 198
Shelley Potteries *43*, 125
Sheraton furniture 16
Sheringham, George 37, 39, 49
Shocking Life 194
Sickert, Walter 129
Silver Collar Boy 135, 181–2
Simonson, Lee 21
Simple Schemes for Decoration 75
Sir John Vanbrugh 135
Sitwell family 199
Sitwell, Osbert 166
Skeaping, John 63
Slade School, London 133
Slater, Humphrey 63
The Sleeping Beauty 104
Smyth, Urquhart and Marckwald, Inc. *164*
The Snake Charmer 128
Soane, Sir John 21
Sobey, James Thrall 137
Socard, Jacques 99
Socard, Tony 99
Société Industrielle d'Art, Paris 111–12, *111*
Sognot, Louis 11
Sorine, Sovely 147
Southern Railway 164
Spectator 57
Spry, Constance 90, *156*, 159
Staite-Murray, William 127
Steel furniture 15, 91–4
Stein, Gertrude 173
Stein, Leo 173
Steuben *121*
Stevens, Robert Mallet 15
Stevens and Williams 123
Stiebel, Victor 160, *194*
Stock Exchange, New York 10, 24, 30, 129, 172
Stockholm 106
Stoke-on-Trent 126
Stone, E., and Partners 41
Strachey, Lytton 86, 165, 166
Strand Palace Hotel, London 45, *46*, 91
Studio 18, 19, 20, 23, 45, 50, 52, 53, 57, 63, 67, 71, 76, 114, 123, 162, 177
Studio Athelia 111
Studio Year Book of Decorative Art 35, 96, 111, 122, 123, 124, 159
Subes, Raymond 27, 51
Sue, Eugène 11
Sue, Louis 173, 174, *174*
Sullivan, Sir Arthur 39
Surrealism 149–62

Surrealist Exhibition, 1936 149
A Survey of British Industrial Arts 51
Sutherland, Graham *43*, 50
Swansea 132
Swanson, Gloria 108
Sweden 48
Swedish Exhibition, 1930 48
Sydney, Silvia 199
Symphonie Fantastique 145, 147, 151
Szecsi, Ladislas 85

Tabard, François 106
Talbot, Suzanne 90
Tanguy, Yves 150, 159
Tapestries 104, 106
Tate Gallery 133
Tatlin, Vladimir 12
Taube, Kerstin *113*
Taxi Pluvieux 150
Tchelitchev, Pavel 136, 148–9, 175
Teague, Walter Dorwin 23
Temple, Shirley 149
Templeton 132
Templier, Raymond 86
Terry, Emilio 148, *148*
Textiles, interior design 99–106
Thamar 12
Theatres 39–45
Thonet *14*, 91
Thorpe, Dorothy *112*
Thorvaldsen, Bertel 22
Three Clowns 106
Tiepolo, Giambattista 159
The Italian Girl in Algiers 159
The Times 58
Tisserand, Ernest 15
Tissot, James 169
Tokyo 70
Tonks, Henry 133
Tonny, Kristians 136
Town and Country 25, 137
Tree, Sir Herbert 86
Tree, Iris 86
Trent & Lewis *202*
Trocadero Restaurant, London 45, *47*
Trotter, Dorothy Warren 166
Tube Investments Ltd 91
Tucson, Arizona *164*
Tudor style 16, 29, 94, 181
Tutankhamun 84
Two Seated Women 106
Tyler, Parker 136

Unit One 162
Urban, Joseph 21, 108, 118

Valloton, Suzanne 136
Les Valses de Beethoven 148
Vanbrugh, Sir John 135
Van Cleef 185, 189
Van Doesburg, Theo 12
Velasquez, Diego Rodriguez de Silvay 196
Venice 136
The Venus de Milo of the Drawers 193
Véra, Paul 104
Vernon, Lord *37*

Veronese, Paris 98, *98*
Versailles 138
Victoria, Queen of England 159
Victoria and Albert Museum 71, 79
Victoria Regina 136
Victoriana 60–1, 142, 152, 165–9
Vitroflex 112, 115
Vitrolite 111
Vogue 60, 81, 86, 133, 145, 160, 161, 164, 167, 169, 194
La Voix Humaine 145
Von Shirach, Baldur 163
Vorticism 18–19
Vuillard, Edouard 136
Vulliamy 189

Wadsworth, Edward 63, 162
Wadsworth Atheneum, Hartford 161
Wagner, Richard 45
Wales 180
Wales, Prince of, *see* Edward VIII
Wall furnishings 95–6
Wall Street, Crash 10, 24, 30, 129, 172 *see also* Depression
Walsh and Walsh *121*
Walton, Allan 103, 139, *144*, 162
Waring and Gillow, London 33, 62, 65
Waters, Billie *80*
Watts, Arthur 49
Waugh, Evelyn 165, 195
Weber, Jean 104
Wedgwood 70, *124*, *125*, 126
Wedgwood, Josiah 50, 126
Weeden and Mather *44*
Wegely 124
Weiler, Paul Louis 159
Weimar 14
Weisweiler 70
Wellesley, Lady Gerald 64
Wellesley, Lord Gerald 36–7
West, Mae 84, 153, 157, 199
Whistler, Laurence 135
Whistler, Rex 58, 68, 133–6, *134*, 182
Whitehall Theatre, London 41
Wild, Evelyn 86
Wilde, Oscar 165
Wilkinson, A.J., Ltd 50, 126
Wilkinson, Norman 163
Wimperis, Simpson and Guthrie 41, 44
Winchcombe Pottery 127
Winchester 137
Windsor Castle 49
The Wise Virgins 135
Within Four Walls 116
Woman and Beauty 125, 198
Women, art déco directed at 12
World War I 10–11, 127
Worth, Jean 167, 187, *196*
Wright, Constance 135, 181
Wrought iron 15

Yardley 70, *71*, *201*

Zinkeisen, Anna 164

Illustration acknowledgements

Photographs of objects illustrated on pages 43 *top*, 52, 100 *right*, 103, 120, 121 *left*, 123, 178, 179 *top*, 201 *top* (except for the 'mouth' button) are reproduced by courtesy of the Victoria and Albert Museum, London, Crown Copyright Reserved; photographs on pages 35, 36, 38 *top*, 40, 44, 47, 66, 109 *top*, 152, 153, 154, 155, 203 by courtesy of *Architectural Review*; on pages 41, 78 courtesy of the Mander and Mitchenson Theatre Collection, London; photograph on page 131 courtesy of the Glynn Vivian Art Gallery, Swansea, on page 156 *top* of the Musée Christofle, Paris. Photographs on pages 9, 42, 43, 50, 52, 72, 74, 80, 98, 105, 111, 116, 117, 122, 128, 130, 139, 178, 179 *top*, 201 by Deste Photography, London; on pages 29, 38 *bottom*, 54, 55, 76, 82, 88, 89, 110, 121 *right*, 134, 156 *bottom*, 168 by Millar and Harris, London; photograph on page 46 by Tim Street-Porter, London. All line drawings by Martin Battersby.